108 Hikes Out of Steamboat Springs, Colorado

HIKING THE 'BOAT II

by

Diane White-Crane

Aspen Tree Press
P.O. Box 775051
Steamboat Springs, CO 80477
http://www.llamalady.com

Cover photos: Front: Gilpin Lake, taken by Don Crane
Back: At Gold Creek Lake, taken by Diane White-Crane

Printed in the USA by Versa Press, Inc., East Peoria, Illinois

Library of Congress Conrol Number: 2001-126493

ISBN: 0-9631322-2-9

First printing: May 2001
Second printing: July 2003

Please Note:
Aspen Tree Press and the author assume no responsibility for the safety of users of this book. Hiking and mountain biking in the backcountry entails a certain amount of risk, and no guidebook can prepare readers for each and every danger that might potentially be encountered in the backcountry. The readers of this book are entirely responsible for their own actions, and neither the author nor the publisher is responsible for any erroneous information, if any, contained herein, as well as changes to roads, trailheads, trails, or any other features, by any individuals, government agencies, or nature. Use of the information in this book is at the sole risk of the user, and neither the author nor the publisher can be held accountable for any injuries, accidents, property loss, or any other problems that may result from using the information in this book.

This book is dedicated with love

to my FAITH in God,

to my FAMILY,

and to the FRIENDS

~both two and four-legged~

who made these hikes with me.

Even the songs of the birds proclaim your praises, O Lord!
And the heavens and earth beneath them;
Green trees that reach towards you,
White fluffy clouds in a deep blue Colorado sky,
Colorful wildflowers glowing in beauty
All proclaim your glory, O Lord.
Cool mountain breezes, green hills and soaring mountains,
Deep valleys and plains, lakes, streams and rivers
All magnify your powers and splendor, O Lord,
And proclaim your greatness and love for mankind.

Find us on Facebook **Visit Hiking the 'Boat on Facebook!**

Before heading out on a hike, visit us on Facebook for any recent updates to trails and conditions. Visit us after your hike to share your photos and stories of your hiking adventures! Check to see if others have offered updates or comments on your trail of interest – posts about any changes resulting from blowdowns, beetle infestations, forest fires, avalanches, closures, etc. For example, signs blown over, moved or changed, trailheads get moved or re-routed, trails get covered by falling and dead trees. You can also check for changes with the U. S. Forest Service: Steamboat Springs: 970-879-1870; Walden: 970-723-8204; and Yampa: 970-638-4516. Happy trails (on line) to you!

My sincere thanks and great appreciation goes to all those who helped me prepare this book for your use:

- My husband, Don Crane, who provided encouragement and many of the photos, including the front cover shot; to our daughters, Sarah and Claire, who made many of these hikes with me over the years;
- John and Mary Ann Duffey, friends who introduced me to the joy of llamas and then gave me two of my own;
- Heleen DeKoning-Adler, who did the design and desktop publishing and her husband, Jon, who provided some of the photos and watched their children;
- Karen Vail who generously wrote all the Yampatika Notes;
- All the many family members and great friends who made these hikes with me over the years – you know who you are because you're in all the photos!
- And special beyond-the-call-of-duty friends, Renny "Map Man" Daly for hike [57] and Jain Himot, who, even on the hard hikes, stays positive, laughs with me, and always dreams up marvelous backpack meals – and Pat Wessel who was brave and/or crazy enough to take the last hike in the book with me [108]; and Barb Yarnell: on a trail or off a trail, a friend indeed!
- John Fielder for some photo advice and lending me a few of his poems;
- And with very special thanks to the U.S. Forest Service Personnel who generously took the time to make helpful suggestions, additions, corrections, and reviews:
  Hahn's Peak/Bear's Ears District: especially Dan McIntyre and Ed Patalik,
  Jon Halverson, Ray George, Janet Faller, Diann Pipher, Kathy Foster,
  Joanne Sanfilippo, Sue Struthers, Rob Bringuel, Angie Krall, and Kirk Wolff.
  Parks Ranger District: Hal Wentz and Fran Bourbeau
  Yampa Ranger District: John Anarella
- And last – but not least – to my two wonderful woolly buddies, Dudley and Sammy, who haul all my supplies, keep me company, inspire my stories and songs and delight me to no end – Oh, you gotta llove a llama!

Also by author:

• Hiking the 'Boat

• Stop Spitting at Your Brother!
Life Lessons of a Rocky Mountain Llama

• Songs for Llama Lovers ~ Young & Old (CD)

The Hikes

Close-in Hikes

Hikes accessed via Buffalo Pass

Hikes accessed via Wyoming Trail 1101

Hikes accessed via Rabbit Ears Pass

Hikes accessed South of Oak Creek

Hikes accessed from Sheriff Reservoir

Hike accessed from Crosho Lake

Hikes in or near Northeast Section of Flat Tops

Hike accessed via California Park

Hikes out of Hahn's Peak - Steamboat Lake - Columbine

Hikes in N.W. Routt National Forest Area

Hikes accessed from Clark & Seedhouse Road

Hikes accessed from eastern (Walden) Side of Mt. Zirkel Wilderness

*How beautiful
on the mountain
are the feet
of those who bring
good news, who
proclaim peace,
...who say to Zion,
"Your God reigns!"
~ Isaiah 52:7*

Introduction

Steamboat Springs and The Routt National Forest

Known as "Ski Town U.S.A.," Steamboat Springs, Colorado, is best known for its world-class ski slopes and deep champagne powder skiing. The area receives on average 355-inches of snow each year. But when the snow melts, a magical myriad of recreational opportunities open up, including hundreds of miles of superb high country hiking trails. Each summer, Steamboat's surrounding forestlands become a paradise for hikers, backpackers and fishermen. And because Steamboat Springs is a bit isolated and off the beaten path, these trails generally seem to be far less crowded than those around I-70 towns like Breckenridge, Vail and Keystone.

Except for a few trails on State-owned lands, all of the hikes in this book take place in the Routt National Forest, a high-elevation forest straddling the Continental Divide, which includes 1,126,346-acres of land within its boundaries. In 1905, President Theodore Roosevelt, who used to hunt in the area, established the Park Range Forest Reserve. This later became the Routt National Forest, named after Col. John N. Routt, the area's last territorial and Colorado's first state Governor.

Steamboat Springs lies nestled against the western ridge of the Continental Divide, about 165-driving miles northwest of Denver. The Continental Divide and the spectacular peaks of the 160,568-acre Mt. Zirkel Wilderness divide the major watersheds of the Routt National Forest. On what locals call "the Walden side," as in Walden, Colorado, the North Platte River, a tributary of the Missouri and Mississippi Rivers, drains the North Park region on the east. And on the western "Steamboat side" of the Divide, the Yampa River begins in the Flat Tops and flows through downtown Steamboat Springs, eventually to the Green and Colorado Rivers.

On the southeastern corner of the Routt National Forest, the Sarvis Creek Wilderness offers yet another 47,140-acres of beautiful, primitive forest, streams and wildlife. And southwest of Steamboat Springs, the Routt National Forest also claims a northern section of the Flat Tops Wilderness, the other part of which is in the White River National Forest.

Elevation and Weather

Elevations in the Routt National Forest range from 7,000' in the river valleys to almost 13,000' atop the Divide. Very heavy snows blanket the area in the winter, and spring and summer seasons are relatively short. Summer days are usually warm, averaging around 70 degrees, with frequent afternoon thunderstorms. Evenings in the high country are generally cool to downright cold, and water bottles have been known to freeze in early and late summer weeks. Snow can begin to fall even as early as September (see hike [108]). Autumn weather is generally more stable, with clear, cool days and often freezing temperatures at night. In heavy snow years, trails often don't open until mid-July, and even then some. Many lakes aren't free of all ice until mid-to-late July, and streams and creeks can be very difficult to cross in summer's early weeks. When planning an early-season hike or backpack trip, it's always best to check on trail openings ahead of time with the Forest Service (970-879-1870).

Mt. Zirkel Wilderness

The majority of the hikes in this book are located in or adjacent to the Mt. Zirkel Wilderness, which is 160,648-acres in size and straddles thirty-six miles of the Continental Divide. Within its boundaries lie parts of the Park Range, the southern end of the Sierra Madre Range, the craggy-spired Sawtooth Range and the headwaters of the Elk, Encampment and North Platte Rivers. Fifteen peaks in the Mt. Zirkel area reach elevations near 12,000', with the highest being Mt. Zirkel itself at 12,180'. Broad valleys, rugged cirques, and more than seventy named sparkling alpine lakes, along with hundreds of creeks, streams and smaller unnamed tarns–all carved out by glaciers many centuries ago–lie nestled within its wilderness boundaries. (Use Trails Illustrated maps 116 and 117 and Routt National Forest map.)

Created in 1964, the area was enlarged in 1980 to 139,098-acres, and then increased by another 20,752-acres in 1993.

Multiple Trail Use

The Routt National Forest provides almost eight hundred miles of maintained trails, including a section of the Continental Divide Trail. Many trails outside the Wilderness Area accommodate more than just one use and must be shared by hikers, mountain bikers, and dirt bikers alike. More than 1,800 miles of roads–ranging from paved to four-wheel-drive dirt paths–provide many points of access into the Forest.

Wildlife

The varied terrain of the Routt National Forest provides excellent habitat for a wide range of wildlife, including threatened and endangered species such as the sandhill crane and the greenback cutthroat trout. Elk and deer are often spotted in their summer range. Other species common to the area include coyote, fox, black bear, bobcat, pine marten, mink, weasel, beaver, snowshoe hare, pika, marmot, porcupine and over two-hundred species of birds. Visitors on more rare occasions see moose and mountain lions.

The numerous streams, creeks, reservoirs and lakes challenge fishermen with their native Colorado River cutthroat trout, brook trout, mountain suckers and mountain whitefish, as well as other nonnative trout. In the fall, elk hunters flock to the area in droves.

I know every bird in the mountains, and the creatures of the field are mine. Psalm 50:11

Trees and Plants

The mountain areas of the Routt National Forest are blanketed by huge timberlands of lodgepole pine, Engelmann spruce, sub-alpine fir and Douglas-fir. Interspersed with these forestlands are large expansions of open meadows and parks containing gorgeous stands of aspens, meadow grasses and wildflowers, which, especially in early July, carpet the meadows with a vast array of fabulous colors.

Between 7,500 and 9,000 feet, the drier, south facing slopes are covered with sagebrush, Gambel oak, serviceberry and chokecherry, while the north facing, moister slopes nourish thick stands of green conifers.

At treeline, spruce and fir trees become stunted and windblown, taking on strange, contorted shapes. Many of these "krummholz" trees, meaning "twisted wood," can be hundreds of years old and provide shelter for ptarmigan birds and other small animals living in this harsh environment.

Above timberline, at about 11,000' in this area, the severe conditions of the alpine tundra offer only tiny, low, ground-hugging "belly flowers" and plants, named that because a person needs to get down on his or her belly to closely study them. These brave plants somehow survive shallow, rocky soil, a very short growing season, high, cold winds, and ultraviolet radiation, yet they can easily be destroyed by just one heavy, misplaced footstep.

Wildflowers

There are many good wildflower identification books for the Steamboat Springs area. If you don't want to lug along a whole book, a great pocket folder guide to area trees and wildflowers is "Rockies Trees and Wildflowers," available for purchase at the Forest Service office on U.S. 40, across from the Holiday Inn.

My own personal favorite is Guide to Colorado Wildflowers ~ Vol. 2, Mountains by G. K. Guennel. The most common wildflowers found in the Routt National Forest are: Bellflower – Columbine – Dogtooth Violet – Early Larkspur – Firecracker Penstemon – Fireweed – Fringed Gentian – Indian Paintbrush – Leafy Cinquefoil – Monkeyflower – Monkshood – Mountain Lupine – Mules-Ears – Pasque Flower – Pearly-Everlasting – Shooting Star – Showy Daisy – Sky Pilot – Wallflowers – Wild Geranium – Wild Onion – Wild Flag – Wild Rose – Yarrow.

Early-day Inhabitants

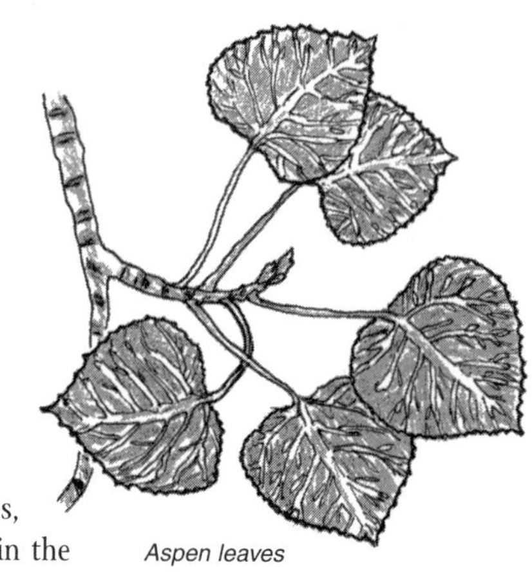
Aspen leaves

The first humans to inhabit the area were nomadic hunters and gatherers who lived off the abundant plant and animal resources in the mountains. As early as the 1300's, American Indian tribes, especially the northern Utes, began to make more permanent year-round settlements near major river drainages, which provided them with easy hunting and fishing accessibility. Because of the access to these area resources, Ute, Arapaho, Gros Ventres, Souix and Cheyenne Indians often intermingled in the area.

For many hundreds of years, the Utes hunted in the surrounding mountains, plains and plateaus of what is now Colorado. When Colorado became a state in 1876, the Ute reservation spanned much of the western part of the state, including what now is the Routt National Forest. Following the killing of a U.S. Government Indian agent and ten of his employees by Ute warriers, sadly the entire Ute tribe was relocated to a reservation in Utah. Read more about the Utes @: www.krma.org/byways/utes1.html

During the fur trapping years between 1825 and 1845, what is now the Routt National Forest became popular trapping grounds. In the late 1860's, gold and silver miners flocked to the area, and mining towns seemed to spring up almost overnight. The Forest still contains the remains of many old log cabins and mining excavations. (See hike [92]) Settlers soon flocked to the area to take advantage of the natural resources available for ranching, timbering and agriculture. Early-day relatives of present-day owners homesteaded many of the ranches located in the area today.

How to get to Steamboat Springs: From Denver, it's a beautiful 3-hour, 165-mile drive. Take I-70 west to Silverthorn; take Colorado 9 north from Silverthorn to Kremmling; take U.S. 40 west from Kremmling, over Rabbit Ears Pass, to Steamboat Springs.

Need more information?

- Steamboat Springs Visitor's Center: 970-879-0880; www.steamboat-chamber.com
- Routt National Forest –Hahn's Peak/Bears Ears Ranger District:970-879-1870; www.fs.fed.us/mrnf/hpbe.html
- Routt National Forest Headquarters, Laramie, WY: 970-745-2300.
- Routt National Forest-Parks Ranger District, Walden, CO: 970-723-8204.

- Routt National Forest-Yampa Ranger District, Yampa, CO: 970-638-4516.
- Steamboat Central Reservations: 1-800-922-2722 or 970-879-6111.
- Colorado Division of Wildlife: www.dnr.state.co.us/wildlife.
- Rocky Mountain Elk Foundation: 1-800-225-5355, ext. 401
- Recorded fishing information for northwestern Colorado: 303-291-7537
- Colorado State Parks: 303-866-3203
- Information on trees and plants: Routt County extension Service: 970-879-0825
- More information about viewing moose: www.dnr.state.co.us/wildlife
- Colorado State Forest Service: 970-879-0475

Aspen Trees

by Diane White-Crane

The ivory bark and apple green leaves of the aspen
lighten up the somber dark hues of the conifers,
as they shimmer and quake in mountain breezes.

These pioneer trees fill the air with a sweet tannin-rich aroma,
brightening up the forest world, as they rustle and
send out peaceful, trembling melodies on the soft winds.

Lovely deciduous trees, aspens thrive in mountain meadows,
where they shade and nourish exquisite wildflowers,
mountain grasses and an array of cavity-nesting birds.

Black knots on their white trunks look like thousands of eyes
watching and welcoming a myriad of visitors
who arrive in their groves on wings, hooves, feet and paws.

And in the golden sunshine of fall,
these graceful trees set whole mountainsides ablaze—
sparkling in reds and glimmering in yellows,

Thrilling our eyes and our hearts and our souls!

Wilderness Ethics - Leave no Trace

Hiking in the mountains around Steamboat Springs, Colorado, can be an exhilarating and joyous experience. There is endless beauty to behold, day after day of sunshine, dark blue skies with white, billowy clouds, fresh air to breathe in, and trails which will take you into an almost "other" world, one full of God's wondrous creations of nature. All of this exists here for us to freely enjoy. And then, after a long, exhausting hike on an area trail, you can end your day by soaking tired muscles in the wonderfully healing waters of one of the local hot springs.

Explore our Creator's glorious mountains, revel in their serenity and beauty, and let them renew your spirit. But always remember to appreciate and respect these special gifts by striving to have as minimal an impact on the environment as possible. Leaving no trace of your presence doesn't mean just packing out your litter, but rather a real attempt on your part to leave your campsite so that others might not know you were ever even there. Follow these rules of Leave No Trace advocated by the U.S. Forest Service so that our grandkids will enjoy what we now have:

Leave No Trace is more than a technique or a set of rules defining appropriate behavior in the wilderness; it is an attitude, a land ethic that respects the wilderness, recognizes its fragility and the need to protect it. In years past, we spoke of people's ability to survive the wilderness. Now we speak of wilderness as the land's capability of surviving human use. The best way that you can help the land survive is to make the least possible impact on the environment. The principles of Leave No Trace are:

- Plan ahead and prepare. Know the area and what to expect when packing and hiking. Give yourself time at the end of each day's travel to find a suitable camp. Find a dry, screened area well away from the trail. It is required that you camp at least 100 feet away from lakes and streams to prevent pollution from dishwater, human waste and manure.

- Camp and travel on durable surfaces. Whenever possible, choose an established site that will not show signs of additional use. Avoid any heavily used campsites that have been posted as revegetation sites. This will allow these areas to heal. Pack a portable water jug to carry water to camp, thereby reducing trips to lakes and streams. Before you leave, put rocks back in place and scatter needles or brush over any bare areas at your site.

- Minimize use and impacts of fire. Use a gas stove instead of building a fire.

- Leave what you find for others to enjoy. Camp lightly and take only pictures. Refraining from outdated practices such as trenching around tents, building structures, putting nails in trees, and collecting from the forest will help to protect the resources. Your site should need no modification. Good campsites are found, not made.

- Properly dispose of what you can't pack out. Scatter wastewater away from camp and water sources. Use a digging tool to bury human waste.

- Pack it in, pack it out. Reduce litter at its source. Simplify by packing with reusable containers. Before leaving camp, take one last look around. Have you packed all of your trash and left your site in its natural condition?

- Bury human waste at least six-inches deep and at least 200 feet away from water or dry waterways. Wash yourself or camp utensils at least 200 feet away from water, using biodegradable soap, if any.

- Don't carve on trees, take erosion-causing shortcuts off established trails, or trample on fragile vegetation.

- Before making a campfire, check for wind conditions, overall fire danger and any administrative restrictions. Use only existing fire rings – don't build new ones. In pristine areas, careful use of a mound fire, a pit fire or a fire pan will allow you to leave no trace. Gather only dead and down sticks from the ground small enough to break with your hands. Don't cut or break branches off standing trees. Burn only wood or paper in your fire. The use of campfires at and above tree line is strongly discouraged to help preserve the limited deadwood and alpine landscape. MAKE CERTAIN fire is completely out and scatter the cold ashes over a large area, well away from camp.

- In the wilderness areas, group size is limited to a combination of 25 people and livestock, with a maximum of 15 humans and 10 pack animals.

- Obey special 0.25-mile restrictions on certain lakes in the Routt National Forest – such as Gilpin, Gold and Three Island Lakes. Violators will be ticketed. ~ U.S.F.S.

For more Leave No Trace information: 1-800-332-4100 or http://www.lnt.org

At the trailheads, please take the time to read all wilderness regulations and updated information, and also sign in at the registers.

Backcountry Safety

Please Note: Especially if you're a novice hiker: find, print out, read and digest a copy of the Mountain Rescue Association Training manual:http://www.mra.org/traininfo.html It's free and available to all.

After you've brought up the site, click on "General Backcountry Safety Student's Workbook" by Charley Shimanski. It covers in greater detail backcountry preparedness, clothing for backcountry travel, what to do if lost, and the hazards of nature and how to avoid them.

I also highly recommend that you purchase and study a copy of BACKCOUNTRY FIRST AID and Extended Care, by Buck Tilton, Director Wilderness Medicine Institute; about $5 – 1-800-359-1646. This small, well-written guide will fit into your first aid kit and teach you all you'll probably ever need to know about giving first aid in the wilderness.

This section is not meant to scare you away from the joys of hiking. You may never have to use much or any of the information that follows. But as invigorating and rewarding an experience as high-altitude hiking can be, you'll enjoy it far more if you're well prepared for any emergency. Life-threatening situations can and do, from time to time, arise, and it's much better to know how to avoid them in the first place–as well as how to deal with them–should they occur.

Remember, unless you're lucky enough to be just in the right place, on top of a high ridge, where a cell phone may work in the mountains, there is no 911 to call in the backcountry! By the time this book is reprinted, technology will probably have improved the use of cell phones in remote places. But even if you do manage to reach 911 on a cell phone, it could be hours before help arrives. Therefore, you'll have to rely on preparation, planning, knowledge, experience and precaution to help keep you safe and having fun on your wilderness trips. According to a U.S. Forest Service brochure, "It is (the hiker's) responsibility to know the hazards involved in your activities in the Forest and to use the proper safety procedures and equipment to minimize the inherent risks and hazards related to your activity."

Always take along the essentials

On each and every hike, take along your common sense, a good compass and the appropriate Trails Illustrated or U.S.G.S. map. DO NOT rely on the hand-made maps in this book! They are not meant to be field maps. Also take along extra clothing – wool hat, gloves, jacket and rain gear, a first aid kit and a good pocket wilderness first aid guide. In addition, assemble the following items, put them all in a large tin can or small cooking pot, call it your Emergency Survival Kit, and always keep it with you when hiking: Waterproof matches – candle – fire starters – hard candy – raisins – bouillon cubes – packs of sugar – several tea bags – two envelopes of dry soup mix – whistle – small flashlight with extra batteries and bulb – two emergency blankets – signal mirror – plastic spoon and cup – string or cord – safety pins – small pad of paper and short pencil – clean red neckerchief – 2 large, plastic leaf bags – 1-1/2' duct tape rolled around a foot of rolled up picture-hanging wire – pocket knife – a tiny radio and extra batteries (for psychological comfort, should you become lost). If you can afford one, a GPS is an invaluable tool for knowing exactly where you are at any given time.

The prudent see danger and take refuge, but the simple keep going and suffer for it.
~ Proverbs 27:12

Lightning

When hiking in the mountains, *never* take chances with lightning. To quote Mark Twain, "Thunder is good. Thunder is impressive; but it is lightning that does the work!" Unfortunately, each and every summer, people are killed by lightning while hiking in Colorado, so it's best to be very cautious.

Electrical storms usually prefer early afternoons, so try to begin high altitude hikes early in the day. Avoid going up on open ridges, passes or summits during a storm. If you are already there and a storm begins to brew in the area, don't wait for the lightning to begin. Start down immediately. Storms build very rapidly in the mountains, often with little warning. They usually don't last very long, but they can bring in very severe weather–including rain and lightning, and even hail and snow in mid-summer. If you go to a lower ravine or valley, be alert for possible flash floods.

Never stay out in an open field in a storm, and stay away from single, isolated trees. Seek shelter in a low area, under a larger growth of smaller trees. Wherever possible, "head for the woods" and get yourself well into the trees. Don't sit out a storm in a shallow cave or stand at the base or edge of a cliff.

If you're caught out in an open area during lightning and can't make it to shelter, don't be the tallest object around. Get down, but minimize your contact with the ground by kneeling–preferably on a foam pad or on your daypack–and keep your head down and hands on your knees until the storm passes. Remove any metal pack frames or metal objects from your body and place them away from you. If caught out in a boulder field, stay down, crouched between the rocks. In an open scree field, stay close to the smallest rocks. Stay away from all sources of water–an excellent conductor of electricity. Spread large groups of people out to reduce multiple risks to the whole hiking party. Your tent provides no insulation from lightning–don't remain in it if it's out in the open or under the taller trees in an area. Count how many seconds it takes to hear thunder after seeing lightning, divide the total by five, and that's approximately how many miles away the lightning is. If both bolt and thunder are simultaneous–usually very loud–you're immediately below the storm. If your hair stands on end, a lightning strike is imminent. Immediately crouch down and cover your ears!

Hypothermia

In the backcountry, hypothermia is the most common killer. In the summer, especially early and late in the season, it's most often caused by a deadly combination of wet, cold and wind. When exposure to these weather elements lowers your body's core temperature so much so that the body is no longer able to warm itself, you are experiencing hypothermia. Falling into an icy stream or getting wet from rain can have very serious consequences in the wilderness, especially when combined with a cold wind. Although most summer hypothermia cases happen when the air temperature is between 30 and 50 degrees, hikers can become hypothermic even in higher temperatures, especially if also exposed to cold water and wind. Wind-chill can lower the body temperature enough to deprive a victim's brain of proper judgment and reasoning power. At this point, the victim will show some or all of the following symptoms: uncontrollable fits of shivering; vague, slow, slurred speech; memory lapses; incoherence; immobile, fumbling hands; frequent stumbling or lurching gait; drowsiness; exhaustion or inability to get up after a rest.

If weather turns bad, stop and put on warm clothing and rain gear *before* you get wet and cold. Wet clothes lose 90% of their insulating value. Wet wool retains heat better than wet cotton or down. Invest in good rain gear. Garbage bags won't do. Ponchos or rain jackets which cover heads, necks and trunks are a must, and rain pants are worth their weight in gold if you're caught out in severe weather.

If your hiking party is exposed to wind, cold and water, watch yourself and others for symptoms of hypothermia. If any are present, stop to treat the victim before the situation turns serious. Don't continue hiking until exhaustion sets in. If you or a member of your party should fall into a stream or become soaked from rain, stop your hike and concentrate on getting the victim warm and dry. Get out of the wind and rain, and remove the wet clothes. Use supplies in your emergency survival kit (see above) to build a warming fire and to make hot drinks. If a victim still remains hypothermic, is semi-conscious or worse, try keeping him or her awake, and at this point, use another person's body to warm the victim up, preferably with direct skin contact inside a sleeping bag or collection of warm clothing. But the best way to deal with hypothermia is to prevent it in the first place!

Wildfires

The danger from wildfires in the Routt National Forest is real, especially in drought years, and especially since the 1997 Blowdown. If you spot or smell a wildfire in the area, evacuate. Leave this hike or camping trip for another day. Be certain to notify authorities of spotted fires as soon as you have an opportunity. When campfire restrictions are placed on an area, obey them! And always, always, always be especially careful with your own campfires.

Altitude Sickness

Newly arrived visitors to Steamboat Springs unused to high altitude will from time to time get altitude sickness, a condition caused by a lack of oxygen. As you go higher, there is less oxygen in each breath you take. Especially if you are coming to Steamboat from sea level, it takes two or three days to acclimatize yourself to the high altitude, so try to enjoy activities around town for a couple days before heading up on the trails. Complaints may include severe headache and nausea, and those affected may exhibit a cough, staggering gait and a loss of appetite. To prevent these symptoms, try to drink lots of water, not just during a hike, but several days before heading up a trail. Eat salty snack and high-energy foods. About a week before your hike, eat carbohydrate-rich, low-fat foods. After you've become totally acclimated to Steamboat's 7,600' altitude, try not to ascend more than 1000' a day.

If a person becomes ill, get them to rest, breathe deeply and eat quick-energy foods like candy or dried fruit. Aspirin can be given for the headache. If there isn't a very quick improvement, get them down to a lower altitude as quickly as possible, before they become too weak or sick to travel on their own.

If symptoms continue, and especially if the person also begins to have symptoms similar to pneumonia or exhibits bizarre behavior, *get immediate medical assistance,* since High Altitude Pulmonary Edema (HAPE) and High Altitude Cerebral Edema (HACE), two much more serious and life-threatening conditions, can develop very quickly–symptoms usually develop in 6 to 36 hours after arriving at high altitude. With HAPE, the lungs fill up with fluid, and the person drowns. Symptoms include shortness of breath, weakness, coughing, gurgling sounds and a feeling of tightness in the chest. The cough is persistent and often irritating. Pulse becomes rapid and respiration rapid and constant. The patient's anxiety level usually increases these symptoms. With HACE, the victim has severe headache, unrelieved by rest and medication, bizarre changes in personality and possible coma. Both of these illnesses can be fatal, so if any of the above symptoms present themselves, the victim needs to quickly be taken to a lower elevation and given medical attention, including medication and the administration of oxygen, both essential to survival.

Dehydration, heat exhaustion and heat stroke

When hiking in hot weather, if you don't drink enough fluids, you will become dehydrated. Symptoms include dizziness, headache, a hot, flushed feeling, weakness and nausea. Even if you aren't thirsty, make it a habit to carry and drink lots of water. If streams and lakes are available along the way, carry a water filter and stop to replenish water bottles. Try to eat salty snacks on the trail, such as nuts or pretzels. A person hiking on a long, difficult trail at high altitude on sunny days should drink at least three to four quarts of water during the day–and as much as possible back at camp before the next day. Treat suspected dehydration with water, diluted sport drinks and shade. When hiking, make children drink often, even if they say they aren't thirsty. Aspirin should be given for headache.

Heat exhaustion may follow dehydration, when a body cannot cool itself. The victim is first weak and may have heat cramps, while sweating heavily. His skin is moist and cool, yet the inner body temperature is still normal. The face will be flushed, then pale, with thready pulse and low blood pressure. The victim usually complains of headache and vomits or becomes delirious. Get the person into the shade and lay them flat on their back. Give them salt water or sport drinks, wet them down and fan them, if necessary. If they are sleepy, let them take a nap. If they don't improve, seek medical help immediately.

Heat stroke, much more serious, often follows untreated heat exhaustion. Now the body begins to heat up far too much and far too fast, up to 105 degrees F. Symptoms include headache, fast breathing, fast heart rate, flushed, red face, clammy (but sometimes dry) skin, disorientation, bizarre personality changes, weakness, nausea and possible delirium and unconsciousness. The body temperature is rising rapidly, pulse begins to pound, and blood pressure rises. Heat stroke is a life-threatening condition. Do not give victim any fever-reducing medication. Put this person in the cool shade, flat on their back, get them to sip cold water, if they are able to drink it, remove clothing, drench head and neck with cold stream water or snow–if any patches of it are left in the trees–and fan them to cool the body off as quickly as possible. Get medical assistance as soon as you can, even if the patient seems to have recovered. Relapse is common.

Drinking Water

To prevent the possibility of ingesting giardia lamblia, an intestinal parasite, you should treat all drinking water taken out of streams and lakes–no matter how clear and clean it looks. Filter water with a hand-held pump, treat with purification tablets, or boil it for five minutes. Make certain the filter you purchase says that it prevents giardia. This condition can be easily treated by a physician, but the possible symptoms you'll experience will make you feel miserable – bloating, gas, diarrhea, appetite and weight loss, nausea, fever, headache, cramps and itching. Symptoms usually don't appear until about two to three weeks after ingesting this parasite. Dogs can get giardia, as well.

Sun Precautions

High altitude sun is far more intense and brutal than it is at sea level! Wear sunglasses, hats with brims, and frequently use sunscreen and sun block chap stick. Don't forget to put sunscreen on noses, ears, back of necks and on the back of legs. You can easily get badly sunburned at high altitudes, even on cloudy, overcast days.

Bugs

Mosquitoes and flies can be very bothersome when hiking, especially in early summer. Always carry bug repellent and use it as soon as you notice the biting insects inspecting you. Don't wait for them to begin feasting on you. In early summer, it's often best to wear lightweight long-sleeved shirts, pants and hats to avoid being bitten. "Afterbite" and antihistamines can be used to relieve itching or allergic reactions from stings, and it's helpful to keep them handy in your pocket.

When children hike with llamas,
there's a special kind of bond.
They share their joy of nature
along a stream or lake or pond.

For the llama is as curious
as a child, in every way.
And the two of them will revel in
the discoveries of the day.

Other Safety do's and don'ts

- Especially when you're making a hike for the first time, plan your trip and study your topographical map beforehand. Begin to use your topo map at the start of the hike and refer to it along the way. Don't wait until you're lost or confused to bring it out.
- Don't let any members of a hiking party split up or wander away from the whole party. If they have to separate, they should do so in sets of two or more. Most people who get lost in the wilderness wander away from the group, and they generally don't have any survival gear or a map and compass with them. So, keep your group together. When a person has to make a toilet trip into the trees, wait on the trail for their return. Don't let them tell you, "Go ahead without me. I'll catch up."
- To help maintain balance, undo hip belts on backpacks before fording streams.
- Generally speaking, unless you're an experienced backcountry hiker who knows the area well, carries survival gear and leaves an itinerary, don't ever hike alone. Don't split up on the trail or go too far off the trail alone. Don't let group members get too far out ahead or too far behind each other on the trail; pace your hike to the slowest hiker in the group.
- By and large, cell phones don't work up in the mountains, except up on some mountain peaks. They are good to have with you, but you can't rely on them.
- Don't glissade down steep snowfields that end in rocks, boulders or atop a cliff.
- Climb rock piles only with care, company, caution and good, supportive shoes.
- Be careful of your footing when crossing creeks on wet rocks and logs– they're often slippery and unstable. Go slowly. Straddle and slide across wet logs on your behind, or crawl on hands and knees if necessary. Hiking sticks and ropes can be useful when crossing.
- Especially in the early season, don't try to cross high-level creeks and streams if the water looks too high or dangerous.
- Waterproof boots before taking a hike – or take along waterproof sock liners in case your Gortex boot linings give out – like mine always do!
- Take along old sneakers or water-crossing shoes for fording creeks and streams. Icy cold water and sharp rocks can be incredibly painful on bare feet and cause you to loose your balance.
- Always, always, always take along rain gear and warm clothes–wool hat, gloves, down vest or jacket and an extra pair of wool socks. Even if you start out on a perfectly sunny day, weather in the high country can change at the drop of a hat, and that perfect day can change rapidly and drastically into a cold torrential downpour or hailstorm. Weather conditions are magnified near the high reaches of the Continental Divide, and area hikers must be prepared for it. Don't learn this lesson the hard way!
- Wear shoes with good ankle support to prevent twisted ankles. Take along an ace bandage for possible sprains. Wear a brace on weak ankles or knees, especially on down part of a steep trail.
- Wear layers of clothing – and put them on and take them off as need be.
- If hiking during hunting season, pray and wear lots of blaze orange!
- Always sign the Forest Service registers at trailheads.
- Always, always, always leave your trip itinerary with a family member or friend, telling

them when you expect to be back and giving them a deadline for your return. Write down the trail you plan to hike, what trailhead you plan to start from, and the year, make, model and license plate number of your car. Instruct your contact person to advise the local sheriff's office (911) if you are overdue, and their office will alert or activate the local Search and Rescue. Leave information on your hiking plans on the dash of your car–especially if you change plans at the trailhead or if you haven't bothered to leave it with anyone at home. Trailheads would be a good place to start looking, if anyone does by chance begin to wonder where you are when you haven't shown up for work in six days!

- Purchase a yearly Colorado Hiking Certificate at sporting good stores. For $3 per year, the certificate insures that, should you become lost or injured in Colorado's backcountry, all costs associated with your search and rescue will be paid for by the Colorado Search and Rescue Fund. For more information, call 970-248-7310.

You who dwell in the shelter of the Lord, who abide in his shadow for life,
say to the Lord "My refuge, my rock in whom I trust!"
He will cover you with his feathers, and under his wings you will find refuge;
His faithfulness shall be your shield and rampart.
You will not fear the terror of the night, nor the arrow that flies by day...
If you make the Lord your dwelling and refuge, then no harm will befall you,
no disaster will come near your tent. For he will command his angels concerning you,
to guard you in all of your ways. They will lift you up in their hands,
so that you will not strike your foot against a stone.
~ From Psalm 91

If you become lost

If you discover that you're lost in the backcountry, fear and panic may threaten to quickly overcome you. That's the time to make yourself immediately S T O P: Sit–Think–Observe–Plan. Don't begin to run! Rather, calm yourself and use your head instead of your feet! Make yourself breathe deeply. Assess your situation. Immediately yell, "Help!" or "Hello!" three times, or blow your whistle three times, and listen to hear if anyone from your party answers. If they do, even faintly, keep yelling, but stay put. Let them come to you. Chances are, they're still on the trail, and they'll help you find your way back to them. If nobody answers, yell in different directions for a period of time. If you're separated from other members of your hiking party, or if you've left an itinerary with someone at home, hug a tree and remain where you are. Someone will eventually come looking for you, if they aren't already. Periodically, blow the whistle, holler loudly, clap your hands three times or bang a branch against a tree trunk three times. Keep away from noisy streams so that you can hear a reply. If you are the person or people doing the finding, be certain to mark well your way back to the trail as you go, or there may be more than one person lost that day.

If you've been hiking alone and haven't left your itinerary with others and have become lost, now, at least, would be a good time to start using your head! In this case, if nobody will be looking for you, use your compass and map, trying carefully to retrace your steps as best you can. Go to a high point and look for familiar landmark features, trails or streams. Try to remember how you got to your present location, and plan your route of travel from up there. Then proceed slowly. If you find a trail or a road, stay on it. If you remain lost, follow a drainage downstream. It most cases, it will eventually bring you to a trail or a road, where chances are good that you'll eventually bump into someone or it will eventually lead you to some sort of civilization.

However, in all circumstances, if it's dark out or the weather is bad, stay put, dig in, keep warm and wait for daylight. If you have found the trail again but it's getting dark, you can probably hike it–proceeding slowly and carefully–if you have a flashlight and good batteries. Use your best judgment about this. But when you aren't on an established trail, *never* try to bushwhack in the dark, even with a flashlight. You won't know you've walked off a cliff until it's too late! (See hike [72]).

The backcountry manual cited in the beginning of this section offers many more suggestions for people who are lost and haven't left an itinerary with anyone, and I strongly recommend you take the time to look it up on the Internet and read it. It also offers suggestions on how to safely search for a lost member of your hiking party. But better yet, always leave an itinerary, always carry survival gear, and don't split up on the trail! Don't later have to say, "Shoulda, woulda, coulda!"

If you have to spend the night outside, put on all of your clothes and try to keep yourself warm and dry. Use your emergency survival kit supplies to light a fire for warmth, making hot drinks, creating smoke for signals and for psychological comfort. Use pine needles or dry brush to make a nest to protect you from the ground's chill, sit on your pack and use your emergency blankets to insulate you from the cold and wind. If it's raining or windy, rig up a shelter or wind block using tree branches and the large, plastic garbage bags in your emergency kit. Use the string, safety pins, wire and duct tape to help secure the bags. If you have no survival gear with you, use pine branches, hollow logs, large boulders, pine needles–anything you find–to help you keep yourself sheltered and as dry and warm as possible.

As often as you can, try to generate three distress signals–three whistle blasts, bangs on a tree, shouts, flashes of light, signal mirror flashes or puffs of heavy smoke. If you are the person doing the finding, signal back two times, letting them know that you hear them and are on your way to them. Then mark your way back to the trail as you search. At night, make three flashes on your flashlight while blowing your whistle or banging on a tree. In the daytime, if you hear rescue planes in the area overhead, go into open areas and try to signal them–using colorful clothing or the red neckerchief in your emergency survival kit, mirror, smoke signals, shiny pot or can–or even an aluminum foil gum wrapper. If you start a fire for warmth or signaling, keep it totally under control at all times. You don't want to ever compound your situation by also starting a wildfire!

Keep in mind that you can generally survive three days without water and three weeks without food. Keep your wits about you and use what you have to best advantage. When any of the six basic fears enter your mind – fear of being alone, of inconveniencing others, darkness, animals, suffering and death – deal with them one by one. Keep yourself calm throughout the night with prayer and/or meditation. Sing songs or hymns, even if you have to make up the words as you go. Stay positive and determined. Lock out negative thoughts. Picture spiritual beings nearby, watching over you, keeping you company, and offering you comfort. Recognize that you have personal strength within you, and don't let your imagination and the darkness distort the situation. In daylight, the forest is a lovely, lovely place, and it remains so in darkness, even if you can't see it.

Remember that in the backcountry around Steamboat Springs, being alone in the darkness won't kill a flea, much less you, as long as you stay put somewhere. Animals are always far more afraid of you than you should ever be of them in this area, even at night! Unless you're badly injured, you won't have to suffer. And you won't die unless you give up or panic and do something totally careless.

Wild animals

In all my many, many years of hiking in western Colorado, I have never had a bad experience with wild animals. There are no Grizzly bears in Colorado. I've had black bears come into my camp from time to time, and I've met a few on the trail. But I almost always cache food up in trees, keep a clean camp and never keep food in my tent, so the visiting bears have left empty "handed." Choose cache trees at least two-hundred feet away from your tent, and suspend the food bag on a rope at least ten-feet off the ground, five feet away from the trunk of the tree, and four feet below the limb on which it hangs. Pitch your tent at least 125-feet away from your cooking area.

Don't try to run away from a black bear – they can very easily outrun you, and your running may trigger an attack. Pick up and hold small children so that they don't panic and run. Clap your hands and talk to the animal in a calm, assertive, low voice while slowly backing away. If by some long shot a black bear attacks you on a trail or in your tent, fight back. Throw everything you can get your hands on at the aggressor. Try never to get between a mother and her cubs.

Bull elk are more common in the area than moose, but moose sightings are happening more and more often in the Routt National Forest. (see hike [106]) Never approach a bull elk or a moose too closely. Watch and photograph them from a safe distance. Move slowly and not directly at them. Back off if they exhibit signs of aggression, such as the hair standing up on their neck, licking their snouts, cocking their head, or rolling their eyes and ears back. If a moose or a bull elk attack, get behind a tree and use it as a shield.

People rarely see mountain lions while hiking in this area, but they are sighted from time to time, and it only takes once! Don't ever let children run ahead of you on a trail. If by some very small chance you encounter one, never approach it, especially one that is feeding or with her kittens. Most mountain lions will try to avoid a confrontation. Give them a way to escape. If you meet a lion, stop, stay calm, talk calmly yet firmly to it, and back away slowly, if you can do so safely. Running may stimulate a lion's instinct to chase and attack. Face the lion and stand upright. Do all you can to appear larger. Raise your arms. Open your jacket. If you have small children with you, protect them by picking them up so they won't panic and run. If a lion behaves aggressively, throw stones, branches or whatever you can get your hands on without crouching down or turning your back. Wave your arms slowly and speak firmly. What you want to do is convince the lion that you are not prey, and in fact, you may be a danger to them! If one attacks you, fight back with rocks, sticks, caps, jackets or even bare hands. Remain standing, or if knocked down, try to get back up.

Please follow the following suggestions for insuring the well being of animals in the wild:

- Never feed them. Human food may harm a wild animal's digestive system.
- Always keep dogs on a leash. They often chase, stress out, and even kill animals, and larger animals may kill them. Dog/porcupine encounters can even lead to a dog's death.
- Keep a clean camp – mishandling garbage and food supplies can promote dangerous bear encounters. Pack out everything you pack in.
- Properly dispose of human waste to reduce the chances of giving an animal an infectious disease.
- Leave what you find. Deer and elk antlers provide calcium to other smaller animals, and downed woody debris commonly used for campfires provides habitat for many animals. So, please limit your consumption of wood products.
- Leave wild animals alone. Never harass, attempt to capture, domesticate or feed them. Travel quietly. Respect the animals' needs for undisturbed territories. Give wildlife plenty of space, for their safety and yours.
- Many amphibians live in our Forest, so keep an eye out when traveling near water sources.
- Always leave injured or young animals alone. Nature will take its course. For more information about Colorado wildlife, log onto: www.dnr.state.co.us/wildlife.

Maps and Compass

The hand-drawn maps in this book are not meant to be used in the field. They are mainly just to give the reader an overall sense of the trail–its location, length, and so on. To help insure your backcounry safety, you should purchase and utilize five Trails Illustrated maps that go with the hikes in this book: 116-Hahn's Peak/Steamboat Lake; 117-Clark/Buffalo Pass; 118-Steamboat Springs/Rabbit Ears Pass;119-Yampa/Gore Pass; 122-Flat Tops N.E./Trappers Lake. If you plan only to make a few hikes in the book, purchase just the maps listed with those hikes.

In Steamboat Springs, Trails Illustrated maps are for sale at many outlets–bookstores, nature stores, sporting goods stores, among others. There are a number of hikes in the book not covered by Trails Illustrated maps, and in those few cases, I cite the appropriate U.S.G.S. maps to use, which can be purchased at Off the Beaten Path (879-6830), Ski Haus (879-0385) and Straightline (879-7568). U.S.G.S. maps can also be purchased directly from the Western Distribution Branch of U.S.G.S., Box 25286, Federal Center, Building 41, Denver, CO 80225 – 303-202-4700.

Trails Illustrated maps may also be purchased directly from Trails Illustrated, P.O.Box 3610, Evergreen, CO 80439-3425–1-800-962-1643.

Although the Trails Illustrated maps don't show as much detail as the U.S.G.S. maps, they each cover the equivalent of eight U.S.G.S. maps, are made out of water and tear resistant paper, and unlike the U.S.G.S. maps, they are frequently updated. By and large, I have found them to be very accurate and reliable, though if bushwhacking off an established trail, I prefer having the additional detail provided by the U.S.G.S. maps.

I also recommend purchasing a Routt National Forest map from the Forest Service, 925 Weiss Drive, Steamboat Springs, 80487, across from the Holiday Inn on U.S.40.–970-879-1870. They offer many other helpful free brochures and maps as well. The Forest Service map also provides an index to all the U.S.G.S. maps that cover the whole Routt National Forest area.

If you don't already know how to use a topographical map and a compass, take some time to learn how before you start hiking. Neither is very difficult, and there are numerous good "how to" books in the library, in bookstores, and sites on the Internet that will teach you. Before venturing off on a long hike, practice your newly found skills on easier hikes. Regularly using your topo map and compass is fun, and doing so will give you a good overview of where you're heading, what the terrain is like up ahead, how much further you have to go, the vertical feet gain and loss, forests and vegetation, and what side trips you might like to make. If you become lost, your map and compass will help you become correctly oriented. Teach these skills to your children and other hiking companions, making a game out of matching up the terrain with what's on the map. If you can, learn how to use a GPS and take one along.

Caution: *Trailheads sometimes get moved, signs fall down or disappear, trails get re-routed or disappear under snowpiles, or fade away in wet meadows, cairns get knocked over, and unexpected events like blowdowns or forest fires can destroy trails altogether.*

The trails covered in this book were last hiked in the summers of 2000 and 2001, and my descriptions are as accurate and up-to-date as they can be at this printing. But passing time, man-made changes and nature always take a toll on guidebooks. So, if you have any doubts, especially when planning a backpack trip, please call the Forest Service first and check for any changes or updates. Steamboat: 970-879-1870; Yampa: 970-638-4516; Walden: 970-723-8204.

The thing to remember when traveling is that the trail is the thing, not the end of the trail. Travel too fast and you miss all you are traveling for.~ Louis L'Amour.

Hiking with Children

Each hike in this book has a "With Children" paragraph suggesting how appropriate that hike may or may not be for youngsters. When I first began hiking around Steamboat Springs, our children were very young. There was no hiking guide for the area, nor had there ever been one. So our children and we had to learn, sometimes the hard way, if any given hike was a good one for kids. When I wrote the first hiking guidebook for the area in 1991, my offspring became the guinea pigs for that endeavor. But now, as young adults, they still love hiking, so my "Mommy's forced marches," as they once called them, couldn't have been too awful!

If you hike with your own children, be certain to make a stop at Yampatika Nature Store, 10th and Lincoln. They are filled-to-the-gills with marvelous naturalist books and toys for children, which will enhance your time with them on the trails. Off the Beaten Path Bookstore, 7th and Lincoln, also carries good nature books.

Even when just day hiking at high altitudes with young children–ages toddler to ten–you'll need to carry much more weight than usual, being especially prepared for any and all emergencies by carrying extra food, water, a very thorough first aid kit, warm clothes and a complete emergency survival kit. Small children need to be kept warm and dry. If they fall into a stream or get wet from rain, they'll have little tolerance for being cold. You'll find it difficult to make them keep moving if they're cold, exhausted or hungry.

Little hikers often bound up a mountainside, full of energy and enthusiasm, only to be totally exhausted halfway back down on the return. Be prepared to carry them some or all of the way back! If they become wet, cold or hungry, the situation can become serious. Always set your mileage goals with this in mind. Remember, you don't always have to reach the lake to have a good hike. Often, just playing along a creek half way up to that lake will provide a wonderful experience for small children. Singing songs along the way can help keep children moving right along. If you have only one child, let them bring a friend along. Encourage games of imagination that work into the context of your hike.

Little ones like to stop and smell the roses along the way, collect things, and investigate what's on the trail, asking a thousand questions as they go. Encourage their curiosity and slow down to enjoy their pace. As they get older and stronger and attain more hiking experience, you'll find them eventually able to meet, and then exceed, your hiking goals.

As a rule of thumb, two-to-four-year-olds can hike one-half to 2-miles on their own, stopping every 10 to 15 minutes to rest. Ages 5 to 7, children can hike over easy terrain for about one to three hours every day, covering three to four miles, resting every half-hour to 45-minutes. Children 8 to 9 can generally hike a full day at an easy pace, covering about 6 to 7 miles over variable terrain.

Dehydration has a way of sneaking up on everyone, especially on hot, longer hikes. Make certain you take more than enough water, or a good filter if there will be water sources along the way. Children need lots to drink on hikes, but they don't always realize it. Insist that they stop to take drinks along the way, even if they say they aren't thirsty. If they don't drink enough, they'll soon be complaining of headaches, weakness and nausea.

Put rain gear on children as soon as the skies threaten rain. Don't wait until their clothes are wet before digging out the gear. It's easy enough to take it all off if the clouds don't open up. Take extra wool socks for small, wet feet. Rain jackets and pants protect children better than ponchos. If you're planning to do much hiking with children, matching rain jacket and waterproof pants are well worth the investment. REI carries reasonably priced ones, which can double for use on rainy days at the school bus stop. Rainproof boots will keep little feet warm and dry and are well worth bringing along. Duck boots work especially well.

A child shouldn't carry more than 20% of their body weight in a daypack.Even on overcast days, don't forget to have children wear hats and use sunscreen, especially on noses, ears and necks. Have them wear T-shirts which cover their shoulders well, and get them to use lip balm often to prevent chapped lips. If the area is buggy, apply bug repellant on children before they get bites. Have them wear sunglasses on sunny days.

Children often get slivers, so keep a tweezers in your first aid kit. Carry Jr. Tylenol tabs, as well, for all sorts of junior aches and pains. Benedryl tabs are useful if children react badly to bug bites or stings, or become allergic to various plants.

Children should be taught to stay on the trail and within your eyesight. Have a child wear a whistle around their neck, and teach them to blow it three times if they become lost. Tell them you will answer them with two whistles to let them know that you hear them. Teach them to hug-a-tree and wait for you to come find them. Let them carry an emergency blanket in their pack and a flashlight. Don't try to cross fast-flowing streams with small children unless there are at least two adults along, with the adult who carries the child wearing protective water crossing shoes on their feet. If children do somehow get wet and cold, stop immediately and warm them up–one way or another–before moving on. This may entail getting dry clothes and wool hats and gloves onto them, and even stopping to make a fire for warm drinks. Children can become hypothermic very quickly. They also generally don't tolerate pain, cold, hunger or exhaustion as well as adults do. They're used to being taken care of and can psychologically and physically fall apart if they become too stressed in any of these areas. Anticipate their abilities, their special needs and any possible consequences or emergencies, and be well prepared for them. Then all concerned will always have a wonderful and safe hiking experience.

Suggested day hike and camp activities to do with children include: sketching – fishing – fish counting or "watching" in the clear streams and lakes – collecting "specimens," like beaver chips from tree stumps, seeds, pine cones, etc.; (bring plastic containers or baggies to collect them in) – making a young naturalist notebook, using books from Yampatika (10th and Lincoln) or from the library – observing things through a magnifying glass – identifying birds, trees or wildflowers – studying life in and around a beaver pond – learning map and compass skills – junior photography: give them a disposable camera – pressing wildflowers, far away from trails where there are billions.

When backpacking, children love evening campfires, so bring popcorn, oil, salt, pot holder and the makings of S'mores for treats. Also compile and bring along song sheets with words to their favorite camp songs, as well as little flashlights for reading them. Other fun lightweight camping items include: a backpacker guitar, frizzby, backpacker kite (available through most outdoor catalogs), a tennis ball, small travel games, and a pack of playing cards.

Especially when hiking with children, please remember that life is a journey, not a destination.

Hiking with Llamas

If it weren't for my llama friends, Dudley and Sammy, this edition of my hiking book would have only about a third as many hikes in it as it now does. Carrying a heavy pack on my back for overnight trips is no longer an option for me. After a certain age, it seems that hips, backs and knees often give out. You may notice that, in general, the backpacking population includes very few middle-aged people. But luckily for me, about the time I began to physically fall apart, my friends, John and Mary Ann Duffey, gave me two wonderful woolly llama friends who now carry all the things I used to carry on my own back, and more. With Dudley and Sammy's help, I am able to visit and explore the wilderness beyond a day hike range. The llamas also are wonderful company. They are intelligent, curious, hard working, humorous and a total delight to be around. As long as my legs and lungs remain in good shape, with my llamas, I can continue to go almost anywhere in the wilderness and remain for longer periods of time. And best of all, I can even take along my Baby Taylor guitar!

Patient, gentle and sure-footed on rocky trails, llamas make perfect pack animals. They aren't for carrying people, though they will happily carry small children or about seventy pounds of your hiking and camping gear. Since like deer and elk they eat grasses and leaves, llamas don't need to carry their own food. Their toughened, leathery soles allow them to hike very quietly along with you without grinding the trails into dust, as do pack horses and mules. A U.S. Forest Service study showed that llamas have less of an impact on a trail than do people, and far less than the heavier horseshoed pack animals. Except for their occasional and delightful hum-

Llama Trekking ~ Paige McGrath '97
www.llamalife.com

ming noises, you'll hardly know there's a 350-pound animal hiking right behind you.

Even pre-schoolers can be quickly taught how to lead these gentle, sociable creatures. Although they do occasionally spit at each other when angry, jealous or threatened, well-trained llamas are taught not to spit at humans. I can honestly say that my two good-natured buddies have never spit on me, or even at any other humans, as far as I know.

In 2000 - 2003, Dudley and Sammy and I were featured thirty-five times on the Discovery Network's Animal Planet channel. During three long days of filming for the program, "the boys" co-operated beautifully for the entire time, greatly impressing the film crew.

For a more detailed, fun look at Dudley and Sammy's life, please read my children's book, *Stop Spitting At Your Brother! Life Lessons of a Rocky Mountain Llama*, available in Steamboat at Off the Beaten Path Bookstore, Yampatika, and at the Clark Store, as well as from every major retail or on-line bookstore in the country. The book delights all ages, since it's a funny look at life as seen through the eyes of Dudley the Llama. It also teaches children lessons about caring and tolerance.

I've also recorded a children's album called, "Songs for Llama Lovers ~ Young & Old," which was nominated in 1999 for a WAMMIE award, "Best Children's Recording, 1999." Both the book and CD are also available from my website: www.llamalady.com, as well. In Steamboat, the CD is available at Off the Beaten Path Bookstore, Yampatika and the Clark Store.

In the Steamboat area, the Pyramid Llama Ranch leases and sells trained llamas, and offers guided llama treks into the Flat Tops Wilderness Area: 970-276-3348. For lists of other breeders and more information about packing with llamas, visit the Rocky Mountain Llama Association: http://www.rmla.com/.

To learn more about llamas in general, besides my own website, please visit these two excellent websites: www.llamalife.com and www.llamapaedia.com.

Update: *In 2003, we welcomed Isaiah and Jeremiah to our llama family (see top of page 298).*

Yampatika Notes

__Karen Vail__, who grew up in the Yampa Valley, wrote the Yampatika Notes in this guidebook. Karen is respected in the area for her extensive naturalist knowledge, and her summertime "Flower Walks" are legendary. The organization she works with, __Yampatika__, is a not-for-profit organization dedicated to providing an understanding of the natural and cultural resources of Northwest Colorado and a sense of place through education, communication, participation and example. The organization represents a collaboration of organizations supporting the use, preservation, conservation and ecology of the natural and cultural resources of Northwestern Colorado. Through memberships, donation, grants, special events and its retail outlet, Yampatika is able to provide environment education and interpretive programs for children and adults, as well as sponsor a variety of volunteer programs and projects. Members receive a newsletter and merchandise and program fee discounts. For complete details on their excellent Partners in Interpretation program and schedule, call 970-879-8140.

Biking the Hikes

Although this book is for hikers, since many trails are multi-use trails, mountain bikers may find my directions to the trailheads and my trail descriptions very useful. I have not personally ridden on many mountain bike trails, so I'm simply listing the 55 hikes in this book which allow biking, and as one who hikes these trails and doesn't bike them, I'm giving my best 'guesstimate' on how difficult it might be to ride a bike on a given trail. But remember, this is only a hiker's guess. If you're planning to ride on any of the more advanced trails, please check with people in the know – either the Forest Service or one of the area bike shops – before heading out on that trail. They can tell you better than I can. Also, please read and observe all the backcountry safety information presented in this book.

For more expert information on area biking, I suggest you purchase a copy of Tom Litteral's *Mountain Biking in the High Country of Steamboat Springs* or Tom Barnhart's *Single Tracks*. Both books are available at Off the Beaten Path Bookstore, Ski Haus and Sore Saddle Cyclery.

Please remember that current etiquette dictates that bikers and hikers both yield to horses, and bikers yield to hikers. If you come upon a horse party, please get off and walk your bike slowly past the horses, on the lower side of the trail. Llamas are seldom skittish like horses, but it's also not often easy to move them quickly out of the way of an out-of-control biker. So please ride safely, and don't barrel downhill on multi-use trails, especially on hike [11].

Ratings:

W = Official Wilderness Areas; no biking allowed.
Unofficial ratings:1 = easy; 2 = moderate; 3 = advanced.
Please ask for more specific information at Forest Service or area bike shops.

Hike Number:

1. *The Yampa Core Trail ~ 1*
2. *Seven Springs Tour of Steamboat Springs ~1*
3. *Historic Walking Tour of Steamboat Springs ~ 1*
4. *Fish Creek Falls – Parking area to overlook ~ No bikes.*
5. *Fish Creek Falls – Parking area to Lower Falls ~ Walk bike to trailhead.*

6a. *Fish Creek Falls-1102 – Parking area to Upper Falls ~ 3 from the trailhead.*
6b. *Fish Creek Falls-1102 – Parking area to Long Lake ~ 3 from the trailhead.*

7. *The Uranium Mine ~ 3 (very rocky)*
8. *Howelsen Hill ~ 2-3 (pick up a brochure with map at the base area)*
9. *Emerald Mountain Quarry ~ 2-3*
10. *Spring Creek Children's Hike (from High school to gazebo) ~ 1*
11. *Spring Creek to Dry Lake Campground ~ 2*
12. *Mt. Werner-Storm Peak ~ with ticket or pass, can ride gondola up; 3 up; 1 down on a bike.*
13. *Bear Creek Trail-1206 ~ 2-3*
14. *Mad Creek–Swamp Park Trail-1100 ~ easy up to Wilderness boundary*
15. *Saddle Trail-1140 ~ 1*
16. *Red Dirt Trail-1171 ~ 2-3 up to Wilderness boundary*
17. *Strawberry Park Hot Springs Tail-1169 ~ 1-2 down; 2-3 up.*
18. *Soda Creek Trail ~ Restricted*

19. Jonah Lake ~ W
20. Grizzly Lake-1101 ~ 1
21. Lake Dinosaur ~ (probably too wet for bikes)
22. Fish Creek Reservoir to Long Lake ~ 1
23. Fish Creek Reservoir to Round and Percy Lakes-1102 & 1134 ~ 1-2

24.-35. Hikes 24 through 35 are all in the Wilderness Area ~ no biking.

36. Harrison Creek Fisherman Trail ~ 2
37. Rabbit Ears Peak ~ 2-3
38. Six Fishing Lakes: Fishhook, Lost, Elmo, Round, Percy, Long-1101 ~ 1
39. Windy ridge Indian Quarry ~ 1 (leave bike at base area of quarry)
40. Routt Divide Trail-1108 ~ 1-3 (have to carry bike through steep boulder field, if using whole trail)
41. Walton Peak ~ 1-2
42. Sarvis (Service) Creek Trail-1105 ~ W
43. Silver Creek Trail-1106 ~ W

44a. Stagecoach Reservoir-Elk Run ~ 1

44b. Stagecoach Wetlands Angler's Trail ~ No bikes.

45. Morrison Divide Trail-1174 ~ 3
46. Tepee Creek Trail-1173 ~1-2
47. Black Mountain Creek Trail-1117 ~ W
48. Four Fun Lakes: Spring, Camel, Crater & Sand-1123 ~ 1-2
49. Bunker Basin Trail-1109 ~ 1-2
50. Allen Basin Trail-1181 ~ 1
51. Harper Reservoir ~ 1
52. Heart Lake-1110 ~ 2
53. Mandell Lakes and Pass-1121 ~ W
54. Smith Lake-1194 ~ 1 (Wilderness beyond Lake)

55.-58. Hikes 55 through 58 are all in the Flat Tops Wilderness Area ~ no biking.

59. California Park to Sugar Loaf Mountain-1114 ~ 1-2
60. Pearl Lake ~ too difficult to ride around lake
61. Steamboat Lake – Tombstone Nature Trail ~ No bikes.
62. Steamboat Lake – Willow Creek to Marina ~ 1
63. Prospector Trail-1156 ~ 3
64. Prospector Extension ~ Northwest ~ 1
65. Prospector Extension ~ East ~ 1
66. Hahn's Peak Lake Trail-1191 ~ 1
67. Hahn's Peak Summit-1158 - last section too rocky for bikes.
68. Manzanares Trail-1204 ~ 3
69. Hare Trail-1199 ~ 2
70. Encampment River Loop-1153 & 1152 ~ W
71. Nipple Peak Trail-1147 ~ 3
72. Bowhunter's Trail-496.1A ~ 3
73. Sand Mountain-1175 ~ 1-2 - up to official trailhead
74. Saddle Mountain View Trail ~ 1-2
75. Greenville Mine Road ~ 1
76. Coulton Creek Trail-1188 ~ 3
77. Hinman Lake and View-1177 ~ 2
78. Hinman Creek Fisherman Trail ~ 1
79. North Fork of the Elk River – eastern side of river-1101 ~ 1-2
80. North Fork of the Elk River – western side of river ~ 1-2
83. South Fork of the Elk River~1101 & 1100-1A ~ 1-2
94. Percy, Round and Longs Lakes-1134 (east to west) ~ 2

Hikes 81 and 82, and hikes 95 through 108 are all in the Mt. Zirkel Wilderness ~ no biking.

Fishing Notes

Many years ago when I lived in Aspen, I used to fly fish a bit. Without knowing too much about what I was doing, I still seemed to be able to successfully "match the hatch." Later, when our children were little, I fished with them on backpack trips. But I have not fished since that time. The fishing information I present for each hike was garnered from various different knowledgeable sources.

However, please be aware that, sadly, Whirling Disease, a parasitic infection of trout and salmon – as well as recent reduced capabilities to stock high altitude lakes, streams and ponds – will no doubt continue to negatively affect the overall fishing quality available in the Routt National Forest. To help prevent the spread of Whirling Disease, please follow these precautions: clean all equipment, especially wading boots, with a mild solution of chlorine bleach; wash mud off all fishing equipment that can hold the parasite; drain any equipment which held water, such as boats, coolers, etc.; when fishing different sections of a drainage, begin at the headwaters or upstream and move downstream – not vice versa; it is illegal to transport fish from one body of water to another; don't dispose of fish entrails or byproducts into or next to any body of water or sink; never transport aquatic plants and make sure all equipment is cleared of weeds after every use.

Catch and release fly-fishing techniques are encouraged in this area, especially where there are Colorado River Cutthroat trout. Returning fish alive is not as simple as it sounds. Mishandling can kill them.

- Fish only with flies or lures. Fish caught with bait rarely survive! Nine out of ten caught on flies generally survive.
- Use barbless hooks, or bend down the barbs on your hooks.
- Remove the hook gently. If you can't remove it without harming the fish, cut the line close to the mouth. Eventually, the hook should dissolve itself.
- Leave the fish in the water while you are unhooking it, and use a pair of forceps or a needle nose pliers to reduce the risk of harm.
- Land the fish as quickly as possible. This is less tiring for the fish.
- Handle the fish as little as possible. Do not squeeze the fish or place your fingers in its gill.
- Release the fish only after its equilibrium is recovered. If necessary, gently hold the fish facing upstream and move it slowly back and forth. Release fish in quiet water.

You can get a wealth of additional information from local fly fishing experts at:

Straightline – 744 Lincoln;
Matt & Bryan's – 730 Lincoln;
Steamboat Fishing Company – 635 Lincoln.

What to take on a Day Hike

Musts:

Day pack, appropriate Trails Illustrated or U.S.G.S. map, a good compass, poly bottles of water, water filter if hike has water sources, top-notch rain gear, first aid kit (see below), emergency survival kit (see section on backcountry safety), insect repellant, sun glasses, visor or brimmed hat, food, toilet paper and trowel, stream-crossing shoes, appropriate warm clothes (see below), wallet or more lightweight baggie (with driver's license, cash, change, AAA card, major credit card, local address and emergency information), drinking cup, watch, sunscreen, lip balm, pocket knife, this guidebook – or Xeroxed copies of appropriate pages – and an extra set of car keys. Show members of the hiking party where you'll hide the extra set of keys outside the car. If you have and know how to use one, a GPS can be a lifesaver.

Optional:

Camera equipment, camcorder, nature books: wildflowers, birds, mushrooms, etc., fishing pole, license and equipment, sketching materials, family dog with leash and small water bowl, if sharing your water.

First Aid Kit:

Moleskin and blister gel pads, aspirin, liquid or chewable Tylenol (if taking small children), band-aids of all sizes, antiseptic ointment, ace bandage, triangular bandage for slings, gauze, tape, steri-pads, safety pins, small scissors, needle, tweezers, eye wash, antihistamine, small bar of soap, burn ointment, salt tablets (enteric coated), Benadryl itch relief spray, anti-acid, ibuprofen (Advil), acetaminophen (Excedrin), necessary prescription medication, and a wilderness first aid guidebook. (See section on backcountry safety, page 8).

Emergency Survival Kit:

See page 8.

Clothing:

If dressed in T-shirt and shorts, in addition, take a long-sleeve shirt, sweater or sweatshirt, down vest or jacket, waterproof windbreaker and good rain gear – coat and pants; wool ski hat and gloves, wind pants or jogging pants, extra pair of wool socks and blaze orange clothing if hiking during hunting season.

Footwear:

Some of the easier hikes in this guide can be made wearing a pair of good athletic shoes, but overall, lightweight hiking boots are always preferred on all hikes. They will help keep your feet warm and dry, provide you with better ankle support and traction, and cushion your feet bottoms. Break in new footwear beforehand. Use moleskin (Dr. Scholl's section of drugstore) or blister gel pads on the first sign of irritation. Don't wait for it to turn into a blister! Carry a small hand towel and old tennis shoes or water shoes with you for stream crossings, especially in the early weeks of summer. When backpacking, the water shoes can double for comfortable camp shoes.

What to add if you're Backpacking

Additional items needed for overnight trips:

Backpack, ground sheet, tent, sleeping bag and foam pad, long underwear, extra socks and underwear, one-gallon collapsible water container, backpack stove and extra fuel, folded-up paper towels, a couple sheets of folded-up aluminum foil, lightweight cooking pots and pans, bowls and plates, utensils (spoons, forks, knives), small spatula, extra waterproof kitchen matches, pot scrubber, meals, snacks, seasonings, camp flashlight and extra batteries, candles, Swiss Army knife, biodegradable soap, toiletries [toothbrush and paste, comb, moisturizer, wash cloth, soap, antibacterial wipes, dental floss, camping mirror], sewing kit, small plastic grocery bags for trash and dirty laundry, extra zip-lock bags for leftovers, fire starters.

The 1997 Blowdown and Subsequent Wildfires

There is a time for everything, and a season for every activity under heaven:
a time to be born and a time to die; a time to plant and a time to uproot;
a time to tear down and a time to build.
~ Ecclesiastes 3:1-3

In the early hours of October 25, 1997, winds in excess of 120 miles per hour blew from the east over the Continental Divide. Over four million trees were flattened in an area five miles wide and thirty miles long in the Routt National Forest. The majority of the blowdown occurred

Aftermath of 1997 Blowdown.

north of Steamboat Springs in the Mount Zirkel Wilderness. Nearly 13,000-acres of spruce and fir trees were blown over, roots and all, or snapped off at the trunk in patches of up to four thousand acres.

The summer after '02 wildfire, Lindsey and Jennifer visit a fire-damaged area, which time and nature will soon begin to heal.

As a result of the ideal habitat created by the Routt Divide Blowdown, spruce beetle populations reached epidemic proportions in 1999. The insect is expected to kill the majority of the mature spruce trees on the forest within a decade, where roughly half the trees are spruce and half fir. Luckily, however, even if the beetles kill all the mature spruce, the fir trees and smaller spruce ~about 8-inches in diameter~ will remain and continue to grow, leaving attractive, functioning forests.

The '97 Blowdown and three subsequent years of drought conditions and bug infestations in formerly healthy trees then set the stage for immense wildfires in the summers of '02 and '03. The huge piles of rotting timber provided ideal fuel for the fires, which closed the forest to hiking for much of those two hot, dry summers.

As of this 2003 printing, area hikers will now see the results of three phenomenon in the Mt. Zirkel Wilderness - blowdown, beetle kill and wildfires. Visitors to the Forest now need to be especially alert and aware of hazards, including stump holes filled with ash, unstable hillsides and snags–trees likely to fall or be easily blown over because of damaged root systems or burnt trunks. Since the fires, rocks and logs once supported by trees and vegetation now have a much greater chance of rolling downhill unexpectedly. As always, campers need to use special care in preventing sparks and campfires from igniting fallen trees, and as always, hikers must be ready to evacuate an area quickly if they smell smoke or spot a fire.

As difficult as it seems to believe, blowdowns, beetle epidemics and wildfires should not be considered ecological disasters, but naturally occurring events that will allow visitors to the forest the opportunity to witness nature's dynamic cycle of disturbances and recovery in action. God willing, in due time, nature will heal and regenerate our beloved forests.

From the rising of the sun unto the going down of the same,
The Lord's name is to be praised. ~ Psalm 113:3

The Core Trail crosses the Yampa River a couple of times.

1. Yampa Core Trail

In the beginning, God created the heavens and the earth
~ Genesis 1:1

Of note: This is a paved, in town, four-mile long, multi-use recreation trail which runs along the meandering, sparkling Yampa River. It begins at West Lincoln Park, along U.S.40, home of Steamboat's huge sculptured elk, "Autumn Majesty," and continues through Old Town to the Walton Creek Road, where it crosses U.S.40 and connects with a more narrowly paved path heading up to the Steamboat Ski Area. The route offers easy fishing access, many wonderful picnic areas beneath cooling, tall cottonwoods, access to a richly overgrown riparian habitat, the Howelsen Hill Ski Area, and the rodeo grounds. Hikers must share this heavily used resource with people on bikes, in-line skaters, and lots of happy K-9's. During mid-summer, unless you're walking in the early morning or later in the day, take along water, sunscreen, hats and sunglasses.

If time allows, be sure to include in your hike a visit to the lovely Yampa River Botanic Park, reached on this route by entering a marked gate, next to Fetcher Park, located between the Emerald Park soccer fields and the Fish Creek Mobile Home Park. This park contains several hundred trees and plants representative of the area's flora, from the Flattops to Buffalo Pass.

Distance: 4-miles each way.

Hiking Time: About 1.75-hours, each way.

Elevation: Trail runs on a very level grade at between 6,700' and 6,800'.

With Children: *This is definitely a family-friendly place; because of occasional inconsiderate "speedsters" on bikes and skates, for safety reasons, you'll want to keep young children and dogs under your control at all times. Take a picnic lunch and stop along the river at a charming gazebo or at one of many picnic tables and benches provided along the way. Engage children in wildflower identification activities in the rich riparian zone or plant life at the botanic garden along the way.*

Fishing: *This route along the Yampa River offers easy public access to some civilized, urban catch-and-release fly fishing; countless pools and eddies provide good habitat for rainbows, browns, whitefish, natives, and even an occasional northern pike.*

Yampatika Notes: *Some of this water in the Yampa Valley began its journey high in the Flat Tops Wilderness to the southwest as snowmelt and springs. Yampa is a Ute word given to a delicious carrot-like plant, highly prized for its small root that tastes like baby carrots. Because the band of Utes summering in the Yampa Valley and surrounding areas used the Yampa extensively, they became known as the Yamparika, or Yampatika, Utes; the "eaters of Yampa." The Yampa River flows into the Green River, then into the Colorado River, and eventually finishes its journey as a mere trickle into the Gulf of California.*

Map: Before beginning this hike, stop in at the Arts Depot off 13th and Lincoln and pick up an "Art Culture Heritage" brochure, which offers a very good map showing the route, as well as the location of delightful works of art you can discover and enjoy along the way. The Depot is located in the old train station, across from the library, near the starting point of this walk.

How to get there: Park in the West Lincoln Park parking area west of the library near 13th and Lincoln. Find the Core Trail by the river and head east.

The Hike: You can enjoy all or any of this route throughout the year, whether you're looking to take just a leisurely stroll or to put yourself through a tougher getting-in-shape workout.

2. Seven Springs Tour of Steamboat Springs

It was You who opened up springs and streams.
~ Psalm 74:15

Of Note: Steamboat Springs takes its name from one of more than 150 thermal mineral hot springs located in the area. The water in these springs is heated many thousands of feet below the city by molten rock, which squeezes up through cracks in the Dakota Formation, heating ground water past the point of boiling and sending it up to the earth's surface. Many years ago, Ute Indians believed that the waters from these mineral springs held medicinal and curative powers, and many of them spent their summers camped in the area.

Legend has it that three French fur trappers in the 1820's came upon one of the springs, which at the time made a loud chugging noise similar to that made by steamboats. And thus came the name, "Steamboat Springs," for an area in the Rocky Mountains that is geographically far, far removed from operational steamboats.

An early-day promotional pamphlet published around 1910 describes the area's hot springs: "...Some mystic power, at the least, has wrought well, for here, and within a few feet of each other, are springs, not only of different temperature, but of different and most delicately mixed mineral constituents. Alkaline, saline-alkaline, iron, sulphur, magnesian in all their various and wonderful combinations are here, besides numerous non-mineral springs delivering water as pure and soft as that from clouds."

This is a hike you can make even in the winter.

An interesting summary of the early and present day history of these springs can be found in reading The Historical Guide to Routt County, available at the library (13th and Lincoln) and also for sale at the Tread of Pioneers Museum, 800 Oak Street, 970-879-2214. Also, a short general history of Steamboat Springs can be found on the internet by logging onto www.steamboat-chamber.com (click onto "Visitor Information" and then "A Brief History of Steamboat Springs.")

Also available at the Tread of Pioneers Museum, as well as from the Steamboat Springs Chamber Information and Visitor's Center 1255 South Lincoln Avenue, (across from McDonald's and Wendy's) P.O. Box 774408, Steamboat Springs, CO 80477, 970-879-0882; is a wonderful free brochure titled, A WALKING TOUR OF THE SPRINGS OF STEAMBOAT – 7 Springs – 2 Miles – 2 Hours. This guide and map will direct you on a delightful tour of seven maintained springs, all within walking distance of each other. It will also describe the history and scientific mineral properties of each spring.

Hiking to these seven springs can also be a marvelous introduction to the city of Steamboat Springs, while at the same time a good way to exercise legs and lungs.

Yampatika Notes: *As you stand at the springs to the west end of town, train your eyes on the valley sides. The bands of rocks running vertically are sediments of limestone and sandstone left thousands of years ago by an inland sea. After this deposition, the land moved and buckled, tilting the layers and creating large faults. These mineral springs were created from such a crack in the earth's crust. Notice how different each spring is in color, odor and temperature. The water pressure in the earth is pushed up through different layers of minerals, which are dissolved and carried up to the springs we now see.*

3. Historical Walking Tour of Steamboat Springs

Architects cannot teach nature anything.
~ Mark Twain

Of Note: This 1.5-mile hike around Steamboat Springs is a perfect way to visit and enjoy thirty historical buildings and sites that will help teach you about the area's rich western history. You first have to stop by the Tread of Pioneers Museum, 800 Oak Street, 970-879-2214, to pick up a free copy of the tour guide, Tread Through Steamboat – A historical walking tour. The brochure contains a condensed history of the city, as well as information about each stop and photographs of the buildings as they looked long ago.

Before heading out on foot, however, to help set the stage for your trek around Steamboat, be certain to first spend some time exploring this wonderful museum. Afterwards, begin your journey around town, and let the guide help you "trace the evolution of Steamboat Springs from a self-sufficient wilderness frontier village and cow town to a farming-ranching-mining community, source of educational opportunities, ski jumping and recreation center and resort town."

A visit to the Tread of Pioneers Museum begins this hike.

View from the Uranium Mine trail, hike 7. of the overview area and the whole Fish Creek Falls and canyon.

4-6a&b. Fish Creek Falls - 1102

4. Parking area trailhead up to overlook view
5. Parking area trailhead down to base of falls
6a. Parking area trailhead up to Upper Falls
6b. Parking area trailhead up to Long Lake

Praise God from Whom All Blessings flow.
Praise Him all creatures here below.
~ Doxology

There are actually four hikes which can be made on the two trails found at this popular trailhead – two easy, short hikes at the beginning – the first on a gentle, paved, interpretive path up to an overlook of the falls, and the second on a gravel path down to the base of the falls, about 0.3 mile, each way. From the base of the falls, the trail continues strenuously uphill through a deeply-cut, high-country canyon to a third and fourth destination – the third being to the glorious Upper Fish Creek Falls, about 2.5 miles past the base, and then the fourth destination being all the way up to Long Lake, yet another 3.5 miles past the Upper Falls. The trip to Long Lake turns the venture into a very long, twelve-mile roundtrip day hike.

Whatever your time and energy, everyone who visits Steamboat Springs during the non-winter months should definitely drive up to see the spectacular Fish Creek Falls, using either of the first two easy routes mentioned above. People who, because of age, disability or health reasons, are unable to walk the steep ten-minute climb down to and then back from the base of the falls, have wheelchair/stroller access on an ADA-access paved path, up to an outstanding overlook of the falls. Either is well worth the effort.

Because of its beauty and close proximity to town, about a 10-15 minute drive, you'll probably have to share your visit to the Falls with large numbers of people. But this impressive destination should not be missed, for the spectacular setting gives everyone a small taste of wilderness. Upper and lower parking areas require a fee. The upper lot offers handicap parking, a toilet, drinking water and a picnic area, as well as access to the four hikes described herein.

Before making any of these hikes, pick up an interpretive trail guide at the kiosk in the upper parking lot. This brochure will teach you much about the area's fascinating history, geology, animal, insect and plant life.

We should be as water, which is lower than all things,
yet stronger than the rocks.
~ Oglala Sioux Proverb

Fish Creek Falls itself is an impressive torrent of foaming water, plunging and crashing down 283 feet over a hanging-valley cliff, through a narrow channel carved into hard gneiss and schist rock, down to a boulder-strewn pool in the canyon creek below. The creek and falls were named "fish creek" because of the abundance of whitefish and brook trout in the waters, which were readily caught and salted for winter eating by early Steamboat pioneers.

The first hike takes you easily up to an overlook view, above the falls, and the second takes

Campfire Song Before Bed

Taps

Day is done
Gone the sun
From the lakes
From the hills
From the sky.
All is well,
Safely rest,
God is nigh.

Fading light,
Dims the sight
And a star
Gems the sky,
Gleaming bright.
From afar
Drawing nigh,
Falls the night.

Thanks and praise
For our days,
Neath the sun,
Neath the stars,
Neath the sky.
As we go,
This we know,
God is nigh.

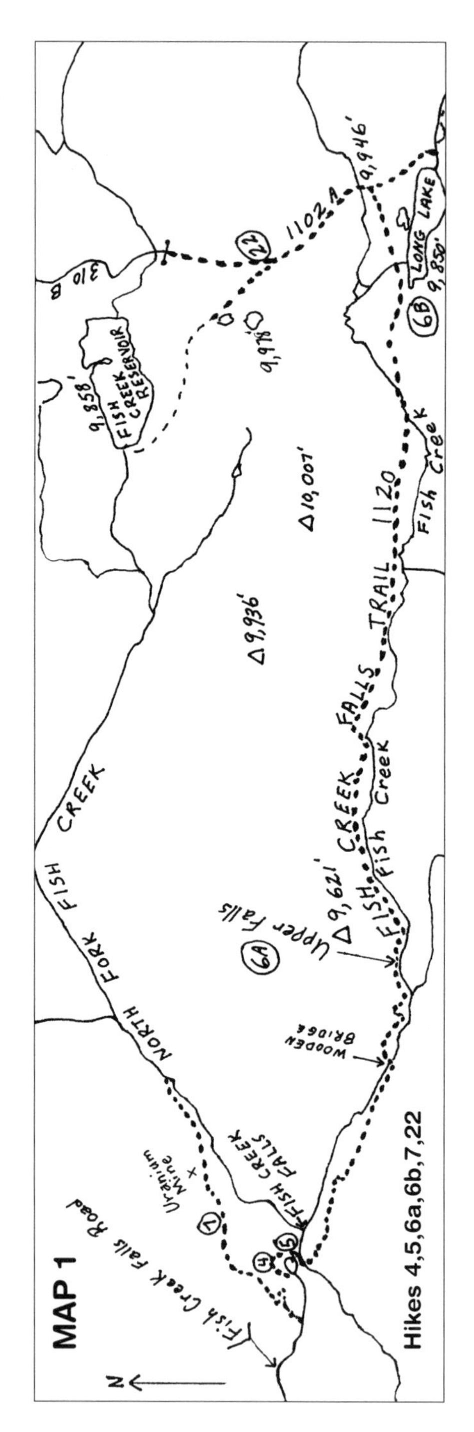

Children, moms and K-9's enjoy playing on the rocks at Fish Creek.

you down – losing about 100 feet in altitude – to the base of the falls, to a scenic, historic footbridge – a marvelous place from which to view and photograph the roaring, thundering falls above. Early in the season, you may be sprayed with a fine, refreshing mist of water. Don't forget to take your camera.

If you're planning to hike past the bridge up to the second falls, or even further on to Long Lake, be certain to take enough drinking water and wear appropriate hiking shoes with good ankle support and sole traction. Bug repellant, sunscreen, hats and rain gear should be carried, as well. For some reason, many people hiking past the base bridge go ill-prepared for the strenuous hike ahead of them, perhaps because their decision to continue on is made impulsively while they are at the base of the falls, rather than planned out ahead of time. Were it allowed, I've often mused that a person could get rich selling maps and cold lemonade to all the thirsty, overheated, sandal-wearing people struggling up this trail, who have with them neither drinking water nor a clue as to where they are really headed!

How to get there: Driving east on Lincoln (U.S. 40), turn left onto 3rd, the intersection just before the big Steamboat Recreation Center swimming pool on the left. Go one block north, and then turn right, east, onto Fish Creek Falls Road. (Don't be confused – the road to the left is called Oak Street, and to the right, Fish Creek Falls Road). Follow this road for 3.2 miles until its dead-end, driving past the lower parking lot on the left, up to the upper lot. If the upper lot is full, return to the lower lot, park and make the short quarter-mile hike up to the upper lot. Both require paying a parking fee. Locals should consider purchasing a Forest Service "season pass," good for unlimited visits. The trailheads for the two trails are well marked at the northwest end of the upper parking lot.

Distance:

4. Trailhead to overlook viewpoint: approximately 0.5 mile, each way.
5. Trailhead to base of Fish Creek Falls: approximately 0.3 mile, each way.
6a. Trailhead to Upper Fish Creek Falls: approximately 2.5 miles, each way.
6b. Trailhead to Long Lake: approximately 6 miles, each way.

Hiking Time:

4. About 15 minutes, each way (easy).
5. About 10 minutes down, a bit longer on the strenuous uphill return.
6a. About 1.5 hours, each way (strenuous, but well worth the effort).
6b. About 3.5 hours, each way (long and strenuous day hike).

Elevation: Trailhead: 7,440'; Base of Fish Creek Falls: 7,340'; Upper Fish Creek Falls: 9,000'; Long Lake: 9,880'

With Children:

4. *Get an interpretive brochure at the trailhead, and use it to teach children about the area's history, geology, animal and plant life along this easy, paved route. Be sure to grab on to little hands before the overlook is approached!*

5. *This hike is a must for kids of all ages! Keep little ones closely supervised along the trail. It is wide and well maintained, but there is a dangerous drop off down to the creek along much of the route. Below the bridge at the base of the falls, children and K-9's will enjoy spending time playing in the boulder-strewn creek – take a picnic lunch and plan to stay a while.*

6a. *In-shape children should be able to make this hike to the Upper Falls, but during summer months, leave early in the day to avoid the mid-day heat, which can quickly wilt even strong young hikers. Make certain you take enough water and remind little ones to take frequent drinks.*

6b. *The hike all the way to Long Lake, a vertical gain of approximately 2440' in about six miles, should be attempted only by older, in-shape children. Even for most adults, this is a very long hike to make in a day.*

Fishing: *later in season, in calmer waters, the creek below the base bridge is good for brook trout.*

The Hike:

4. See "With Children" above.
5. See "With Children" above.

6a. From the scenic footbridge at the base of the falls, the trail now continues a steep climb south and then eastward, along the Fish Creek drainage and up the southern flank of a canyon, traveling through several different ecosystems, including delightful lush groves of aspens and mixes of scrub oak, mountain ash, junipers, Douglas firs and Rocky Mountain maples, which cool and shade hikers much of the way. Depending on the time of the season, expect to discover many varieties of moss and wildflowers along this trail.

A visit to Fish Creek Falls is a "must" for Steamboat visitors.

The Upper Falls is a very special place to visit.

Gradually rising to a level high above the creek, the valley narrows, framed in by giant glacier-carved cliffs of gneiss on either side. Geologists call the rocks along this trail "Colorado's Basement," and they represent some of the oldest rocks to be found in the state.

After about an hour of hiking, many people end the first half of their hike or stop for a rest at a wooden bridge, which crosses the creek. Sit on the large, smooth boulders and enjoy watching the cascading water. But unless you're out of energy, don't quit here. Continue across the bridge and climb through aspens and willows, enjoying the wild roses, bedstraw, sage, juniper and cow parsnip on both sides, eventually coming to a very steep, rocky section where you'll have an excellent view of the beautiful, rugged canyon ahead and the fast-flowing water down far below you.

The trail now turns right and traverses up along the base of a gigantic glacier-carved rock wall, at the top of which you'll be on a plateau, where you'll have wonderful, broad views of the valley below. But don't take all your photos here. A few minutes further, you'll enjoy great picture opportunities of the whole city of Steamboat Springs down below. After a little more switchback climbing up over smooth slabs of bedrock, arrive suddenly at the thundering Upper Falls – you'll no doubt hear it just before you actually see it. A short side path off the main trail to the right takes you over closer to the falls. If you can, plan to spend a little time at this marvelous place – one of my personal favorites.

The upper falls is actually part of a second canyon, and it was created during the Ice Age by the coming together of a smaller, tributary glacier intersecting with a larger, lower down, more permanent glacier. When you sit on some of the highly-polished rocks along this trail, think about how they were deposited and smoothed between 2 million and ten-thousand years ago by rock and grit-filled Ice Age glaciers, which crept slowly downhill from the high peaks above, polishing and cutting their way down the two connecting canyons.

6b. To continue on to Long Lake from the Upper Falls, return to the main trail, turn right and gain altitude up a series of switchbacks. The stream closely parallels the trail, and there will be many smooth, large rocks on which to picnic or sunbathe close to the water. The trail pulls away from the creek and then returns to it a number of times, and you'll get to view many pretty mini-waterfalls for quite some distance. Upon reaching the head of the canyon, the trail will begin to level off for easier hiking through a wide-open, U-shaped valley of alternating lush meadows and woods. The creek itself meanders calmly through willow thickets and marshy areas, and you'll be able to watch brook trout quickly shooting about in the clear pools of water.

About one-half mile before Long Lake, you'll have to cross a large stream. In the early summer weeks, it's best to have a pair of water-crossing shoes for the crossing. Later on in the sum-

Stop to take some family photos on the way up to Long Lake.

mer, you should be able to jump across on the rocks. Continue straight ahead, past the marked intersection with trail 1022, the Mountain View Trail. This trail brings mountain bikers from the Mt. Werner ski area to Long Lake.

On the final stretch, hike through a sub-alpine forest and arrive at the northwestern shore of Long Lake. Two trails on the other end of this lake take a hiker to various other destinations, one to Fish Creek Reservoir, hike [22], and the other to a series of wonderful little lakes – Round, Percy, [23] Little Lost, Elmo, Lost, Fishhook and finally, back to the Base Camp trailhead near the top of Rabbit Ears Pass, hike [38].

Long Lake was man-made in the early 1900's for the purpose of storing water at the headwaters of Fish Creek. Although it is indeed a "long," narrow lake, it was actually named after an early-day prospector whose last name was "Long." Imagine the confusion if his last name had been "Short!"

Yampatika Notes:

5. *Diversity is nature's answer to success. From the upper parking lot, look up the canyon. Notice on the left that the canyon slope is a general silver color, with sparse and short vegetation. On the right canyon slope, you'll see tall conifers, lush and green. Because we are in the Northern Hemisphere, the sun tends to be in the southern horizon as it cruises across the sky. So it will shine more intensely on south-facing slopes, to the left, creating a hot, dry and rocky environment. The north-facing slopes, to the right, are moist, cool and rich. Plants have adapted well to these two extremes.*

6a. *These canyons were created in a very different time, our last Ice Age, called the Pinedale Glaciation, beginning 30-40,000 years ago and ending approximately 12,000 years ago. In the deep canyon of the North Fork of Fish Creek that enters to the left, envision a glacier almost covering the tops of the ridges surrounding you. A much smaller glacier, coming in from the main fork, encountered this deep glacier where the Falls are now.*

What this left was, in essence, a hanging valley: a smaller, shallower valley entering a large, deep valley and leaving a cliff and a waterfall.

6b. *After successfully managing the uphill switchbacks, pause at a flat, narrow section before the second bridge and look across the valley. Pick out the polished, smoothened rock, facing up-canyon, which has been abraded by the descending glacier. Notice on the down canyon side of these outcroppings the abrupt cavities and breaks. This is from plucking by the glacier, pulling large chunks of rock away as the ice passed over the outcropping.*

7. The Uranium Mine hike

The stream uncrossed, the promise still untried,
the metal sleeping in the mountainside.
~ Stephen Vincent Benet

Helen, Dudley, Sammy and Sam follow the old rails to the mine opening.

Of Note: This is a fun, close in hike, on a rocky old jeep road, now closed to vehicles, which will reward you with a spectacular bird's-eye-view of Fish Creek Falls and its canyon valley. Take your camera along.

The road also leads to an interesting, old, abandoned uranium mine, and then down to the north fork of Fish Creek. It's a bit of a steep climb – gaining approximately 800 feet in elevation in about a mile and a half of hiking, and you should definitely wear hiking boots with good ankle support and lug soles, since feet tend to slip on the loose gravel, especially on the down return. It's best to hike this trail in the early part of the day, before it gets too hot. And even though it's a relatively short hike, take water, sunscreen and bug repellant.

On one early June trip up here, I was treated to the aerial antics of about six eagles, which appear to have nests on the boulders high up to the left, as you are hiking up. And the cool, lush woods abound with the delightful sounds and sights of many bird species, making this is a very good hike for birders.

Distance: Approximately 1.5 miles, each way.

Hiking Time: About 45 minutes up, 35 minutes down.

Elevation: 7,200' at trailhead; 8,000' at uranium mine.

Map: Trails Illustrated 118. Also see map 1, hike 4.

With Children: *Because it's a fairly short 1.5-mile hike, in-shape children of all ages can make and enjoy this trip. However, little ones will probably need a helping hand on the trip back down, since some sections will be on slippery gravel. Especially with kids, take water and hike this one in the cooler part of a day. Fun rest stops can be found in the delightful, shaded woods along the way, as well as at the north fork of Fish Creek at trail's end.*

Yampatika Notes: *This mine was named after Ralph Zuschlag, who was instrumental in putting it in. During WWII, uranium and other metals were in high demand. This small mine produced only trace amounts of uranium. The joke during the time was that, because of mine tailings placed near the edge of the canyon, glowing fish could be caught in Fish Creek.*

How to get there: Driving east on Lincoln (U.S. 40), turn left onto 3rd, the intersection just before the big Steamboat Recreation Center swimming pool on the left. Drive one block north, and then turn right, east, onto Fish Creek Falls Road. Follow this road for about 3 miles, until reaching the lower parking area for Fish Creek Falls, on the left. Parking requires a fee. If you somehow end up at the upper parking area, just drive about a quarter-mile back down to the lower lot, now on the right, and park. From the lower lot, walk up the sidewalk for 0.1 mile and look for the trail on the left, next to a very big rock and a sign, "No Motor Vehicles."

The Hike: The trail begins on a series of steep switchbacks, and after just ten minutes, you'll hear and then see the spectacular Fish Creek Falls down far below, to the right. You'll also look down on the overview area (see hike [4]). At this point, you will be at least twice as high above the falls as you would be standing at this observation area down below you. To your right, you'll also have a superb view of the ski runs on Mt. Werner and the Flat Top Mountains. Continue to enjoy these views for the next couple switchbacks, so stop and take some photos.

After checking out the mine, continue on the trail for just a few more minutes to end the first half of the hike down at the fast-flowing north fork of the Fish Creek – a good place to eat lunch. Tighten your bootlaces before heading back down on the loose, gravely trail.

8. Howelsen Hill

Great things are done when men and mountains meet;
This is not done by jostling in the street.
~ William Blake

Of Note: Howelsen Hill is Steamboat's oldest city park, offering an array of recreational activities, both in summer and in winter, as well as easy access to the Yampa Core Trail and the Alpine Slide. A colorful, illustrated summer brochure can be picked up at the parking-area kiosk, near the Tow House. This brochure describes in greater detail the history of the ski hill and offers a detailed map for the many biking, horseback and hiking trails which travel up the ski hill and then continue up Emerald Mountain, above Howelsen Hill. This brochure is also available at the city's Department of Parks and Recreation office on Howelsen Parkway, just past the ice skating arena.

You can make this hike without having to leave downtown Steamboat Springs. The hill itself is the oldest continuing ski area in Colorado, first opened in 1915. The area has sent more skiers to international competition than any other area in North America. Howelsen Hill was named after Carl Howelsen, an early-day Norwegian ski champion who lived in the Steamboat area for nine years in the early 1900's and helped to establish Steamboat as "Ski Town USA."

There is one official hiking trail up to the top of the hill, but you can use the map to plan any number of routes varying in length and difficulty. If time and energy permit, you can also continue from there up to the top of Emerald Mountain for a bigger challenge and an even better view of the city and valley below. Take your camera!

Distance: About 0.75 mile via the hiking trail; about 2.5 miles to the top of Emerald Mountain.

Hiking Time: About 20 minutes up to the top of the jump area, via the hiking trail; about 2 hours to the top of Emerald Mountain.

Elevation: Base: 6,696'; top of hill: 7,136'; Emerald Mountain: 8,252'.

Looking down the ski jump.

With Children: *The trip to the top of the hill makes a short, fun hike for all but the very youngest child, who would need quite a bit of help on the first steep sections. Children endure no long car ride to get to the trailhead, and families can enjoy the views and have a picnic near the top of the ski jump and wonder why anyone would ever want to fly off something like that on skis! Especially with children, remember to take drinking water, and try to hike it in the cooler part of the day.*

Yampatika Notes: *For such a small ridge of land, this area is one of the most diverse in the valley. Of special interest, look for very large Gambel Oak on the lower slopes. This gnarled tree is our only native oak to the area, and it produces the typical, albeit small, acorn. Also, look for Rocky Mountain Maple, which is very large in this area. These maples are actually shrubs, not trees, and they have the typical maple leaf with a red petiole, turn yellow in the fall, and produce the fun "helicopter seeds" known as samara.*

Map: Summer Trail Map – Howelsen Hill Park (see 'Of Note' above)

How to get there: Driving or walking west on Lincoln (U.S. 40), turn left onto 5th Street, cross the bridge and the railroad tracks, and turn right onto River Street. When you reach the gazebo, turn left, drive past the ball field on the left and park in the lot near the lodge. Pick up a brochure/map at the kiosk.

The Hike: The official hiking trail begins by walking northwest from the parking lot, between the SSWSC Training Center and the Tow House, onto a road at the base of the jumping area, which turns first south, and then southeast. Climb uphill just past the K60 jump on the left, until the final right-side entrance into the woods – which is marked "hiking trail." Don't turn right until this marked route. The route now changes from a road into a steep dirt path, climbing up into the woods. The hiking trail is not well marked from this point on, so at the first fork, continue to the right. A sign at the top will tell you not to climb on the jump. On your return, make certain you don't try to walk down any marked ski runs, which might look like inviting shortcuts, but may prove too steep for people to safely hike on.

There are many additional routes up Emerald Mountain, which you can discover on the map. However, the most direct hiking route to the very top of the mountain begins under the power line behind the jump area, follows the road a bit to the left, and then heads straight up, alongside the power lines to the top, a gain of about 1,500' from the base. The last couple hundred feet of this direct route travels straight up on slippery gravel, so this is not a good route for children or if you lack shoes with good traction.

9. Emerald Mountain Quarry

Listen to me, you who pursue righteousness and who seek the Lord:
look to the rock from which you were cut and to
the quarry from which you were hewn... ~ *Isaiah 51:1*

Of Note: Here's a quick climb up a road, gaining about 1,000-feet in two miles, which will give you a good workout and take you high above Steamboat Springs, where you'll have an out-

Enjoy a fantastic view of the whole city from the quarry.

standing panoramic view of the whole city below – from Sleeping Giant (Elk Mountain) all the way to Rabbit Ears Pass, and everything in between. And you don't even have to leave town to reach the trailhead. This is a "hot" hike, since it neither follows a stream nor ends up at a lake, like most of the trails in this book do. The trees along the way, first scrub oaks and then aspens, are small and offer next to no shade. So, it's best to hike early in the morning or on a cool day. Many bike riders also use this road to access the myriad of bike trails in the area.

The destination end point of this hike is an old sandstone quarry on the east shoulder of what we now call "Emerald Mountain," although maps still list it as "Quarry Mountain." Some of the very first buildings in Steamboat were made from sandstone from this quarry during the 1900's, including the Routt County Courthouse, the train depot and founding father James Crawford's home. The old dirt road up to the quarry, Blackmer Drive, now closed to general vehicular traffic, was named after an early-day Steamboat doctor.

Take a panoramic camera with you to capture some pretty impressive views.

Distance: About 2 miles, each way.

Hiking Time: About 45 minutes up and 35 minutes down.

Elevation: Gain 1,088' going up.

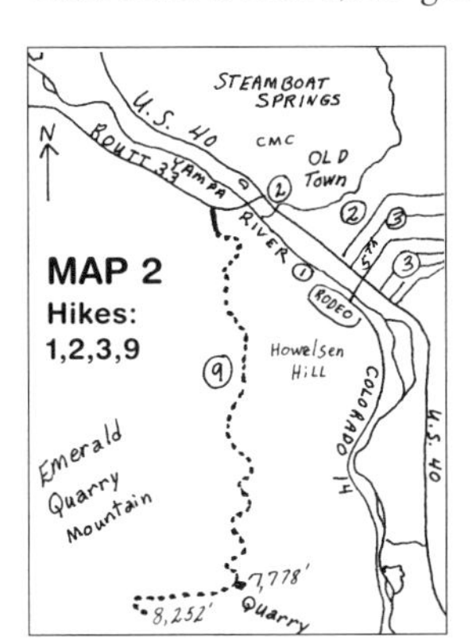

With Children: *Even though this hike isn't a long one, it is steep and hot, and thus not a good hike for most young children. Because it's only a couple miles each way, older, in-shape children should be able to make this climb fairly easily, but they'll complain less if you make it before the hottest time of the day. Take plenty of drinking water.*

Yampatika Notes: *Dakota sandstone was quarried for its fine white quartzitic sandstone, a fine building material. Stones were taken down from the quarry by wagon, which was rather difficult, so enough stone was taken out for several local buildings, and then the quarry was abandoned. In the 1930's, local residents began to call Quarry Mountain "Emerald" Mountain because of its lush green color.*

Map: Trails Illustrated 118. Book map 2.

How to get there: Drive west out of town on U.S. 40 until 13th Street. Turn left onto 13th, drive over the bridge which spans the Yampa River, and make a left onto Gilpin; turn left onto Saratoga Avenue (which becomes Fairview Drive), and make a quick right onto Routt Street. Drive to the trailhead, which you can see straight ahead of you, and park at the trail marker.

The Hike: You'll begin and remain the whole time on a dirt road; ignore the many spur bike trails which seem to go off in every which way. After about 15 minutes, you'll pass on your left the backside of the Howelsen Hill Ski Area (hike [8]) and the Alpine Slide. Along the way, don't be tempted to take what look like shortcuts, for you may end up far away from your destination. Wherever the road splits, always remain right. The views increase in beauty the higher up you go. The aspens grow bigger, and the surrounding groves become lusher, and you'll begin to hear the sounds of birds common to aspen groves. After about 45 minutes, the road dead-ends straight ahead at a rock cliff, although it will also fork uphill to the right and branch out into two gated roads. Walk straight ahead at this point, eastward, toward the view of the Steamboat ski runs, which you'll see directly ahead of you. At the cliff's edge, the quarry will be just up to your right. Be very careful if you do any climbing at the quarry since the dirt and rocks tend to slip, and be especially protective with children and K-9's near the dangerous cliff drop-offs. Take marvelous photos here and note, unless you're new to the area, how much Steamboat has grown in the last ten years!

If you have more time and energy, continue up to the top of Emerald Mountain by following the gated road on the left, just after you leave the quarry to begin your return.

10. Spring Creek Children's Hike

11. Dry Lake Campground via Spring Creek

But blessed is the man who trusts in the Lord, whose confidence is in him.
He will be like a tree planted by the water that sends out its roots by the stream.
It does not fear when heat comes; its leaves are always green.
~ Jeremiah 17:7-8

Of Note 10: Spring Creek Children's Hike: A delightful, easy, short hike for young children can be made along the first section of Spring Creek – first up a jogging/exercise trail and then up a gravel road to a wonderful covered picnic shelter, a city park and reservoir. This is also a good hike to take in the early spring, when snow still blocks the high country trails, for a quick evening walk, or if you'd simply like to study birds, butterflies, or flowers without too much effort. Since it begins right in town, there's no long drive to a trailhead.

On the road section, be especially alert for occasional cars and descending bike riders, some of whom, unfortunately, travel far too fast down this route.

Bring a picnic to eat at the shelter.

The best remedy for those who are afraid, lonely or unhappy is to go outside, somewhere where they can be quiet, alone with the heavens, nature and God. Because only then does one feel that all is as it should be and that God wishes to see people happy, amidst the simple beauty of nature.~ Anne Frank

Of Note 11: Dry Lake Campground via Spring Creek: Hiking along this very heavily-used, longer section of the crystal-clear Spring Creek does not include the exercise trail mentioned above, but rather, it begins on the Spring Creek Road and continues past the picnic shelter, up the Spring Creek drainage, ending where the trail meets the Buffalo Pass Road. This hike crosses over the scenic creek eleven times, but because bridges have been constructed, you shouldn't have to worry about getting wet feet. I recall years past, before the bridges were in place on this trail, when I spent half my time changing into and out of water-crossing shoes.

If you choose to make it simply a one-way up or down hike, you can use two vehicles, leaving one at both ends of this hike.

Because this hike is at a lower altitude than most others in this guide, and because much of the trail is out in the sun, it's better to avoid hiking uphill during the hottest part of a mid-summer day. Remember to take plenty of drinking water or a filter. If you need to re-supply at the top, there's a cold-water pump in unit #4 at the Dry Lake Campground.

In late June and early July, more than eighty different kinds of vibrant wildflowers can be identified along this route, and lovely mixes of ferns, aspens, serviceberry bushes, willows, pines, firs, and spruce provide a lush environment and sometimes, when you're lucky, shaded canopies. Take your wildflower/tree identification books along with you.

It's best not to make this hike alone, since a Forest Service sign cautions hikers about possible mountain lion encounters in the area: "If you encounter one, stop, don't run, don't crouch, stay calm, make yourself look big by holding your arms or a stick up over your head, and if attacked, fight back." But speaking from personal experience, I personally believe that the larger danger to hikers on this trail is the occasional out-of-control mountain biker, who comes barreling down the trail. Unfortunately, although the on-foot hiker supposedly has the right of way, you need to anticipate this risk and be ready to jump out of their way, since they often can't stop in time to miss you!

Distance: 10. About 1.2 miles, each way.
11. About 4.5 miles, each way.

Hiking Time: 10. About a half-hour, each way.
11. Approximately 2.75 hours up and 2.5 hours back down.

Elevation: 10. Gain about 400' from parking area on 2nd Street to picnic shelter.
11. Spring Creek Trailhead: 6,800'; Dry Lake Campground: 8,000'.

With Children: *At this writing, because of the large number of mountain bikers on this trail – some at the upper, more narrow sections, riding far too fast on the descent, I would suggest taking young children only on the first hike, [10]. This lower-down section along Spring Creek, behind the high school and up to the picnic area and reservoir, provides an excellent kid's hike. Take along a picnic lunch, toy boats on strings, fishing poles, wading shoes and a towel for lots of water fun at the sandy beach area on the far side of the upper reservoir. There are toilets and handicap car parking near the shelter.*

Yampatika Notes: *Spring Creek Canyon is an experience for the senses. Feel the coolness on your skin as you enter the narrow canyon. Compare that with the open, sunny road above the reservoir. Close your eyes down in the lower section and listen to the stream trickle by, the songs of the chickadees, yellow warblers, and American dippers, and the rat-a-tat-tat of woodpeckers. Stop to smell the soft pink roses, sweet anise and bedstraw. Feel the smooth bark of red-osier dogwood, and notice its vivid red color. Note the soft down of cottonwood tree catkins, seeds, and the rugged bark of conifers along the way.*

In the spring and fall, look and listen for elk. The Spring Creek drainage is a valuable winter foraging area, and elk will stay into spring and return early in the fall. Look for their large oval, two-toed prints, and their dark brown oval droppings. In the fall, listen for the strange bugle of bull elk, as they are in the fall rut. The canyon is closed in the winter to help protect the elk from undue stress as they forage.

Fishing: *Fun fishing for brook trout in the reservoir.*

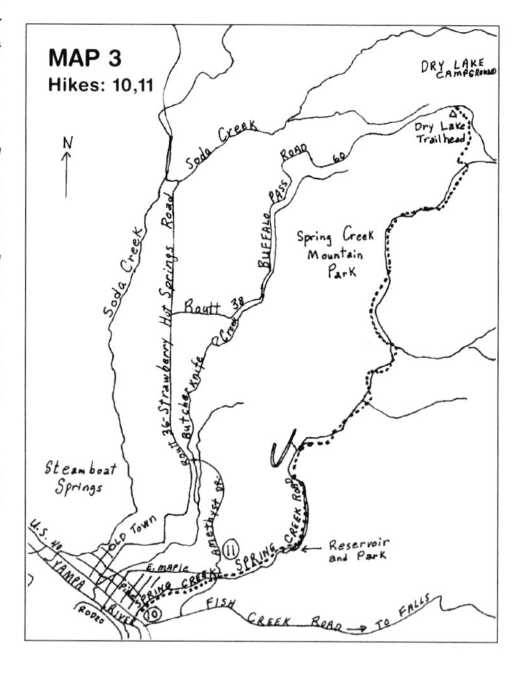

Map: Trails Illustrated 116 and 117.

How to get there:

10. From Lincoln (U.S. 40), turn north onto 3rd Street and drive two blocks. Turn right onto Pine, and go one block. Park just south of the high school, in the parking area at the intersection of 2nd and Pine; cross on the bridge straight ahead, turn left and walk along this jogging/ exercise trail.

11. From town, on Lincoln Ave., turn north onto 3rd, go one block and turn right onto Fish Creek Falls Road. Drive 0.3 mile to Amethyst; turn left onto Amethyst and drive 0.4 mile to the Spring Creek Road/Routt 34, on the right. Park here along the dirt road.

The Hike:

10. Hike along Spring Creek, behind the high school to the left and private homes up above, to the right. After about 10 minutes, you'll meet Amethyst Drive; turn left here, walk a bit to the intersection of Amethyst and Maple; cross Amethyst here, being careful of cars, and now hike for about 0.5 mile up the dirt road, Routt 34, along Spring Creek, until you reach the picnic shelter. Take some time to read the information presented at the pavilion – it teaches all about the area's rich variety of plant and animal life. Explore the trails heading through surrounding woods and around the park and reservoir areas.

11. Follow the road, on up past the picnic shelter and reservoir park. The route now becomes a 4WD road and splits further up; watch for a sign to the right, beginning the official Forest Service trail #1160. The road now becomes a path which climbs moderately at first, and then more steeply towards the end, gaining about 1,200-feet in about 4.5 miles. You'll cross Spring Creek on bridges a total of eleven times before finally arriving at the Dry Lake Campground parking area on Buffalo Pass.

Spring Creek to Dry Lake Campground is a good hike to make early in the season.

12. Mt. Werner - Storm Peak

I listened to the music of the night wind in the pines,
I saw the quiet splendor of a field of columbine.
I skied on crystal pathways to a mountain peak so tall,
and I walked the mighty summits with the One who made it all.
~ Tracey Wickland

Of Note: A hike up and/or down the main ski mountain in Steamboat Springs is an enjoyable and worthwhile one to make. Your efforts will reward you with wonderful views of the Yampa Valley, the ski area and the downtown area. And, with the help of the Silver bullet Gondola, you can make such a hike as easy or challenging as you'd like. If you have cranky knees, it's better to hike up than down this trail. Also, you should not hike down without supportive hiking boots or shoes with good traction, water and rain gear. Lightning storms often come up in the afternoon, so plan to hike early in the day.

Originally named Storm Mountain, Mt. Werner was renamed in 1965 for Buddy Werner, a local native and hero who was one of the top American skiers in the 1950's and 60's. Werner died tragically in an avalanche in Europe at the age of 28. The Bud Werner Memorial Library was named for him, and his story is featured in the library's lobby, 13th and Lincoln.

Near the top of the gondola, the Vista Nature Trail offers a one-mile interpretive trail, which teaches about the area's wildlife habitat and native vegetation. It also provides scenic vistas of the Yampa Valley and the ski area. Picnic tables are provided, and guided interpretive nature walks are scheduled. You can also access the trail near the Thunderhead Lift.

Llamas imitating a gondola on the hike up Mt. Werner.

There are many options for hiking this mountain, and all the information will vary, depending on which option you choose:

1. Hike up to mid-way (2,200' vertical gain) and hike back down.
2. Hike up to mid-way, and then take the gondola down (free going down).
3. Ride the gondola up to mid-way (requires a ticket purchase), and then hike back down the 3-mile-long Thunderhead Hiking Trail. This is what most hikers choose to do. This downhill hikes take about an hour-and-a-half.
4. Take the gondola up to mid-way, then hike to the top of Storm Peak, and then either hike the return all the way to the bottom, or hike to the gondola and take it the rest of the way down.
5. Hike from the base to the top of Storm Peak and all the way back down again – a fun, challenging 3,700' vertical gain, 12-mile roundtrip trek to take after your legs and lungs are ready for it.

Enjoy lunch at the Thunderhead before hiking down Mt. Werner

Distance: There are many options for this hike, and all the hiking information will vary depending on the option you choose.

Hiking Time: This will totally depend on which hike you choose, what shape you're in, and how often you stop to rest or take photos, etc. Making this hike with llamas, as I do from time to time, takes hours, because people stop me a dozen times along the trail to ask me all about my woolly friends.

Elevation: Base area: 6,900'; Top of gondola: 9,100'; Top of Storm Peak: 10,600'.

***With Children**: Many families, even those with young, in-shape children, take the gondola up and hike down. Make certain you're all wearing good hiking shoes and take rain gear, sunscreen, bug repellent, and lots of drinking water for the kids. During season, a restaurant serves lunch at the Thunderhead, and you can re-fill water bottles inside, as well. There's also a short, interpretive nature walk outside the Thunderhead.*

***Of Special Note:** At the publication of this book's first edition, you will begin to see spruce trees dying on the ski mountain, victims of the spruce beetle epidemic caused by the 1997 Blowdown. Expect this condition to worsen over the ensuing years.*

Map: Stop at the base area and pick up a free summer map.

How to get there: Drive east out of town on U.S.40, Lincoln, for 1.8-miles to the Mt. Werner/Ski Area exit on the right. Turn left at the stop sign, and follow Mt. Werner Road. Park as close to the Gondola Building as you can. If you're planning a downhill hike only, purchase a ticket and ride the Gondola up. However, if you're planning to hike up the mountain, walk to the base of the mountain, under the Gondola and look for the hiking trail sign.

The Hike: In 1997, a new and greatly improved 3-mile hiking trail was built on the mountain, for hikers only. From the Thunderhead, the trail moves down the mountain into the aspen woods off of Valley View ski run, and it meanders through the woods, up to the saddle near the top of the structure for the Christie lifts. Catwalks take the hiker the rest of the way down to the base. The present trail is much less steep and downhill than the old one, and it zigzags back and forth across the mountain through a number of shady, cooling woods. The vegetation along the route includes aspen, scrub oaks, a small wetland area, a dry section and lodgepole pines. In July, the trail abounds with colorful wildflowers.

If you hike the trail from the bottom, begin far to the right at the base, even to the right of the gondola. Follow the hiking signs carefully so that you don't get on the bike paths by mistake, which can be a dangerous mix.

There is a charge to ride the Gondola up. However, as of this writing, people who hike up may ride the gondola down for free. And as long as they are on a leash, dogs are allowed on the gondola. Hopefully, these policies won't change.

If you wish to hike all the way up to the top of Storm Peak from the Thunderhead, follow the catwalks to the left, all the way to the top. Watch out for bike trail intersections and motor vehicles. Don't hike this section without having the trail map with you – and take a camera and lots to drink. Please stay on established trails and roads to prevent erosion.

13. Bear Creek Trail - 1206

Wilderness to the people of America is a spiritual necessity, an antidote to the high pressure of modern life, a means of regaining serenity and equilibrium.
~ Sigurd Olson

Of Note: This is an excellent, more-difficult climb, up along a busy creek to a splendid, boulder-strewn high meadow park with uplifting views. Nature lovers will enjoy the plentiful variety of birds and early-appearing wildflowers along the way. Because the snow pack generally melts sooner on this trail than it does on most of the higher elevation trails, this is a good hike to make early in the season.

Distance: 5.2-miles, each way.

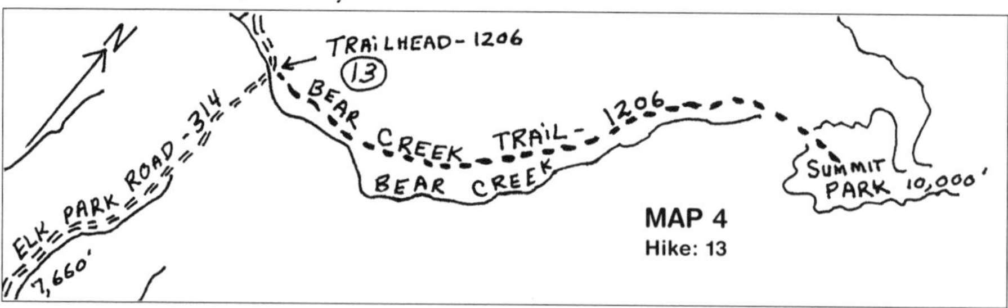

Pretty views, meadows and aspen trees await you in 10,000' high Summit Park.

Hiking Time: About 2.5-hours up and 2-hours coming back down.

Elevation: Parking area: 7,660'; Summit Park: 10,000'.

With Children: *Because it's a 2,340' climb up to the park, few youngsters can make this hike. However, if you can split the mileage in half, this trail makes a good two-day family backpack trip, if your children are game. There are many good campsites and water sources along the way.*

Yampatika Notes: *Black bear, red fox, mule deer, elk and many other animals love this habitat, called the mountain shrub lands. Located between 6,500' and 7,500-feet in the Yampa Valley, this area is full of acorns from Gambels Oak, seeds from Rocky Mountain Maple, and berries from Chokecherry, Serviceberry, Snowberry and others, which in the fall, provides food for animals on which they fatten themselves for the winter months.*

Map: Trails Illustrated 117; Book map 4.

How to get there: From town, on Lincoln Avenue, U.S. 40, turn north onto 3rd, go one block and turn right onto Fish Creek Falls Road. Drive 0.3-mile and turn left onto Amethyst. After 1.6-miles, the road comes to a fork with hwy. 323. Stay right at this road and drive 6.2 miles to the new trailhead. Park in the small turnoff on the right.

The Hike: From the new trailhead, hike about 2.5 miles until the intersection with FSR 314. At this intersection of 314 and the trailhead for 1206, just after fording Bear Creek, there's a large park with excellent campsites straight ahead, where the difficult four-wheel drive road continues north. However, for the purposes of this hike, you'll now head east on what begins as a double track, climbing through meadows, pines and aspens.

Be alert! When you reach a fork in the trail, don't continue on the wider two-track heading northwest, to the left, but rather, choose the narrow, steep, and more faint single track up to the right, heading northeast. Be watching for this change – it's easy to miss. Keep your compass handy if you need reassurance. As long as the creek remains close by, on your right, you should be heading on the correct path. If you're hiking away from the creek, you've probably made the wrong choice.

Enjoy the impressive green ferns mixed with more-heavily wooded sections of aspens, fir and spruce. Cross a smaller tributary creek, and then continue along Bear Creek for a bit longer; cross another tributary, bushwhack around a few downed trees, ford the main creek on a log, and soon arrive at the gorgeous huge mountain valley park. Enjoy photographing pretty views of the Steamboat Ski Area and the Flat Top Mountains, which early in the season, will still be snowcapped.

14. Mad Creek Hikes - 1100
15. Saddle Trail - 1140

While there may be no "right" way to value a forest or a river, there is a wrong way, which is to give it no value at all. How do we decide the value of a 700-year-old tree? We need only to ask how much it would cost to make a new one, or a new river, or even a new atmosphere.
~ Paul Hawken

Of Note: Because the Mad Creek Hikes trailhead is only 5.5-miles from Steamboat, hiking on it seldom offers solitude. Since there is an early snowmelt on this lower-down trail, it's a good hike to make in the early part of a season. The trail offers a marvelous array of almost 100 different species of wildflowers, and mid-June through early July is the most ideal time to go searching for them in this area.

This hike will initially take you up a gravelly path, along a south-facing canyon wall, to a shelf high above the splashing Mad Creek, and then lead you gradually back down to it.

There are actually four hikes that can be made via this trail. Most people choose to take a short 1.5-mile hike just to where the trail meets the creek, and then return on the same route. But there are also three longer loop hikes that can be made on this trail, as well, all worth three separate days of your time if you're staying in the area.

The Swamp Park Trail – 1100 was heavily damaged in 1997 Blowdown, but it has been cleared. The sections of 1100 that make loops with the Saddle Trail (see hike [15]) and the Red Dirt Trail, (hike [16]) were not seriously damaged, and you can still hike these loops. Crossing over Mad Creek on a bridge and connecting up with an old jeep road provides yet a third loop option.

From time to time, rattlesnakes are spotted on this hot, rocky trail. So keep youngsters and K-9's under close supervision, and watch where you're placing hands and feet. If you happen to spot one, walk slowly away, studying it from a safe distance of at least four feet.

Distance: Trailhead to Forest Service Guardhouse (the "Mad House") area: about 1.5-miles,

A torrant of water pours down Mad Creek.

each way; trailhead to junction with Saddle Trail-1140: 1.75-miles, each way; trailhead to junction with Red Dirt Trail-1171: 5.5-miles, each way; FSR 128 loop hike: total of 4.5-miles.

Hiking Time: Varies with the hike chosen. The hike on 1100 just to the Forest Service guard house, a/k/a "The Mad House," takes about one hour; the hike on 1100, just to the junction with the Saddle Trail, takes about 1.25 - hours; the hike on 1100 just to the junction with the Red Dirt Trail takes about 2.5-hours; the whole loop hike using FSR 128 takes about 3-hours. You'll need to tack on additional distance and times, depending on which loop you choose.

Elevation: Trailhead: 6,763; F.S. Guardhouse: 7,200'; junction with Red Dirt trail: 8,600'.

With Children: *Younger children will enjoy hiking to the point where the trail meets the creek, near the first gate. Hiking a bit beyond this point, to a bridge which crosses over the creek, will also be a good destination with kids. Both places offer creek-side water fun – fishing, picnicking, rock hopping, stone throwing, etc. This can be a very hot hike, so make it early in the day, and take plenty of water or a filter. You can point out animal prints on the first part of the trail, and if you watch carefully, you're likely to spot interesting snakes and lizards – though, hopefully not a rattler!*

I have probably hiked on the Mad Creek Trail at least forty times over the years, and I have spotted only one rattlesnake. He was easy to spot and stay away from. Just in case, though, children and K-9's should be closely supervised, especially on hot days when snakes like to sunbathe on rocks.

Yampatika Notes: *The Mad Creek Valley was glacially carved out, and as you enter the open meadow at the Mad House, notice the big round, smooth boulders scattered throughout. These are glacial erratics, or "glacier poop," as they are humorously known – basically waste materials from the glacier. The rocks through the lower canyon, mostly gneiss and schist, are Precambrian, about 1.7-million years old. Gold has occasionally been found in Mad Creek – watch for garnets. Mad Creek was named such by locals in 1877 because a traveler nearly drowned while crossing the creek, and his horse was beaten to death on the rocks by the angry, fast-flowing torrent of rumbling water.*

Fishing: *Mad Creek offers good brook trout fishing and easy access to the water.*

Map: Trails Illustrated 117. See also book map 5.

How to get there: Drive west out of Steamboat on U.S. 40, Lincoln, for about 1.3-miles past 13th to the Airport/Clark turnoff, Routt 129. Turn right here, north, and drive for 5.5

miles. Look for the large buck-and-pole-fenced parking lot on the right. The trailhead sign says "1100 – Swamp Park Trail." Toilets are available.

The Hike: 14. Mad Creek Hikes trail - 1100:

The trail begins with a steep climb up along an exposed hillside, high above Mad Creek, where you can look over the side to enjoy views of the river rushing down the ravine. The first 15-minutes will be the hardest on a hot day. But after you climb up about 0.5-mile and turn the corner, you'll probably encounter cooler breezes and some tree shade. After hiking for about 45-minutes, begin to descend, and in a short while, you'll be down in a lush meadow. Open and close the Forest Service gate at this point, and climb the fence on the right, if you want to go down to the creek for a picnic, fishing or a quiet sit by the creek.

If you'd like to make the loop hike with the Saddle Trail, then traveling back down on part of the Red Dirt Trail, after the gate watch for a sign at a fork, directing you left, to the Saddle Trail. (see hike [15].)

If you'd like to picnic near the bridge or make the loop hike using FS 128, continue on the trail after the gate, going through another gate and through a grassy meadow, around the Mad House. From there, follow an old jeep road down to the right, to a bridge at the creek. This is a great place to picnic, fish and enjoy the creek. When you want to complete the loop, follow the road across the bridge and hike through lovely, open meadows and aspens.

Toward the end of this route, you'll be treated to a marvelous, expansive view of the beautiful Elk River Valley down below. When you reach Routt 129, you'll have to turn right, north, and walk carefully along the highway for a few minutes, over the Mad Creek bridge, returning to the parking area.

To make the very long loop with the Red Dirt Trail, from the first gate, follow the trail around the fence of the Mad House. You'll see a sign, "Swamp Park," which you'll follow. The old road now becomes more of a single track around an old pasture. Stay left at the fork with the split-rail fence, which curves right. Continue hiking northeast up the lush valley, walking parallel with Mad Creek, through some very old stands of tall aspens, the leaves of which will be spectacular come late September. You'll see signs of old and new beaver activity along this part of the route. Leave the meadow and travel through more stands of cooling aspens, mixed in with scrub oaks – an unusual sight. The trail follows closer to the creek at this point.

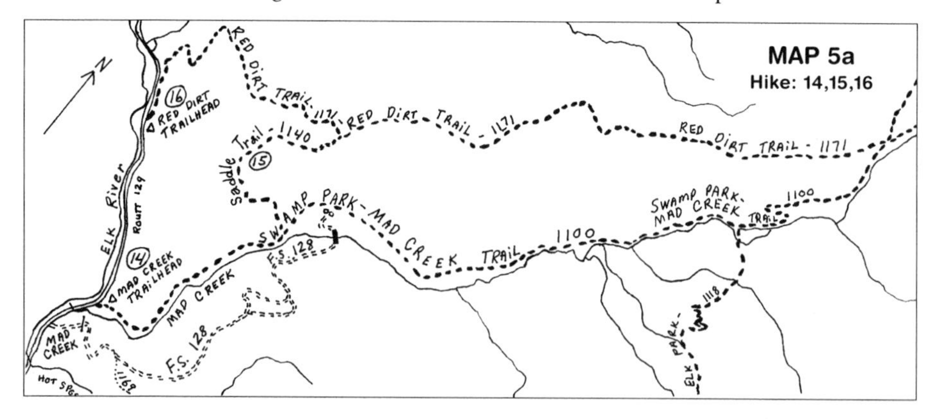

The barn by the Mad House

After hiking about four miles from the trailhead, you'll come to the Mt. Zirkel Wilderness Boundary sign. Continue a moderate climb for about 15-minutes, and then go slightly down to another meadow, where you'll soon encounter three stream crossings. You'll need water-crossing shoes here. After the first crossing, look for a sign, "Elk Park Trail-1118." Remain left of this sign, staying on 1100. Begin a longer climb and some steep switchbacking, until you reach the intersection with the Red Dirt Trail-1171. Follow this trail back down to Routt 129 (see hike [16]), where you'll then have a nasty 1.2-mile walk along the busy highway to return to your car at the trailhead parking lot. This is the only downside of making this loop hike. In fact, if you have the use of two cars, it's worth leaving one at either parking area to avoid this unpleasant walk along the dangerous, busy highway at the end of your long loop hike.

The Hike: 15. Saddle Trail - 1140:

You'll need to reach this trail via either the Mad Creek/Swamp Park Trail, hike [14], or via the Red Dirt Trail, hike [15]. This is a 1.1-mile long section that connects those two trails together, forming a loop, which can be hiked from either end. To avoid having to walk the unsafe 1.2-mile section along the highway at the end, leave a car at each end. The last downhill section of this hike may be too big a challenge for people with cranky knees.

To reach the Saddle Trail via the Swamp Park Trail, read the directions in hike [14] above to arrive at the intersection of those two trails. Once there, turn left onto the Saddle Trail, which then makes quite a few directional changes until it meets the Red Dirt Trail. It begins going northwest – then southwest – then northwest again – and then north – northeast – and finally, north! But the trail is so well defined, these directional changes won't confuse you.

If you need to filter water, do so out of Mad Creek, before you go onto the Saddle trail, since once you leave the Swamp Park Trail, there are no other water sources along the way.

From the Swamp Park Trail, the Saddle Trail starts out on an old jeep road, winds up a ridge through thick aspens, skunk cabbages and scrub oak, to a single track at the top of the saddle, where you'll enjoy a wonderful view of the whole Mad Creek Valley. After 1.1-miles, you'll see a marker for the Red Dirt Trail. Turn left and enjoy a delightful climb down through scrub oaks and cooling spruce, pines and firs. This loop trail offers a marvelous variety of wildflowers and birds.

16. Red Dirt Trail - 1171

The guardian angels of life sometimes fly so high as to be beyond our sight, but they are always looking down upon us.
~ Jean Paul Richter

Praise to thee, my Lord, for all thy creatures, but above all for Brother Sun, who brings us the day and lends us his light.
~ St. Francis of Assisi

If using the Red Dirt trail for the loop hike, use it on the downhill return.

Of Note: The best two features of this hike are first, the vistas at the beginning of the beautiful ranching Elk River Valley, and then, upon arriving at the destination, the views of the magnificent Mad Creek River Valley. Unfortunately, you'll have to huff and puff a bit in between, climbing about 2,000' to the highest point of the hike. If you're into photography, the photo opportunities are definitely worth the effort.

If you're going to use this hike as part of either the Mad Creek loop or the Saddle loop (hikes [14] and [15]), I suggest using it as the return route. You'll still get to enjoy the beautiful views, but you'll be able to hike down #1171, instead of up the hill. The down section of this hike may be hard on creaky knees. Heading up this route can be a very hot, dry climb, especially on a sunny day, so take plenty of water with you, even for your dog, since there is no suitable source along the way.

Distance: About 5-miles, each way.

Hiking Time: About 3-hours, one-way up; less coming back down.

Elevation: Trailhead: 6,800'; high point of trail: 8,800'.

With Children: *This is not a very good hike for very young children. It climbs and climbs and is hot and dry. Especially on a sunny day, little ones may whine and melt along the way. On a cool day, however, older children who enjoy climbing would enjoy the challenge of this trip. Take along lots of drinking water, and buy a disposable camera for them to take some excellent photos for their scrapbook.*

Yampatika Notes: *Visit this south-facing slope in the spring, and you are in for a treat! Large sunflower-like blooms of Arrowleaf Balsamroot and Mules Ears, dark purple Larkspur, vining Wild Sweet Pea, shy lavender Waterleaf, and stunning white Evening Primrose are just a few of the wildflowers taking advantage of the early spring sun.*

Map: Trails Illustrated 117; Book map 5.

How to get there: Heading west out of Steamboat, drive 1.3-miles from 13th Street until you get to the Airport/Clark turnoff, Routt 129. Turn right, north, here, and travel 6.65-miles to the trailhead. Watch for the sign on the right for trail #1171. There is room for several cars to park at the trailhead.

The Hike: From the Elk River Road, begin a long, steep traverse up the mountain, to the northwest, and switchback up a brush-covered hillside. Very quickly, enjoy great views of the Elk River Valley below. After about five minutes of hiking, notice the dark red color of the dirt ahead of you. Seeing this red earth, Spanish explorers first called this area "Colorado," which means "the color red," and the name stuck a century later.

The trail alternates between open areas and wooded areas, through aspens, lodgepole pine, firs, ferns, scrub oaks and a goodly variety of lovely wildflowers, when in season. Here and there, the trail levels off a bit through the woods, giving you a brief respite from the sun and the climb. Along the way, you'll soon recognize Hahn's Peak off in the distance.

After about an hour's hike, you'll see the trail sign to the right for the Saddle Trail. If you're making a loop with that trail, turn right here; otherwise, continue hiking straight ahead. Another hour and forty-five minutes of hiking will bring you to the official Mt. Zirkel Wilderness regulations sign.

The hike for the next fifteen minutes will treat you to outstanding views of the whole Mad Creek Valley down far below. Enjoy this walk until the trail starts to descend. For the purpose of this hike, stop before descending and return on the same route. The trail continues all the way toward Swamp Park, which was heavily damaged by the '97 Blowdown. But to make a loop with the Swamp Park Trail, you will continue down until you reach the junction with 1100, and then turn right and take 1100 south/southwest back to the Swamp Park Trailhead parking lot, where, hopefully you'll have a second car waiting to drive you back to the trail-of-origin Red Dirt trailhead – otherwise, it's a nasty 1.2-mile hike back to your car along a busy highway 129 – something you should try to avoid.

17. Strawberry Park Hot Springs - 1169

When the well's dry, we know the worth of water.
~ Benjamin Franklin

Of Note: This single-track trail climbs gently up along Hot Springs Creek, which flows down through a narrow, steep forested canyon. The trail hugs the north side of the creek, taking you from the Elk River Road 129, up to the delightful Strawberry Park Hot Springs. In the 1880's, a large sawmill operation existed at the lower end of this canyon, processing old timber, some of which had been burned by local Indians, and the lumber it produced was used in many early-day area barns. The trail often slopes precipitously close to the creek in places, and hikers need to be cautious of ledge drop-offs and descending mountain bikers.

The Strawberry Park Hot Springs are located in a secluded setting on the eastern end of this trail, just north of Steamboat Springs. Naturally-heated scalding water, at 146 degrees F, tumbles down a mountainside, where it then mixes with cold stream water and is channeled into four rustic, man-sculpted masonry pools. The temperatures in the pools vary from 105 degrees to 85 degrees. In the summertime, the springs can be reached easily on a gravel road via car, thus making these picturesque springs a very popular area for Steamboat tourists. There is a charge to enter the facilities. Bring a towel, bathing suit, water shoes (a must!) and a picnic.

Distance: 3-miles, each way.

Hiking Time: About 1.5-hours, one-way up; less time going down.

Elevation: Bottom trailhead: 6,700'; Top of trailhead: 7,800'.

With Children: *This is not a difficult trail for most in-shape children; however, because of the descending bikers and unstable ledges in a few places, children should be well supervised on the trail. A great kids' hike would be to have someone drive you up to the hot springs, where the children can spend some time soaking. Afterwards, hike for three-miles one-way, downhill to the bottom, where a car and driver wait to pick you up. Since much of this trail is at a lower elevation, it can be quite hot on sunny days, so if you're making the climb up, try to do it with children earlier in the day.*

Yampatika Notes: *In the early years of Steamboat Springs, during the late 1800's and early 1900's, ladies in long woolen skirts, men in woolen knickers, and kids all bundled up would ski up from Steamboat Springs on long wooden skies for a day's outing at the Strawberry Park Hot Springs. They would bring up eggs and vegetables, and cook them with fish they would catch in the creek in the 147F degree waters running down the mountainside. In the Yampa Valley, there are only two true "hot springs," those with temperatures above 90F degrees – Strawberry Park Hot Springs and the Heart Spring, which heats the local swimming pool. As surface water percolates down through rock layers, it may come close to magma chambers, extremely hot pockets of liquid rock. Some of these magma chambers can be very close to the surface. The magma heats the water,*

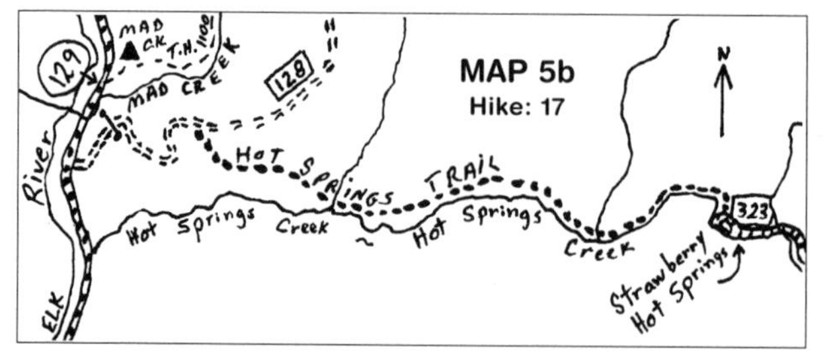

The wonderful hot springs pools await hikers at the end of this trail.

forcing it to rise up through layers of rock. Eventually, the water finds a place to bubble out of the ground, and, "wal-la!" We have a hot springs!

Map: Trails Illustrated 117; Book map 5.

How to get there: Drive west out of town on U.S. 40 for 1.3-miles past 13th Street. Turn right, north, at the Airport/Clark turnoff – Routt 129 and drive 5.5-miles. Park in the Mad Creek 1100 trailhead parking lot on the right. Walk carefully along the highway south for about 400 yards to FDR 128. Walk up this dirt road for about a half mile, making sure to close all gates, until you see the hot springs trail cutting off to the right. There should be a sign directing you. The road dead-ends at the springs.

From the other end, to drive the seven miles by car to the hot springs, go north on 7th Street and follow the "Strawberry Park Hot Springs" signs to Routt 36 and then FDR 323, a dirt road which dead ends at the hot springs.

The Hike: The trail heads out across a lovely meadow and closely follows the stream, gaining altitude at a moderate rate. There are several small side streams that are preferable to the main stream for filtering water, since the main stream comes from the hot springs above, where people soak in the water – wearing bug repellant, suntan lotion, deodorant, and who knows what else.

At about mile two, you'll see the remains of two old cabins off to the right. After another mile, arrive at the Strawberry Park Hot Springs. Change into your bathing suit and water shoes, and enjoy a hot soothing soak.

18. Soda Creek Trail

Each blade of grass has its spot on earth whence it draws its life, its strength;
and so is man rooted to the land from which he draws his faith together with his life.
~ Joseph Conrad

Of Note: Soda Creek was so named because it runs down into town next to the Soda Springs, from which local children used to take bubbling water to add to flavored drinks, making their own version of "soda pop."

The trailhead for this hike is only about 10-miles from downtown. It's an excellent easy hike for visiting relatives unused to the altitude, or for hikers just starting to get their hiking legs. In early July, you may be treated to thick meadows of splendid, eye-catching purple/white columbine flowers. Please read Yampatika Notes below, and do your part to protect fenced-off fragile areas by keeping away from them.

Distance: About 1.0-mile to the junction with Soda Creek; after this, the trail continues up a valley, paralleling the creek for about two more miles. But you can travel any part of this distance and have a good hike.

Hiking Time: Variable. About 0.5-hour to reach Soda Creek; another forty-five minutes to reach a large meadow turn-around area.

Elevation: Trailhead: 8,200'; at junction with Soda Creek: 8,000'.

With Children: *This is the perfect hike to take with young children. The first mile down to the creek will be a little easier than the hike back up this section, but after the junction with the creek, it remains pretty gentle. You'll have much to see and explore with children, perhaps including beaver ponds, wildflowers, and ripe, purple serviceberries in August. Pick them and make serviceberry jam with the kids after you get home. Please read Yampatika Notes below, and keep away from all fenced-off areas.*

Yampatika Notes: *The geographic term, "riparian" means the area along the banks of a body of water, such as streams, rivers, lakes and ponds. The rich riparian area in the Soda Creek drainage is valuable habitat for a wide diversity of species. Domestic pets, livestock and humans can trample precious vegetation needed to shade and protect species, introduce pathogens into waterways and move species away from prime areas for shelter, feeding and breeding. There are several areas fenced off in the drainage. Respect this closure to ensure protection of this valuable riparian habitat and the many species found here.*

Map: Trails Illustrated 117; Book map 6.

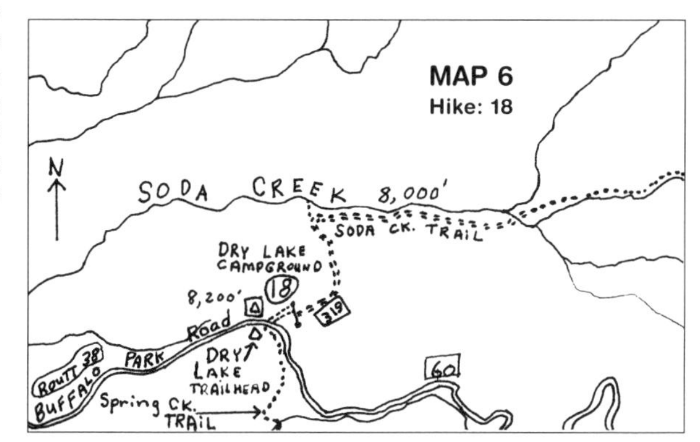

There are many great spots to stop for a rest along the family friendly Soda Creek. Please respect fenced-off, closed areas.

How to get there: From town, on Lincoln Avenue, turn north onto 3rd, go one block and turn right onto Fish Creek Falls Road. Drive 0.3-mile until turning left at Amethyst. After 1.6-miles, the road comes to a fork with Hwy. 323 – the Strawberry Park Road. Stay right, going onto this road, and then drive 2.4-miles until Routt 38, Buffalo Pass Road. Turn right. The road very soon becomes dirt but is car accessible. Drive 5.8-miles to Dry Lake Campground on the left. Park in the parking area across the road, and then cross back to the campground area. Look for a small "Soda Creek Trail" sign.

The Hike: Walk around the barrier and head on down the remains of an old jeep road, descending gradually through lovely stands of aspens, firs and spruce. In late June through early July, you may see spectacular whole meadows of columbine flowers, if grazing sheep haven't found them first!

Walk for about twenty minutes until you come to an unmarked junction. Stay left and hike about another 200 feet to come to a fun rest spot at the stream, where you can take a break or let the children throw rocks into the water.

Afterwards, return to this junction, and now turn left, east, paralleling the creek, and hike as far up the canyon as you wish. In early summer, there may be many small streams through the woods to cross, so take water shoes and extra dry socks for the kids.

At about mile three, come to a large meadow and marsh where you can climb or sunbathe on huge granite rocks. The trail eventually fades, but you can bushwhack up the canyon for as long as you desire.

19. Jonah Lake

Then they took Jonah and threw him overboard, and the raging sea grew calm.
At this, the men greatly feared the Lord and they offered a sacrifice to the Lord and made vows to him.
But the Lord provided a great fish to swallow Jonah, and Jonah was inside the fish three days and three nights.
~ Jonah 1:15-17

Of Note: The trail to Jonah Lake begins at Summit Lake, so named because it's located at the top of Buffalo Pass on the Continental Divide. This is a very quick hike, plummeting down about 120' in elevation in a very short distance. But it goes to a pristine lake, and it's a good way to get away from the usual crowds of people visiting Summit Lake. From Jonah Lake, several other wonderful lakes can be easily accessed.

Distance: About 0.25-mile, each way.

Hiking Time: About 10-minutes, one way down; a bit longer coming back up.

Elevation: Trailhead: 10,320'; Jonah Lake: 10,200'.

With Children: *Although it's a somewhat steep hike, with a bit of help, even very young children should be able to make this trip because of its short distance. Kids would also enjoy fishing in Jonah Lake.*

Yampatika Notes: *Ray Peck and Percy Paxton, the first Forest Rangers on the Routt Forest, named Jonah Lake in 1911 or 1912, while they were drawing timber reconnaissance maps. The name came from the fact the first planting of trees was not very successful.*

Fishing: *Summit Lake: brook and rainbow; Jonah Lake: cutthroat 8-10" range and a good place to fly fish, especially in early evening hours; Whale Lake: large brook population; Shoestring Lake: good for brookies; Martha Lake: cutthroats in the 10-12" range.*

Map: Trails Illustrated 117; Book map 7.

How to get there: From town on Lincoln Ave., U.S. 40, turn north onto 3rd, go one block and turn right onto Fish Creek Falls Road. Drive 0.3-mile and turn left onto Amethyst. After 1.6-miles, the road comes to a fork with Hwy.323. Stay to the right onto this road, and drive 2.4-miles, turning right onto the Buffalo Pass Road, Routt 38. The road very soon becomes dirt, but it remains car accessible. Drive 13-miles up the pass

Sarah doing her mermaid imitation in cold Jonah Lake.

until you come to the Forest Service sign to the left of Summit Lake. The sign says, "National Forest Campground – Summit Lake." Follow this road around the west side of the lake, staying to the right on the circle. Drive 0.3-mile from this sign, and stop at the first campsite on the right, just before the outhouse. The trailhead is not marked, and it's not easy to see from the road. However, walk through or around this car campsite, if it's unoccupied, and you'll soon discover the trail heading north.

The Hike: Follow the trail down through the woods, soon passing a Mt. Zirkel Wilderness boundary sign. The trail will be snow packed in the early part of the season, so be prepared for possible wet feet. Very quickly arrive at the southeast end of Jonah Lake.

If you're experienced with a compass and topographical map and have them both with you, and if you're wearing good waterproof hiking boots, you may want to continue on, bushwhacking to a series of splendid little lakes: Whale, Shoestring, Martha and George. They are all just a hop, skip and a jump from each other, but there are no well-established trails. Just follow the drainage from lake to lake. Since these lakes are wonderfully pristine, please remember to walk gently, don't camp within 100' of any water sources, don't leave fire rings or litter and keep them unspoiled, so that your children's children will someday be able to enjoy them, too.

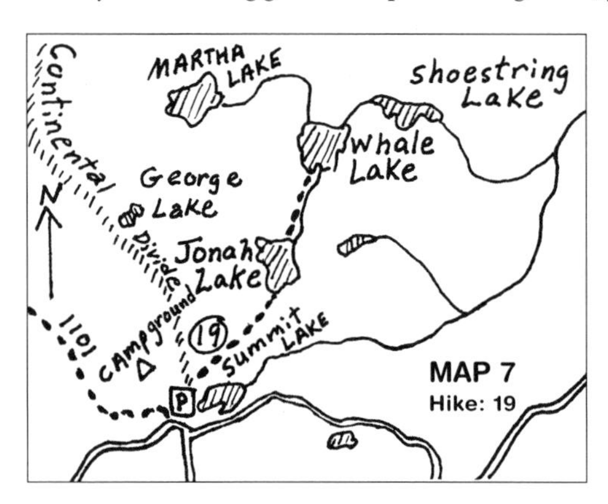

20. Grizzly Lake - 1101

Those who have packed far into grizzly country know that the presence of even one grizzly bear on the land elevates the mountains, deepens the canyons, chills the winds, brightens the stars, darkens the forest and quickens the pulse of all who enter it. They know that when a bear dies, something sacred in every living thing interconnected with that realm also dies.– John Murray

Of Note: After the first half-mile climb, this family-friendly hike to Grizzly Lake meanders atop a very gentle section of the Continental Divide. Instead of the typical above-timberline Divide ascents, this section of 1101 is relatively level and runs through spruce forests thick with trees and vegetation. The many gorgeous wide meadows along the way fill with wildflowers in early July, and to me, some look more like man-made athletic fields and cleared ski runs than nature-made mountain meadows.

This trail also serves as a section of the official Continental Divide Trail, and area backpackers seeking a longer trek often continue on past Grizzly Lake to Base Camp Road, atop Rabbit

Ears Pass, where they can be picked up by a vehicle. There are many good views to be enjoyed along the way, as well as side trips to a series of wonderful little fishing lakes, all worth a visit: Percy, Long, Round, Lost, Elmo, and Fishhook. See hike [38].

Distance: 3-miles, each way, to Grizzly Lake.

Hiking Time: About 1.5-hours, each way.

Elevation: Trailhead: 10,350'; Grizzly Lake: 10,210'.

***With Children**: Although the initial first half-mile of this hike climbs abruptly, the rest of the hike to the lake is fairly gentle. This hike makes an excellent easy family backpack trip. There are many good campsites, ponds and streams along the way.*

***Fishing:** Grizzly Lake is only 5' maximum depth, and thus provides no fishing.*

Map: Trails Illustrated 117; Book map 8.

How to get there: From town, on Lincoln Ave., turn north onto 3rd, drive one block and turn right onto Fish Creek Falls Road. Drive 0.3-mile and turn left on Amethyst. Drive 1.6-miles, until the road comes to a fork with Hwy. 323. Stay to the right, onto this road, and drive 2.4-miles. Turn right onto Routt 38, the Buffalo Pass Road, and drive about 13-miles up this dirt, but car accessible, road until coming to the first parking lot for Summit Lake on the right. Continue past this lot for about 0.1-mile until reaching the large upper parking lot, designated for horse trailer parking. Park here and look for the trailhead sign for 1101 and the CDT.

Llamas help families with young children "travel in style" – here, the Adlers at Grizzly Lake.

The Hike: Immediately begin an abrupt half-mile climb up into the woods, heading in an east-southeast direction. You'll gain the most altitude of the whole hike during the first ten minutes, so don't get discouraged. The trail soon levels out and offers gentle rises and descents along the rest of the way to the lake. Starting out, you'll quickly be treated to eye-pleasing views of Summit Lake and surrounding mountains. After about ten minutes, notice a communications tower, and a bit later, a power line off on the right.

The trail parallels this power line for a while, with a view of the famous Rabbit Ears off to the right, and then it passes under the power line. Watch for a small sign for 1101 at this point. The trail now turns sharply to the southwest (right) and briefly joins a jeep road. Notice the view of the Rabbit Ears now appears on your left. After about an hour from the trailhead, you'll reach a trail sign: "Wyoming Trail 1101-Base Camp Trailhead." From this point, Grizzly Lake is about another thirty-minutes. Pass small lily-padded ponds on both sides, and don't be fooled by a large pond on the left – this isn't the lake yet. You've still got about another half-hour of hiking. After about three miles, look left, northeast, and spot the lake through the trees. A rock cairn along the trail alerts you to your arrival.

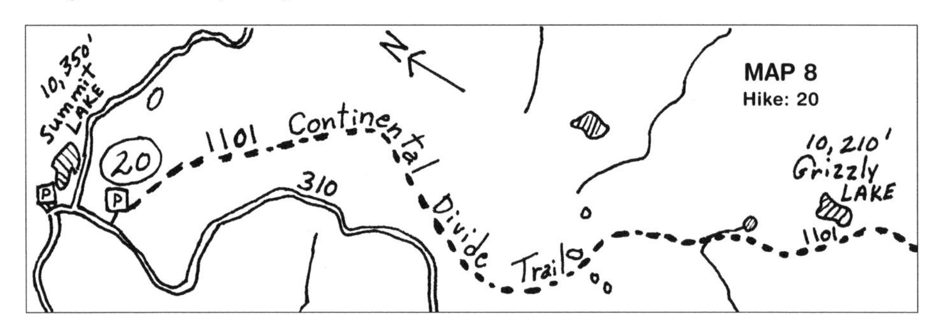

21. Lake Dinosaur

We have eyes, yet we often don't see the beauty that God has given us.
Many place their values on the wonders of heaven that God has promised us.
We need, however, to see the heaven he gives us on this earth.
The wonders of nature, the beauty of the forest, the innocence of a child, and the good of people.
~ Richard Nunes

Of Note: Here is a perfect little hike for visiting relatives whose legs aren't in great shape, or for you if you don't want a real challenge. The trail takes you quickly up to a most-charming lake. Popular with local fishermen, the lake is 9.4-acres in size and twenty-seven feet in maximum depth. It was named many years ago by an old surveyor, who on a visit discovered a great many salamanders. To his co-workers, he jokingly referred to the tiny reptiles as "dinosaurs." Large granite boulders jut into the lake and offer perfect perches for fishing and sunbathing.

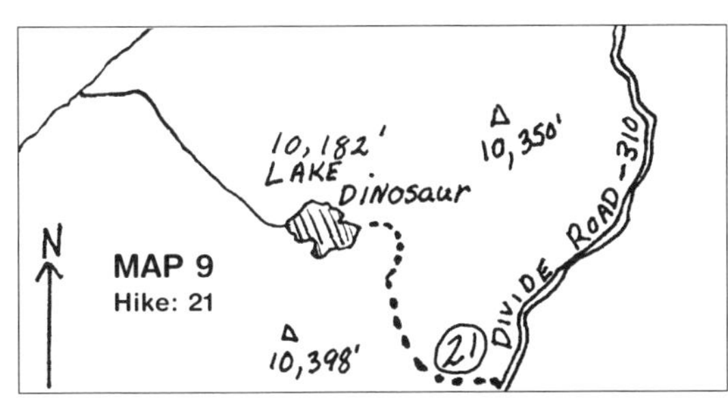

Distance: About 0.75-mile, each way.

Hiking Time: Approximately 20-minutes, one-way.

Elevation: Trailhead: 10,020'; Lake: 10,182'.

With Children: *On one of my first hikes up here many years ago, I came across a group which had easily managed to transport up to the lake five adults, two babies, one toddler, three dogs and one canoe. So this is definitely a family hike! There are good camping sites at the northern end of the lake for an easy backpack trip. The lake itself is a delight, with many large rocks on which to perch for fishing and picnics.*

Yampatika Notes: *During season, this walk is a pure wildflower paradise, with open meadows brimming with flowers in late July and early August, coniferous forests with hidden beauties, and rich riparian areas full of colors. Tread extremely carefully and lightly, as you explore the riparian areas around the lake. You'll be rewarded with Ladies Tresses Orchid, White Bog Orchid, Fringed Gentians, Little Red Elephants, Swamp Laurel, and the very seldom seen Purple Cinquefoil – right at the lake's edge. Please protect this very fragile area by staying on existing trails and watching where you put your feet. Do not collect any of these plants.*

Fishing: *Good for fat brookies in the 6 – 8" range.*

Map: Trails Illustrated 117; Book map 9.

How to get there: From town, on Lincoln, turn north onto 3rd, go one block and turn right onto Fish Creek Falls Road. Drive 0.3-mile and turn left on Amethyst. After 1.6-miles, the road comes to a fork with Hwy. 323. Stay right, onto this road, and drive 2.4-miles. Turn right onto Routt 38, Buffalo Pass Road, which becomes dirt but is car accessible. Drive about 14-miles to Summit Lake. Turn right at the parking lot, and then, just past the parking lot, turn right onto F.S. 310. If early in the season, check beforehand with the Forest Service to see if 310 is open yet – 879-1870. From the open gate, drive 3.3-miles. Park at a rock outcropping on the right where the road was widened. Look for a small stream at this trailhead, which is not marked. The path is found to the right of the outcropping.

Lake Dinosaur is a great place for a quick, easy family backpack trip.

The Hike: The trail heads gently up and through a large meadow, and then up and onto a knoll, where it hangs close to the trees. You will see various trail poles down in the meadow, which indicate the old jeep route. However, stay on the defined path, high and to the far left of these poles, since it is usually very wet down in the lower meadow. After a short time, arrive at the southeastern end of the lake.

22. Fish Creek Reservoir to Long Lake

Lord, you have been our dwelling place throughout all generations. Before the mountains were born or you brought forth the earth and the world, from everlasting to everlasting, you are God.
~ Psalm 90:1-2

Of Note: This is a short, pleasant hike, which takes hikers easily on a level path to a large man-made lake. From there, many options are available for adding on more mileage: you can walk around the long lake or continue on for a short distance to several other lakes – Round and Percy – see hike [23], Little Lost, Elmo, Lost and Fishhook. This can also be a reverse of a hike to Fishhook Lake from Rabbit Ears Pass – see hike [38]. And finally, if you have someone drop you off at the trailhead for this hike, from Long Lake, you can walk down to the bottom of Fish Creek Falls, where your ride can then pick you up.

Expect to find lots of snow along this trail in the early hiking season.

Fish Creek Reservoir draws its water from the Middle Fork of the Fish Creek, and was constructed in the mid-1940's and enlarged in 1973. It is the main water supply for Steamboat Springs, and a popular site for car camping and fishing. During the early summer weeks, mosquitoes can be overpowering here. Long Lake, at 9,880' and 40-acres in size, offers good fishing on some open stretches along its northern shore.

Distance: About 1.5-miles, each way, to Long Lake.

Hiking Time: About 45-minutes, one-way.

Elevation: Reservoir: 9,870'; Long Lake: 9,880'.

With Children: *This is an excellent, short hike for children of all ages. There is very little vertical gain and loss, and children will get to enjoy both the reservoir and the lake, or lakes, should you decide to continue on. There are good car campsites for base camps near and around the reservoir, and excellent campsites at all of the lakes.*

Yampatika Notes: *This watershed supplies drinking water for Steamboat Springs and adds to the Yampa River – and hence, the Colorado River watersheds. Snow is the most important element in watersheds here in the high mountains. In this area, snow pack of well over twenty-feet can build up in the winter. With the spring melt, high mountain snows release their moisture in a torrent of runoff that cleanses streams and river ways and fills up the reservoirs, providing water for the Yampa Valley and beyond.*

Fishing: *The reservoir is stocked; a few hundred yards just north of the reservoir, look for Puppy Dog Lake, which is actually just a shallow pond, good for fly and lure fishing for nice-sized brookies. Long Lake (40 acres, 32' depth) is good for brook trout to 12".*

Map: Trails Illustrated 118; Book map 1, found with hike [4].

How to get there: From town, on Lincoln, U.S. 40, turn north onto 3rd. Drive one block and turn right onto Fish Creek Falls Road. Drive 0.3-mile and turn left onto Amethyst. After 1.6-miles, the road comes to a fork with Hwy. 323. Stay right onto this road and drive 2.4-miles. Turn right onto Routt 38, Buffalo Pass Road, and drive on this dirt, but car accessible, road for about 14-miles until Summit Lake. At Summit Lake, go right past the parking lot, through the gate for FS 310. (Call the Forest Service if early in the season to see if it's open: 879-1870.) From the gate, drive south on 310 for 4.45-miles, until the road becomes 310B. Follow this road for a short distance, until it dead-ends, just south of the turnoff to Granite Campground. Park here and look for a little sign that says 1102A, on the left side of the road.

The Hike: The well defined road, FDR 310.2, climbs gently through fir and spruce for about 15-minutes, and then meets up with the old jeep road coming from the reservoir. Turn left and continue south on this road for about 15 more minutes of hiking, until you meet a trail sign for Fish Creek Falls.

If you want to hike on down to Fish Creek Falls, turn right here and hike past Long Lake, down to the Falls.

If you want to hike just to Long Lake, or to the above-mentioned additional lakes, turn left here and continue on for just a few more minutes, after which you'll arrive at the eastern end of Long Lake and the junction with trail #1102. Turn right for Long Lake, or turn left for 1102 and Round Lake.

23. Fish Creek Reservoir to Round Lake and Lake Percy - 1102 to 1134

We will be known forever by the tracks we leave.
~ Dakota Indian Proverb

Round and Percy Lakes offer great family camping and fishing.

Of Note: Here are two idyllic destinations for a short, easy backpack trip. Both lakes can be reached from several directions–see [38] and [94] – but this route from the north probably entails the least amount of effort. Both lakes offer opportunities for good fishing and camping. Round Lake, almost a perfect circle, is sixteen acres in size and has a level but heavily-forested shoreline. Although this is a good lake for fishing, fir and spruce trees extend all the way to the water's edge on every side, making it difficult to fly fish. Lily pads in the western, shallow section of the lake, also add to a fisherman's challenge.

Right next door to Round Lake, Percy Lake, at 10,033', is only an acre larger and a tad longer than Round Lake. Its northern and western shores are covered with lily pads, and using floating devices can help improve your fishing success here. The eastern bank provides deeper water, and thus improved chances for fishing. Look for good campsites on the southern and northern sides of the lake.

Distance: About 3.0-miles from Fish Creek Reservoir to Round Lake, each way; Percy Lake is located about 0.1-mile from Round.

Hiking Time: About 1.5-hours, each way.

Elevation: Reservoir: 9,870'; Round Lake: 10,060'; Percy: 10,035'.

With Children: *I highly recommend this hike for a backpack trip or a six-mile round-trip with children. These are two family-friendly lakes, with fun campsites and good fishing for pan-sized brookies. Since there is little elevation change, most every child can successfully make the gentle three miles in.*

Yampatika Notes: *Enter the dark, coniferous forests. Conifers are evergreen – needled trees with woody cones. In the sub-alpine zone, you will find three major types of conifers in Northwest Colorado:*

1. *Sub-alpine fir: flat needle in cross-section; can't roll it between your fingers; soft when touched, with silver bark.*
2. *Engelmann spruce: square needle in cross-section; rolls easily, sharp to the touch; rough bark.*
3. *Lodgepole pine: needles in packets of two's; bark rough; hard, woody cone. Remember: firs are flat and friendly, spruce are sharp and square, and pines are in packets.*

Fishing: *Round (40' max. depth): good for brook up to 14"; Percy (23' max. depth): good for brook 10-14".*

Map: Trails Illustrated 118; Book map 1 (hike [4]); map 48 (hike [94]); map 16 (hike [38]).

How to get there: Follow driving instructions for hike [22].

The Hike: Please follow the directions to Long Lake in hike [22]. After arriving at Long Lake, look for a turnoff trail sign on the eastern shore, about a hundred or so feet north of the inlet stream, directing you left, east. After about 0.75-mile, head through a large open meadow and hike uphill into a fir and spruce forest. A quarter-mile after the meadow, reach a four-way junction of trails: 1102, which you've just hiked on, now meets 1134, the Lake Percy Trail, on which you continue. The Wyoming Trail-1101 also intersects north and south at this junction. Continue for a quick quarter-mile to reach Round Lake's northwestern shore. Lake Percy is "just over the hill" to the east, about 0.1-mile further on the trail.

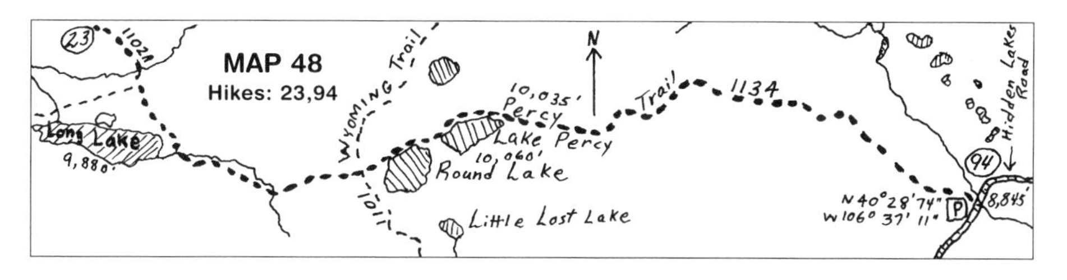

The Lord must have liked us, I say when I see, the bloom of the rose and the green of the tree.
The clover below and the tall pines above – Oh, there's something about us the Good Lord must love.
~ Edgar Grant

omahawk
Ranch

Hikes accessed by Summit Lake Section of the Wyoming Trail - 1101

Even youths grow tired and weary, and young men stumble and fall; but those who hope in the Lord will renew their strength. They will soar on wings like eagles; they will run and not grow weary; they will walk and not be faint.
Isaiah 40:30-31

WARNING: *You should either be an experienced hiker, or be with experienced hikers, if you decide to make any long treks along the Continental Divide. You should have a good compass and the appropriate topographical map along with you, as well as the knowledge of how to use both. You should also be well-equipped for possible bad weather, since storms atop the Divide can be more severe and unpredictable. There are sections of 1101 which are marked only by rock cairns or poles, and late snows often cover trails well into July. Wet, marshy areas can also devour marked trails.*

Of Note: Most of the 49-mile long Wyoming Trail-1101 follows the Continental Divide and offers wonderfully expansive views both east and west into North Park, Rabbit Ears and Never Summer ranges to the southeast, and of the major drainage areas flowing to the west. It also extends for twenty miles inside the Mt. Zirkel Wilderness, much of which is above timberline. It begins on the Continental Divide near Dumont Lake, on Rabbit Ears Pass (hike [38]), and it ends in the Medicine Bow National Forest in Wyoming (see hike [70]).

A number of wonderful hikes in this book are all accessed by the section of the Wyoming Trail-1101 that begins at Summit Lake, atop Buffalo Pass. The first hike presented here is meant to be just an easy day hike on the first two miles, to where 1101 intersects with the upper end of the Newcomb Creek Trail – 1132. The additional hikes north of this point on 1101, presented in this book, generally require backpacking and overnight stays.

This section of the Wyoming Trail-1101 follows an old road along the crest of the Park Range, which in the '50's and '60's, many locals used to jeep all the way to Luna Lake, before the area received wilderness designation and was closed to motor vehicles. The terrain is mostly gentle and rolling, with just a few steeper descents and climbs. The open meadows and parks, guarded by stands of Engelmann spruce and sub-alpine fir, are gorgeous and inundated with wildflowers during July. This area is also prime elk and deer habitat.

Buffalo Pass and its Mad Creek watershed supposedly receive more snow than any other section of Colorado, so you shouldn't try to make any of these hikes too early in the season. Parts of these trails will generally be covered with snow until early July, and even then some. Especially if snow covers the trail, so much so that you aren't sure where you're heading, you should have a compass, a topographical map, and the knowledge of how to use both. If early in the season, call the Forest Service to check if the road to Summit Lake is open yet: 879-1870.

Yampatika Notes: *Up on the Wyoming Trail-1101, you are walking the Continental Divide. This imaginary line divides the Rocky Mountains into the west and the east. If you would pour water on the mountains on the west side, it would run toward the Pacific Ocean or the Gulf of California. On the East slope, the water would run toward the Atlantic Ocean or the Gulf of Mexico.*

About a half-mile from Summit Lake, you'll pass a vast cliff to your right – east. Wander over and look down, and you may see ravens – or sometimes red-tailed hawks, soaring in the deep bowl. They are using the thermals created as winds hit the cliff face and are pushed upward in a strong rush of air. Ravens and hawks are ultimate gliders of the bird world. Sit and watch the ravens play – diving, somersaulting and rolling in mid-air.

How to get there: All of the hikes originating from Summit Lake – [24]-[32] – require the following driving directions to the trailhead: From town, on Lincoln, turn north onto 3rd, drive one block and turn right onto Fish Creek Falls Road. Drive 0.3-mile and turn left at Amethyst. After 1.6-miles, the road comes to a fork with Hwy. 323. Stay to the right onto this road, and drive 2.4-miles. Turn right onto Routt 38, the Buffalo Pass Road. Drive about 13-miles, and just before arriving at Summit Lake, notice the trailhead sign for 1101 on the left. Drive just past it to the parking lot, and then return on foot.

24. Day Hike on Wyoming Trail - 1101

If people destroy something replaceable made by mankind, they are called vandals;
if they destroy something irreplaceable made by God, they are called developers.
~ Joseph Wood Krutch

Of Note: This easy two-mile section will give you a delightful taste of the Wyoming Trail. On one early morning hike on this section, we were fortunate to see a whole herd of elk. You will be treated to views both east and west.

Distance: About 2-miles, each way.

Hiking Time: About 1.25-hours, each way.

Elevation: Summit Lake: 10,320'; Newcomb Park Trail intersection: 10,800'.

This gentle section of 1101 makes it possible for even youngsters to enjoy a short hike up along the Continental Divide – here 8-year old Heidi and mom, Paula.

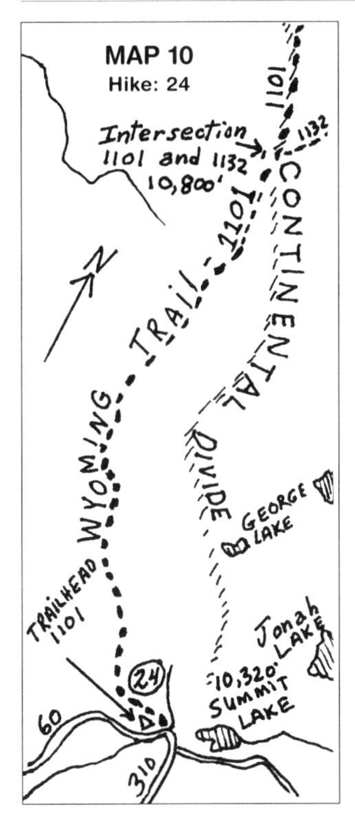

Expect to see left over snow even in July up on the Wyoming Trail - 1101.

With Children: *Every-aged child should love this trail. Until mid-summer, you may encounter big patches of snow and mud, through which kids will probably want to tramp. Be prepared for cold, wet feet. You and they will enjoy the wide-open feeling of the tundra-like alpine meadows, the many tiny wildflowers, as well as the probability of seeing elk and deer if you come early and hike quietly. There are many marvelous photo opportunities up here, as well, of your child on top of a snow pile in July, or with mountain ranges in the background. Please read the information on page 81 about hiking this trail too early in the season.*

Map: Trails Illustrated 117; Book map 10.

How to get there: Please follow driving directions to Summit Lake Trailhead in this section's introduction on page 82.

The Hike: After walking for 0.1-mile, you'll come to the official Wilderness Boundary sign. Climb gradually up the remains of an old jeep road for about 15-minutes, until the trail then begins to level off. The official turn-around for this hike is at about the two-mile mark, where 1101 intersects with the Newcomb Park Trail. (See hike [25]). If you have extra time and energy, you can continue your hike north for however long you care to on this trail, or if early in the season, until the trail becomes snow-covered or faint. If you continue past this point, be certain to have a topographical map and compass with you.

25. Round Mountain Lake - 1132

The time comes when character must be developed. And the wilderness is where it is done...
the wilderness where God appears to be miles away and His promises even farther.
He is, however, close at hand, for He has promised never to leave nor forsake us.
~ John Bevere – "Victory in the Wilderness"

Round Mountain Lake is a favorite fisherman destination.

Of Note: This hike [25] continues where hike [24] ends, so please read the descriptions for that hike first.

Round Mountain Lake, 10 acres in size and 11' maximum depth, is a lovely wilderness lake attracting little traffic. Since some of the trail is marked only by a series of rock cairns, this is not a good early-season hike, when snow hides much of the trail. Even after the snow melts, there will be little, if any, visible path through a marshlands section. And for this particular hike, you need to be "on your toes," even late in the season, or you might walk right past two important trail changes and end up lost.

Fisherman revel in the abundant, large brook trout in the lake, which can also be reached from the eastern side of the Mt. Zirkel Wilderness via the Newcomb Creek Trail–1132 (hike [95]). Outstanding views of North Park await photographers.

A section of the trail near the end is very steep and would be a challenge to people with problem knees. Good campsites abound all along the first two-thirds of the route, and several decent sites exist around the lake itself.

Distance: About 4.5-miles, each way.

Hiking Time: About 2.5 to 3-hours, one way.

Elevation: Trailhead: 10,320'; Round Mountain Lake: 9,860'.

With Children: *On a backpack trip, the first half of the hike in would be relatively easy for older children, but on the uphill return, the steep section near the beginning will be a bigger challenge.*

Fishing: *Good for brook trout to 12".*

Map: Trails Illustrated 117; Book map 11.

How to get there: Please follow the driving directions to the parking lot on Buffalo Pass, near Summit Lake, at the beginning of this section, on page 82.

The Hike: Follow the hiking directions for day hike [24] on 1101, the Wyoming Trail, for two miles, to its junction with the Newcomb Park trail. The Newcomb Park trail sign is on the right.

Turn right, east, onto this trail, 1132. Follow a very old jeep road northeast for about 15-minutes, until reaching a wet marshland. Keep your map and compass handy to insure that you're traveling in the right direction, should the trail become indistinct. Small ponds come into view on your right, and rock cairns should be evident. Approaching to the left of the ponds, keep looking straight ahead for these cairns. When you see the first one, leave the established jeep road and follow a series of cairns across the wet marshes. Early in the season, the trail here will be faint to none. After the marshes, the path will once again become distinct, and then easy to follow. Pass a large pond on the right, and about 0.5-mile from this pond, notice the outstanding views to the left, northwest, of the ragged ridgeline of the eastern outer edge of the Continental Divide.

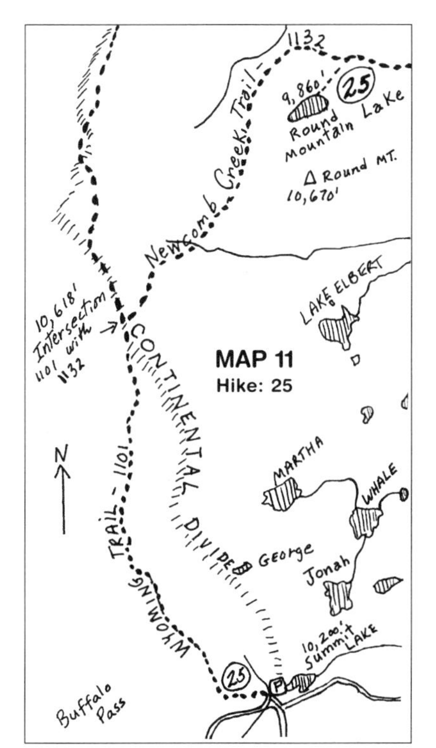

The trail now plunges steeply down through the woods, and then gradually levels out. Shortly after you pass a small pocket meadow on the right, begin to look for a cairn on the right-hand side of the trail, which directs you to the turnoff for Round Mountain Lake. It's very easy to just walk by this cairn, so remain alert. At the cairn, the trail to the lake angles back sharply over your right shoulder. Turn right onto this trail, and hike about another 0.3-mile, arriving at the north end of the lake.

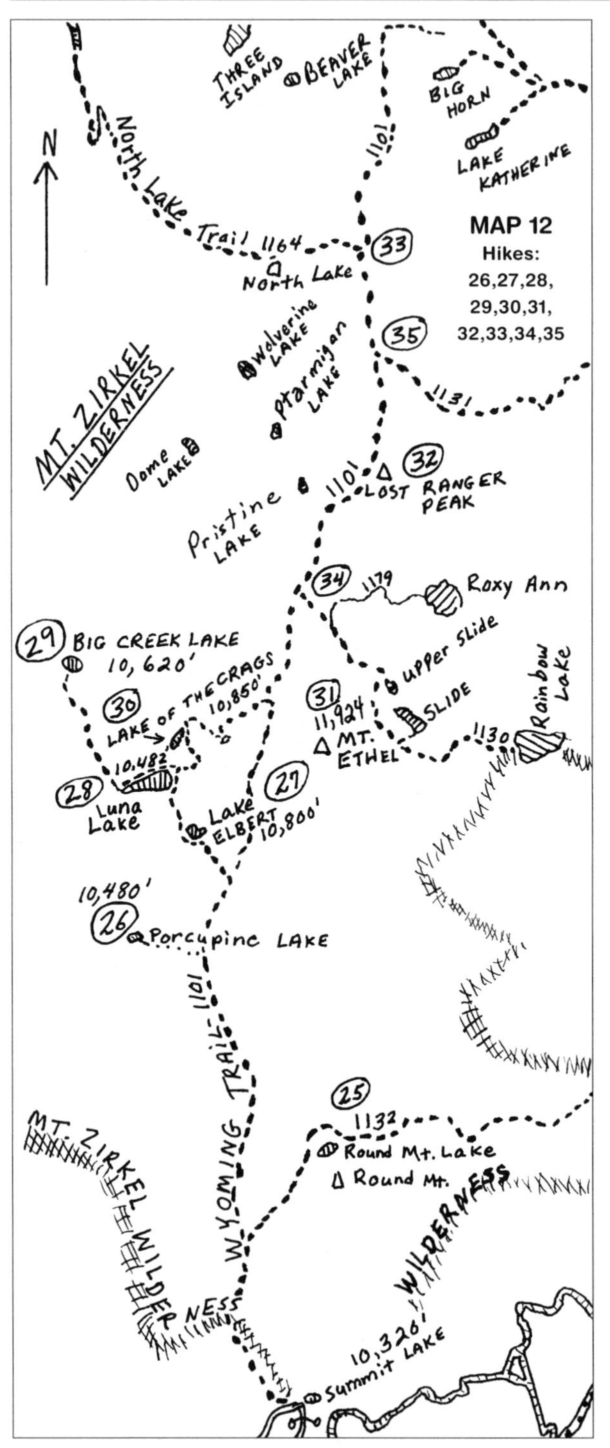

Author's Notes: *The broad high uplands along this 1101 section of the Park Range's western crest are bedecked by a myriad of sparkling alpine lakes – some noted on this map. Thousands of tiny rivulets in this area create larger creeks and streams that in turn flow into and out of these lakes. They then head downhill through vast forests, building in size into larger systems, which flow into the Elk River itself. Finally, the Elk flows into the Yampa River in Steamboat Springs. What an amazing design!*

Boulder-strewn ridges, steep-walled cirques, tarns, arêtes, cols and horns – all created by the erosive forces of long-ago glaciers – are the order of the day up here. Cirques are the scoop-shaped natural amphitheaters on the mountainsides. Tarns are the small, deep lakes lying at the bottom of the cirques. From atop Lost Ranger Peak, you'll easily spot the arêtes of Big Agnes Mountain and the Sawtooth Range – the narrow, jutting ridges made up of a series of high saddles – or cols – plus the intervening saw tooth ridge segments – horns.

Except for the Hahn's Peak area, where by 1874, prospectors had extracted almost $5 million worth of gold, fortunately, they didn't find valuable mineral deposits in this area, which is why it doesn't have a vast backcountry road system in place like we see in so many other areas in Colorado. The Buffalo Pass Road, the access to the trailhead for these hikes, travels from Steamboat Springs to Summit Lake, and then down to North Park. This is the only road that crosses the whole Park Range between Wyoming to the north and Rabbit Ears Pass to the south. This lack of roads, no doubt, is part of why the area eventually became the Mt. Zirkel Wilderness, and aren't we the lucky ones for it!

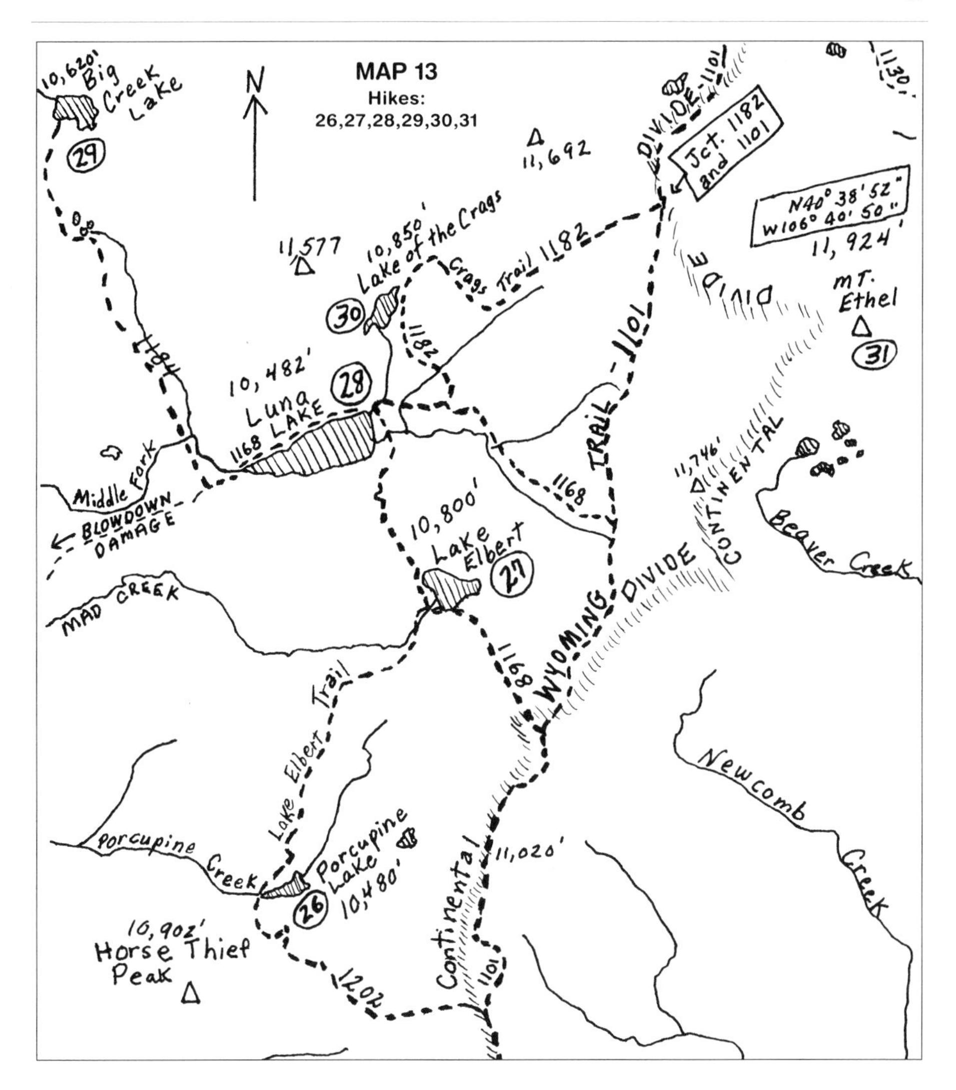

26. Porcupine Lake - 1101 & 1202

Only to the white man is nature a 'wilderness.'
~ Luther Standing Bear, Ogallala Sioux Chief

Of Note: Your chances of finding a spot to pitch your tent in solitude are very high at Porcupine Lake, since few people take the short hike off of 1101 to seek it out. The four-acre lake sits in a small, high alpine, rocky basin, and hot, tired backpackers will find here the makings of a quick, refreshing swim – clear, deep (17' in the middle) water, a sandy bottom and a treeless, sandy shoreline.

The primitive Trail-1202, which leaves its junction with 1101 and passes through a lovely alpine meadow, can become a bit faint in places, especially early in the season, so it's best to keep the map and compass handy, just in case. The Forest Service does not maintain this trail.

For more information about the first six miles of this hike along the section of 1101, please see the introduction to this section on page 81.

Distance: About 7-miles, one-way.

Hiking Time: 3.5-hours, each way.

Elevation: Trailhead: 10,320'; Porcupine Lake: 10,480' (with up and downs along the way, some gradual, some steep).

Map: Trails Illustrated 117; Book maps 12 and 13.

With Children: *This hike requires an overnight, and seven miles is too long for most children to carry a heavy pack.*

Yampatika Notes: *You may come across a porcupine waddling through the forest, or sitting in a tree having lunch. These rotund, sharp-quilled animals are the second largest rodents in North America, with beaver being the largest. They are well built for climbing and feeding in trees. Scaly pads on the soles of their feet provide traction, and their stiff tail helps with balance and bracing. Their summer diet consists of leaves, buds and young shoots of plants, and in winter, mostly the inner bark of trees. Lodgepole pine is their "ice cream" tree, although they will also eat Engelmann spruce, sub-alpine fir and Douglas fir.*

Fishing: *Occasionally stocked, but because of winterkill, don't count on it.*

How to get there: Please follow driving directions for hike [24], page 82.

The Hike: Please read and follow the instructions for hike [24], to the intersection of 1101 and the Newcomb Park Trail, at mile two. Continue past this intersection, remaining on 1101, until at about mile four, just as the trail meets the Continental Divide, watch on your left for an old weathered wooden marker, along with a brass U.S.G.S. survey marker embedded into a rock.

Continue on the old jeep road for another 3-miles, after which the trail leaves the road and descends on a long series of switchbacks. Look to your left, down the valley far below, and you'll be able to spot the Porcupine Lake Trail 1202 heading west. Just before 1101 makes a sharp turn to the right, at the bottom of the valley, 1202 goes off to the left. Be looking for a red blaze on an old spruce tree, and follow it west, through the trees. The trail gradually heads uphill for a bit and then evens out, as it passes through a rocky meadow. Stay alert for the rock cairns, which will guide you through a half-mile-long grassy meadow. At the end of this meadow, watch for two small cairns showing where the trail turns right and heads downhill, through an open area in the trees. Make a steep descent down a grassy slope, and walk through a level stretch. You'll soon be able to see Porcupine Lake down in the valley.

From Porcupine Lake, 1202 continues north for about a mile, to Lake Elbert and the intersection with 1168, which takes you from Elbert to Luna Lake.

27. Lake Elbert via 1168
28. Luna Lake via 1168
29. Big Creek Lake -1184
30. Lake of the Crags -1182

We do not inherit the earth from our ancestors. We borrow it from our children.
~ Ancient American Indian Proverb

IMPORTANT: *Please read the information presented prior to the description for hike [24] on page 81 before considering making any of these hikes.*

Of Note: These four lakes lie in very close proximity to each other, and if they have the time, backpackers often establish a base camp at one lake, and then make multi-day hikes and fishing excursions to all the others. Please follow all Leave No Trace rules at these lakes.

Win and Elaine and their llama buddies up above Lake Elbert, to the left.

27. Lake Elbert via 1168: One of the members of Steamboat Springs' founding families, Logan Crawford, named Lake Elbert after Elbert Husted, whose father once tried to buy the whole town of Steamboat Springs. The lake is less than a mile trek off 1101, and it provides an ideal place to rest your head for a night.

Lake Elbert is a fisherman's joy, where cutthroats and rainbows up to 16" await an angler's tasty-looking fly, and a treeless shoreline eliminates the threat of frustrating limb snags.

At eleven acres in size and 45' in maximum depth, this sparkling, high altitude lake sits near timberline, and outstanding scenery surrounds and delights the visitor in every direction. Good campsites can be found on the lake's southern end.

***Yampatika Notes**: Keep your eyes open along the forested stretches of this trail for a well-camouflaged chicken-like bird, the blue grouse. This plump bird is a mottled brown with a silvery-blue tip along its tail that is very visible when it flies up into the tree canopy. The grouse is also called dumb chicken or dumb hen because it moves very slowly as danger approaches. In the spring, males will set up a territory where they will "boom" or "hoot" to attract females. The first you may sense of a blue grouse is a vibration in your chest or ears from the male's low-pitched hooting calls amplified by special sacs in his neck. See page 2.*

Friends visiting the wonderful Luna Lake. When camping at any of these lakes, please don't camp or have fires within 100' of any lake, stream or trail, and follow all Leave-No-Trace rules.

28. Luna Lake via 1168: Like Lake Elbert, Luna Lake, at 10,482', was also named by the Crawford family in 1875. They thought the lake looked like a crescent moon. Luna is definitely one of the gems of the Mt. Zirkel Wilderness, and because of its special beauty and the excellent fishing in it's deep, 55' maximum-depth waters, it remains a popular destination for local hikers and fishermen.

In the 50's and '60's, locals from Steamboat used to jeep the nine miles from Buffalo Pass all the way to Luna Lake. This ended in 1964, when vehicles were prohibited in the newly created Mt. Zirkel Wilderness. But the old tire tracks still remain and constitute much of this section of the Wyoming Trail-1101. For most hikers, it's too tough a hike to make roundtrip in a day. But for strong backpackers – or for those lucky enough to have the use of llamas or packhorses, which approach the lake from the northern portion of 1168 – this large 38.2-acre lake, one of the largest in the Mt. Zirkel Wilderness, remains a choice destination. On weekends, you're likely to have to share the lake with other visitors, and so it may be a good idea to set your camp up at a nearby lake, saving Luna for a daytime visit.

29. Big Creek Lake-1184: Less than an easy two-miles northwest of Luna Lake lies Big Creek Lake. The trailhead for the well-defined 1184 is located just west of the outlet stream for

Llama trek along 1101.

Luna Lake. The Mad Creek/Swamp Park section of the Luna Lake Trail-1168, was badly damaged by the '97 Blowdown, but it was cleared in the fall of 2000. To use this trail, call the Forest Service for an update: 879-1870.

At 10,620' in altitude and eight-acres in size, Big Creek Lake sits in a basin, guarded on all sides by high ridges. A rocky, grassy meadow lies between the lake and the steep surrounding rock-covered ridges. Fly fishermen enjoy its treeless shoreline, as they cast their line for plentiful 10- to-12-inch cutthroats in this small, 41'-deep fishing hole. Although the lake has shallow edges, it deepens quickly, creating a dark shade of blue in its middle. Good campsites are located along the east, west and south shores of the lake, and because of its relative remoteness, there should be little, if any, competition for these sites.

Be my strong rock, a castle to keep me safe; you are my crag and my stronghold.
~ Psalm 71:3

30. Lake of the Crags–1182 (from Luna Lake): About a mile's hike from Luna Lake, this small, 5.8-acre lake sits nestled below an impressive rock face, which towers dramatically to 11,577' above the lake's western side. The hike from Luna to Crags will offer some outstanding views back down to Luna, and if the sun is right, also a sighting down below of Lake of the Crags doing its fanciful imitation of a shimmering, bright signal mirror.

Wake at sunrise to capture on film the beauty of an illumined sheer rock face rising up behind the glasslike lake's western shore. Relish fishing along the mostly open shoreline for colorful cutthroat trout. Lake of the Crags is yet another excellent place to spend the night, and

Resting along 1101.

you can find good campsites on the southern and eastern ends of the 11'-deep lake.

Yampatika Notes: *Lake of the Crags is a stunning, true alpine lake. Notice there is very little vegetation surrounding the water – no trees, no marshes and very little wetland. The water feeding this alpine lake comes mostly from snowmelt. As the spring surge of snowmelt issues forth, it fills and oxygenates the lake with fresh water. But our snow now has a much higher pollutant concentration than in years past, so as the snow melts, it brings a surge of acidic runoff. The granite rock cannot neutralize this acid, like limestone can, and there is little vegetation to filter out the pollutants. So the acid runoff hits the lakes just as frog and salamander eggs are hatching, producing some unfortunate results.*

Distances:

27. Lake Elbert: 8-miles each way, from the Summit Lake.
28. Luna Lake: 9-miles each way, from the Summit Lake.
29. Big Creek Lake: 11-miles each way from Summit Lake; 1.75-miles from Luna.
30. Lake of the Crags: 10-miles each way from Summit Lake; 1-mile from Luna Lake.

Hiking Times:

27. Lake Elbert: About 4-hours, one-way from Summit Lake.
28. Luna Lake: About 4.5-hours, one-way from Summit Lake.
29. Big Creek Lake: About 5.5-hours, one-way from Summit Lake.
30. Lake of the Crags: About 5-hours, one-way from Summit Lake.

Elevations: The trail from the Summit Lake Trailhead to all four of these lakes gains and loses elevation many times along the route. The altitude at the trailhead is 10,320'.

27. Lake Elbert: 10,800'.

28. Luna Lake: 10,482'.
29. Big Creek Lake: 10,620'.
30. Lake of the Crags: 10,850'.

With Children: *Since these destinations are located in the remote interior of the Mount Zirkel Wilderness, they require backpack trips, too long and difficult for most children to make. If you break the trip up into several days, however, older, in-shape children have been known to greatly enjoy these lakes. Using llamas or packhorses, however, allows all ages to enjoy this area. Please Leave-No-Trace at these pristine lakes!*

Fishing*: Excellent fishing in all four lakes. Please practice Catch and Release fly-fishing.*
27. Lake Elbert: cutthroat and rainbow to 16"; cove on eastern side good for lures.
28. Luna Lake: cutthroat to 20".
29. Big Creek Lake: cutthroat 10-12".
30. Lake of the Crags: cutthroat 10-20".

Map: Trails Illustrated 117; Book maps 12 and 13.

How to get there: See driving instructions before hike [24], and also read more information there about the Wyoming Trail – 1101 on page 81.

The Hikes:

27. *Lake Elbert:* Follow the directions in hike [24] to the intersection of 1101 with the Newcomb Park Trail at the two-mile mark. Through the trees on your right, begin to check out a continuing series of beautiful panoramic views of the Rabbit Ears to the south and of several mountain ranges to the east. There are many good vista view lunch spots along this section.

Continuing north on 1101, and after the first two miles, climb first up a gentle ridge, and then down to a small pond. After the pond, hike gradually uphill through a series of meadows for about two miles, until reaching the Continental Divide at Windy Gap, an abrupt, steep valley named many years ago by local old-timers. On the rocky hillside on your left, look for a brass U.S.G.S. Survey marker cemented to a trailside rock, listing the 10,700' elevation junction with the Divide. This spot also represents the halfway mark for the hike to Luna Lake.

At the top of a series of long switchbacks, the trail now descends fairly steeply for about a half-mile down to a valley, where it then rejoins the road. Cross the spacious valley and then begin a steady two-mile uphill climb back to the Divide. Just before reaching the Continental Divide, you'll reach a fork in the trail where you will leave 1101. The faint trail to the right at this point is 1101, but you should stay left, on the more-defined trail here. Very shortly thereafter, you'll see a trail sign for the Divide – 1101, which also points the way northwest, to Lake Elbert. At this junction of trails 1101 and 1168, follow 1168.

Watch off in the distance for a good view of Hahn's Peak . The trail for the remainder of the distance to Lake Elbert may be wet and fading in spots, especially when going through the sloshy meadows, but check your map, and head toward the lake's south shore, along the outlet stream.

28. *Luna Lake:* the one-mile trail continuing to Luna Lake passes along Lake Elbert's western side and climbs up a ridge between the two lakes. At the top of the ridge, the trail goes through a short meadow and then begins a difficult descent down to Luna Lake, hard on weak knees. The trail then passes through a wet meadow and ends up at Luna Lake's eastern shore.

29. *Big Creek Lake:* at Luna Lake, follow the Luna Lake Trail-1168 along the north shore of the lake until it intersects with the Big Creek Lake Trail–1184, just after crossing the outlet stream coming out of the western end of the lake. There is a sign showing the way, and the trail is well defined. Hike downhill for about a quarter-mile and cross the Middle Fork of Mad Creek. Hike through the rocky meadow, and then climb up two steep switchbacks to the top of a ridge, where you'll then have to watch carefully for rock cairns to direct you through a tricky large open area. Keep your map and compass handy, since the trail becomes very faint, and may even disappear in the grassy meadow area at the north end of the ridge. Head straight through the meadow, aiming at a low spot between rock-covered ridges that surround the northern end of this meadow. The trail then continues to the right of a cairn, close to the trees. Soon after heading down through woods of fir and spruce, you'll be able to see the lake down below.

30. *Lake of the Crags:* Pick up the section of the Luna Lake Trail-1168, which takes you from Luna Lake to the Lake of the Crags, at the stream which flows into the northeastern corner of Luna Lake. At this part of the lake, look for a trail junction sign for 1168 and 1182. Turn left at this sign, onto 1182. Hike up this rocky trail, through patches of fir and spruce trees, passing the remains of an old cabin on the left. About a half-mile after leaving Luna Lake, enter a clear area of huge, rounded rock outcroppings. Stop here for a break and to check out spectacular views of Luna Lake, about 350-feet below. A short time later, the trail brings you to the small picturesque Lake of the Crags.

Special Note: At all of the above pristine lakes, please don't camp or have fires within 100' feet of lakes, trails and streams, and follow all leave-No-Trace rules.

31. Mount Ethel via 1101

You who dwell in the shelter of the Lord, who abide in his shadow for life,
say to the Lord: "My refuge, my rock In whom I trust!"
And he will raise you up on eagle's wings, bear you on the breath of dawn,
make you to shine like the sun, and hold you in the palm of his hand.
~ Michael Joncas - On Eagle's Wings

WARNING: *You should be either an experienced hiker, or be with experienced hikers, if you make any of these long treks along the Continental Divide. You should have a good compass and the appropriate topographical map along with you, as well as the knowledge of how to use both. You should also be well equipped for possible bad weather.*

Even in mid-summer, expect to cross snowfields on your way to Mt. Ethel.

Of Note: If you're base camped in the Luna Lake area off of the Wyoming Trail-1101, atop the Park Range, you do yourself a big favor to include this relatively easy hike from the west up to the large, level summit of 11,924' high Mount Ethel. Staggering views and sweeping vistas await your eyes in every direction – of the jagged-spired Sawtooth Range, the area's highest Mount Zirkel, and of Red Dirt Pass, as well as looking down on Slide and Rainbow Lakes on the eastern side of the Wilderness Area.

Two-miles past 1101's intersection with 1168, the turnoff to Lake Elbert, at the junction of 1101 with 1182, the Lake of the Crags trail, you simply take out your map and compass, face the Mount Ethel summit, and walk up the very gentle slope for less than a mile, and less than a 300-foot vertical gain, to the top.

Head for the rock outcropping along the steep northeast face for the most impressive views. The summit is fairly flat, a typical alpine zone tundra – rocky, open, rolling and sun swept. Although also treeless and windswept, it is graced by natural granite rock gardens of cushion plants, lichens, mosses, and tiny forbs with brilliantly colored, delicate flowers – truly a place where you can drink in the splendor of God's glorious creation.

As always, avoid or leave this peak if storm clouds threaten lightning, and exercise extreme caution around ledge drop-offs.

Map: Trails Illustrated 117; Book map 13.

Yampatika Notes: *As you pass some of the rock piles of Mt. Ethel and other alpine areas, you may be greeted with a loud "nyeeah, nyeeah." That's a pika warning its buddies that you're coming. Also called rock rabbits, cony and chief hare, they are related to rabbits, but are well adapted for life in the tundra – small ears, no visible tail, and a round body to conserve heat. Active year-round, pikas store dried plant materials collected in the summer in hay piles under rocks. The content of these "hay pile complexes" from one pika could fill a bathtub.*

32 - 35 Lost Ranger Peak Hikes

Big Blue Mountain Spirit, the home made of blue clouds...
I am grateful for that mode of goodness there.
~ Apache Chant

WARNING: *You need to be either an experienced hiker, or be with experienced hikers, if you make any of these long treks along the Continental Divide. You should have a good compass and the appropriate topographical map along with you, as well as the knowledge of how to use both. You should also be well equipped for possible bad weather.*

Of Note: There are four approaches to Lost Ranger Peak: two from the western side of the Mt. Zirkel Wilderness – via Buffalo Pass and North Lake – and two from the eastern side of the Wilderness, via Lost Ranger Trail and the Rainbow Lake Trail. Because this is such a "must" destination for serious hikers seeking to truly take in and digest all that the area has to offer, each possible approach is presented in this book. Unless you're Superman, however, all of these hikes must be made as day hikes from a base camp at one of the nearby lakes.

At 11,932' high, Lost Ranger Peak is the highest point along the Wyoming Trail-1101 section of the Continental Divide Trail. The commanding views from the Peak are spectacular in every direction, and they afford a hiker a feeling of standing right in the middle of, and on top of, the whole Mt. Zirkel Wilderness. The only place, which rivals this, in my personal experience, is the top of Mt. Zirkel itself (hike [93]), another "must" hike which allows one to feast on nature's immense beauty, and for me, to re-enforce my own belief that the one who created all of this is truly beyond any mere human comprehension.

The summit of Lost Ranger Peak is a surprisingly flat and tame rolling tundra of lichen-covered rocky soil and plants common to such a fragile alpine ecosystem. Keep alert for belly flowers, miniature arctic zone blossoms that you must lie down on your belly to see and relish.

The views in every direction are thrilling and a topographical map-lover's dream. Unfold and spread out your own map, and easily identify all the major landmarks in the whole wilderness area, including Mount Zirkel, Big and Little Agnes Mountains, and the Sawtooth Range to the north. To the northwest, look down on three of my favorites – Pristine, Ptarmigan and Wolverine lakes. The distinctive, always recognizable Dome looms to the west, and Mount Ethel to the south. But hang onto your map – and your hat – for it's usually quite windy up top!

As always, avoid or leave the peak if storm clouds threaten lightning, and exercise extreme caution around ledge drop-offs.

Yampatika Notes: *Above the saddle leading to Lost Ranger Peak is a look at a rather unusual forest. The spruce/fir form linear, parallel stands called ribbon forest. What causes these parallel lines of growth found at only specific elevations is not exactly known, but wind is probably a major factor.*

Enjoy spectacular views from the top of Lost Ranger Peak.

32. To Lost Ranger Peak (11,932')

from Summit Lake - 1101 (10,320')

The Sovereign Lord is my strength: he makes my feet like the feet of a deer; he enables me to go on the heights.
~ Habakkuk 3:19

Follow the information and directions for hike [24], which covers the area in general, as well as the first two-mile stretch of the Wyoming Trail-1101.

After that, follow the Lake Elbert hike [27] on 1101. When you reach the fork for the turnoff to Lake Elbert-1168, remain on 1101, going straight ahead, following the trail and the cairns.

About two miles past the Lake Elbert junction, pass the turnoff for the Lake of the Crags Trail to the left, continuing north on 1101. At this point, there will be no mistaking the impressive, rocky-crowned Dome on your left and the Lost Ranger Peak on your right, to the north.

About a mile past the junction with the Crags trail, on the right you'll come to, and then pass by, the junction with the Rainbow Lake Trail-1130. Look east, to your right, to see Roxy Ann Lake (hike [98]). From here, 1101 continues to a low saddle, which sits below the peak, and then it follows a series of rock cairns, as it climbs uphill and to the right for about a half-mile, through clumps of gnarled, wind-shocked krummholz trees on the left – an area of austere alpine tundra. The trees suddenly end, and here you'll notice a relatively gentle slope leading up for about 0.1-mile to the Lost Ranger summit. This is where you'll leave 1101, turning west, left, and hiking up for a few minutes to the highest point you can see.

Map: Trails Illustrated 117; Book map 12.

33. To Lost Ranger Peak (11,932')

from North Lake trailhead - 1164 (8,460')

He who forms the mountains creates the wind and reveals his thoughts to man...
~ Amos 4:12

Use rock cairns up on the Wyoming Trail to guide you to the top of Lost Ranger Peak.

Follow the directions to North Lake, hike [85]. After a 4.4-mile hike, arrive at the lake. Continuing east, past North Lake, gently climb for about a half-hour, passing a small-unnamed pond on the left at about mile 5.6, and you'll reach the junction of 1164 with the Wyoming Trail-1101, on top of the Continental Divide. The trail disappears here, so look for a post about a hundred yards across the clearing, and then for a sign about 40-yards further. Turn right, south, and look for a rock cairn about 160-yards away, showing where the now faint trail continues. Continue hiking south, pass a post, and walk through a lovely alpine meadow. At this point, the trail begins to gain altitude, as you see Lost Ranger Peak ahead of you. This trail is marked pretty well along this stretch with rock cairns.

About six-miles from the trailhead, the path turns a bit left, around a grove of brave spruce trees, and then disappears in a large, clear area. Look directly ahead of you, south, to see the next rock cairn. Head for it, and once again pick up a visible trail. At this point, watch for and follow a series of posts. The trail and trees fade out at about the 7.3-mile point, but watch for another cairn and hike to it. From there, another cairn can be spotted on the horizon, a bit to the left. Now, find and follow a very faint trail that ascends to the top of Lost Ranger Peak. Turn around to see a great view of the Sawtooth Range behind you, and then superb views of North Park to the left.

Cairns will guide you where portions of an actual trail seem to fade in and out at will. About eight-and-a-half miles into the hike, the trail levels out, as it reaches the peak's glorious high alpine plateau.

Map: Trails Illustrated 117; Book map 12.

34. To Lost Ranger Peak (11,932')

from Rainbow Lake trailhead - 1130 (8,760')

The day is yours, and yours also the night; you established the sun and the moon.
It was you who set the boundaries of the earth; you made both summer and winter.
~ Psalm 74:16-17

Follow the directions to the intersection of the Rainbow Lake Trail-1130, with the Roxy Ann Lake Trail-1179, hike [98].

At this intersection, instead of heading down to Roxy Ann Lake, continue on 1130 for a steep, one-mile hike up to the Continental Divide, on the Wyoming Trail-1101.

Now follow the directions in hike [32], from the point where the Wyoming Trail-1101 intersects with the Rainbow Lake Trail, all the way up to the top of Lost Ranger Peak.

Map: Trails Illustrated 117; Book map 12.

35. To Lost Ranger Peak (11,932')

via the Lost Ranger Trail - 1131

Please note: *I have not personally hiked trail 1131 yet. The following trail information comes from the U.S. Forest Service, Parks Ranger District: 970-723-8204.*

How to get there: From Walden, take County Rd. 12W west to County Rd. 18, and continue west. Turn right where pavement ends on County Rd. 5 to Delaney Butte Lakes. Go west on County Rd. 20 from Delaney Butte to the Routt National Forest boundary. The Pitchpine Trailhead is just west of the boundary. This trailhead provides access to the Grizzly-Helena Trail. Take this trail (1126) north 3-miles to the intersection with the Lost Ranger Trail near Red Canyon Reservoir.

Attractions: Solitude! The trail is very steep and rough. It is closed to motorized vehicles as almost all of it lies within the Mt. Zirkel Wilderness. Magnificent scenery of Red Canyon is seen from many points along the trail. The large saddle along the Continental Divide provides excellent summer range for elk.

Narrative: Although the Lost Ranger Trail is quite steep and rough, it traverses some of the most interesting country on the Parks Ranger District. To begin, the trail crosses the geological dike formation at the mouth of Red Canyon, which was created as the Roaring Fork carved a passage through this solid rock formation. Both the Reservoir and Falls are on private land, although most maps show them on National Forest. There is no camping or fishing on private land. After dropping into the canyon and crossing the Mt. Zirkel Wilderness boundary, the trail enters an area where hundreds of trees blew down during an ice storm in 1977. A makeshift trail winds through the debris, although recent downfall may occasionally block the trail, which begins to climb steeply along the north side of Red Canyon after crossing the Roaring Fork. The vegetation is very diverse, with rare plants and a scattering of Douglas fir, subalpine fir, Engelmann spruce, lodgepole pine, limber pine, and the only Gambel oak in North Park. As the trail crosses a small open park, a cabin can be seen along Red Canyon Creek, which was probably at one time used by a prospector. The trail becomes steeper and finally switchbacks up to the saddle near the Continental Divide. Spectacular views of the huge red cliffs in Red Canyon are seen along this upper portion of the trail. On top, the trail ambles through high mountain meadows of sedge and delicate wildflowers among scattered stands of dense spruce-fir forests. This saddle provides excellent habitat for elk during the summer and fall, and they may be spotted feeding in the open parks in the early morning or late evening hours. Finally, the Lost Ranger Trail intersects with the Wyoming Trail along the Continental Divide. U.S.F.S.

At 1131's intersection with the Wyoming Trail-1101, it will be about another mile of hiking on, and then just off of, 1101 before you will reach the top of Lost Ranger Peak. After arriving at this intersection, turn left, and head south. The actual trail grows faint-to-non-existent up on this section, but poles and cairns keep you on 1101 until you reach the point where you leave 1101 and walk up the fairly easy last stretch to the top of the peak. Read the last sections of hikes [32] and [33] for additional guidance.

Map: Trails Illustrated 117; Book map 12 and book map 51, page 259.

Everything created by God reflects his glory in some way -
from the smallest microscopic form of life to the vast Milky Way,
from sunsets and stars to storms and seasons.
In nature we learn that God is powerful,
that he enjoys variety, loves beauty, is organized, wise and creative.
~ Rick Warren

teamboat

36. Harrison Creek Fisherman Trail

If people concentrated on the really important things of life, there'd be a shortage of fishing poles.
~ Doug Larson

Of Note: Here's a delightful, easy-to-reach access to a couple gentle streams which feed into Harrison Creek, as well as to Harrison Creek itself, which was named after two early 1870's Steamboat settlers, Charles and Owen Harrison. This hike is a good choice for fly fishermen, or for you if you only have a short time to devote to a hike, since its trailhead is reached after a quick eight-mile drive up Rabbit Ears Pass.

Harrison Creek eventually feeds into Lake Catamount, but this trail follows the creek in an easterly direction. Lovely aspen groves line the trail, and they will provide a good late September easy-to-get-to color show. You should be able to find and feel a bit of solitude here, even though, distance wise, the trail isn't far from U.S. 40 on Rabbit Ears Pass.

Distance: About 0.5-mile, each way, to the creek fording.

Hiking Time: 15 to 20 minutes down; 20 to 25 minutes return.

Elevation: Trailhead: 8,400'; Harrison Creek Ford: 8,200'.

With Children: *The first ten minutes or so drop steeply down to a feeder stream, and young children might need help on the return trip. But even if they make it only to this point, it's a fun, friendly stream with some nice wading pools in which to fish or cool off, on hot, sunny days.*

Yampatika Notes: *The seclusion of this area of Harrison Creek provides wonderful habitat for mink. Related to weasels, this long, skinny animal – up to 24-inches long, peruses the waterways for fish, muskrats and any other meat they can catch. They are dark brown, with a white spot under their chin and chest and a long, skinny tail. Mink is from a Swedish word meaning "stinky animal," alluding to the strong musky scent they produce to mark territory and when they're threatened.*

Fishing: *Good stream fishing for brook and cutthroats in the 6-10" range. Please practice Catch and Release.*

Map: Trails Illustrated 118; Book map 14.

How to get there: Driving east out of Steamboat, on U.S. 40, from the Colorado 131 turnoff, continue up the pass for eight miles.

Later in the season, it's easy to cross at the Harrison Creek ford.

About 0.25-mile past the "Don't Shoot A Moose" sign, look for a small turnout area on the right, just as U.S. 40 begins to curve north, to the left. This is FSR 298. Turn right here and find a place to park your car. Walk on the road for a bit to the last car campsite on the left, where the road dead-ends. The trailhead for this hike begins on the right end of this campsite, and it quickly heads down into the woods.

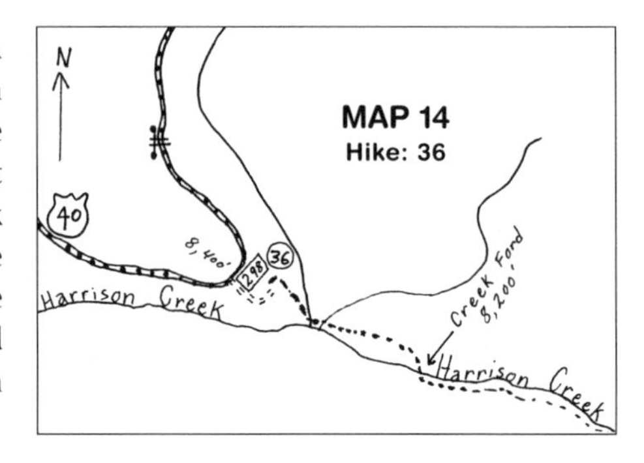

The Hike: Hike downhill in an easterly direction until the trail comes to a stream. Continue on the trail, south/southeast, as it crosses several feeder streams and then meets up with the main Harrison Creek. The wide ford at Harrison Creek is where this short hike turns around, but the trail does continue on the other side of the creek, if you're of a mind to follow it further. It continues to follow the creek and eventually leads to four-wheel drive FSR 303, which then circles north to FSR 251. This rough, dirt road continues north until it ends at its intersection with U.S. 40, across from the Dumont Lake turnoff.

37. Rabbit Ears Peak

In his hand are the depths of the earth, and the mountain peaks belong to him.
~ Psalm 95:4

Of Note: This hike takes you to the eroded base of three independent shafts of rock – 100'-high, rusty-colored pinnacles – two of which are known as "The Rabbit Ears." The twin pillar formation, which stands on the Continental Divide southeast of Steamboat Springs, as well as the pass, was officially named "Rabbit Ears" during a survey expedition in the 1870's because, from a distance, they resemble rabbit ears. Over the years, one has eroded more than the other, making them now look less like ears than they did back then. The landmark is visible along the highway from as far away as Kremmling, and even from the middle of North Park, many miles away.

The route to the summit follows an old jeep road, still used occasionally by people in 4x4 vehicles. You can hike through meadows blanketed in early summer by an unending, colorful crazy quilt of wildflowers – more than eighty species. In fact, during the height of the flower season, generally in early-to-mid July, this will be one of the very best wildflower viewing trails in the whole Routt National Forest. The large meadows are most impressive – overflowing with a myriad of dazzling reds, blues, whites and yellows – all mixed together with a zillion thick clusters of purple-white columbines, the gorgeous, orchid-like state flower. (See page 3.)

The Rabbit Ears Peak hike is one of the best wildflower hikes in Colorado.

The flower's beauty is
so great, it is the choice
within our state.
When friends they ask to
know what's fine,
I often say,
'The columbine.'
~ John Fielder – Colorado
Wildflowers

Tall stands of dark green spruce and fir, along with groves of light-colored quaking aspens, intermix with meadows in a gently rolling terrain. Take your camera, lots of film, a wildflower guidebook, sunscreen and plenty of drinking water. Be prepared for possible bloodthirsty mosquitoes at the top in early summer.

Distance: Approximately 3-miles, each way.

Hiking Time: About 1.5-hours, one-way up, but allow extra time for many photo/flower stops.

Elevation: Trailhead: 9,604'; Peak: 10,654'.

With Children: *This is a wonderful hike for children over mostly open, gentle terrain. Toward the end, there is one tricky steep climb, where the footing for little feet can be difficult. But with adult help, they should be able to manage. Remember to take lots of drinking water, sunscreen, bug repellent, and hats. About two miles into the hike, you'll cross a stream fed by an underground spring. This is a good place for filtering water, if need be. Children will enjoy a short side trip off to the left to follow the stream up to its source, which flows gently out of the side of a hill near the remains of an old cabin. Because of dangerous drop-offs and crumbling rock, don't let children climb up the ears, and be especially careful if you take them with you behind the ears to see the additional views.*

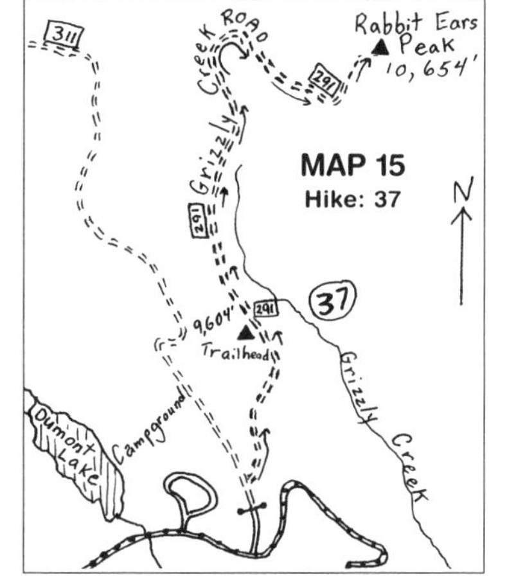

Yampatika Notes: *Between 33 and 23 million years ago would have been a scary time to be in Colorado. Fire in the sky! Intense volcanism produced much of the landscape seen today. The Rabbit Ears are the remains of pyroclastic materials. Some people mistakenly think that the Ears represent the core remains of a prehistoric volcano, but they don't. Instead, they are layers of extruded rock and ash that cooled quickly on the earth's surface, like a many-layered cake, into basalt and breccia. The tiny holes in the basalt were caused by trapped gas within the molten lava. The white mineral calcite cemented all the rocks together in such a way that, over time, as weathering eroded parts of the layers, the cemented harder areas were left intact. And those are the blocks we see today.*

Sit on the base, but it's unsafe to climb up the Ears.

OF SPECIAL NOTE: *Because of its delicate and impressive beauty, the Colorado columbine was decreed to be the state flower in 1899. Exactly 100 years later, in April 1999, horrific, violent events at a high school in Colorado named after the state flower, gave the word "columbine" a totally new and different connotation throughout the whole nation. It is sadly ironic that the name of something so exquisitely beautiful now represents memories of such a terrible tragedy.*

The columbine's blossom has five white inner petals surrounded by five purple-blue outer sepals. Its spurs project backward and hold the nectar that attracts hummingbirds and insects, which then help pollinate this stunning wildflower. *(See page 8.)*

Fishing: *Nearby Dumont Lake is well stocked with easy-to-catch rainbows, using bait or spinners.*

Map: Trails Illustrated 118; Book map 15.

How to get there: Drive 19-miles southeast of Steamboat up Rabbit Ears Pass, U.S. 40. Turn left, north, at the Dumont Lake sign, and follow this old section of the original pass road for about a mile to an old stone monument and historic marker on the left. Turn left here, and drive on the dirt road FSR 131 for about 0.1-mile (if the gate is open) until you see a small, difficult-to-spot marker on the right that reads 291. Park your car here. If the gate isn't open, park at the gate, walk around it, continue on the road until you see the 291 sign on the right. Don't begin your hike until you find the 291 post!

The Hike: Follow the old jeep road, Grizzly Creek Road, toward the ears, keeping left at an early junction with the remains of an old logging road. The Ears will appear to be closer at this point than they actually are, and the views keep getting better and better, as you hike through meadows and clusters of tall fir trees.

About halfway up, the meandering trail begins to climb and level off intermittently. At the end, it climbs a very steep grade for several hundred yards, before suddenly leveling off and ending in woods at the base of the western rock. This is not one of the Ears. A precarious causeway may be very carefully followed to take you closer to the actual Ears.

At this point, you can enjoy spectacular 360-degree panoramic views – of the pointy Whiteley Peak, the Flat Tops to the southwest, the Gore Range to the south, Mt. Zirkel Wilderness to the north, Rocky Mountain National Park to the east, and Walton Peak in the southwest. I recommend against climbing the Ears and suggest using extreme caution if you decide to go close to and behind these brittle volcanic formations to check out all the wonderful views. The rock is old, weathered and crumbly, and there are dangerous drop-offs.

RCA
YOUTH CHOI

38. Six Fishing Lakes:

Fishhook, Lost, Elmo, Round, Percy and Long – Wyoming Trail – 1101

The gods do not deduct from man's allotted span the hours spent in fishing.
~ Babylonian Proverb

The two best times to fish is when it's rainin' and when it ain't.
~ Patrick F. McManus

Of Note: The trip to Fishhook Lake can be an end destination, or the beginning of visits to a series of six delightful fishing lakes – Fishhook, Lost, Elmo, Round, Percy and Long – via a section of the Wyoming Trail-1101. They are all close enough to each other, and on a gentle enough trail, that they can all be visited on a very long day hike. From Fishhook Lake, it will only take a few minutes to hike to Lost, and from there, another mile on level terrain to reach Lake Elmo. Next, after only 0.75-mile more hiking, you'll reach an intersection that takes you soon to Percy and Round to the right, or to Long Lake to the left. See hikes [22] and [23] for other approaches to Percy, Round and Long Lakes. Along the way, you'll pass through dense forests and open meadows.

These lakes provide good fishing and camping opportunities, and any or all of this entire route would be a delightful choice for a family backpack trip.

Distance: 1.5-miles to Fishhook, one way; add on just over another four-miles each way, if you go to all six lakes.

Hiking Time: About 45-minutes to Fishhook, one-way; about 3-hours one way, if you travel to all six lakes and don't remain too long at each one.

Elevation: Trailhead: 10,038'; Fishhook Lake: 9,877'; Lost: 9,900'; Elmo: 10,038'; Round: 10,060'; Percy: 10,034'; Long: 9,880'.

With Children: *This hike is highly recommended for all but very young children. Take boots or extra shoes and socks for possible wet, marshy areas. You can travel to any of these lakes for a fun time with children. Take fishing poles, bait, wildflower guidebook, sketching pad and pencil, plastic containers for nature's treasure finds, etc.*

There are numerous campsites at all of the lakes. It will be wet and buggy in the early part of the season.

Yampatika Notes: *Because of the abundant marshes and stagnant pools throughout this riparian corridor, there are*

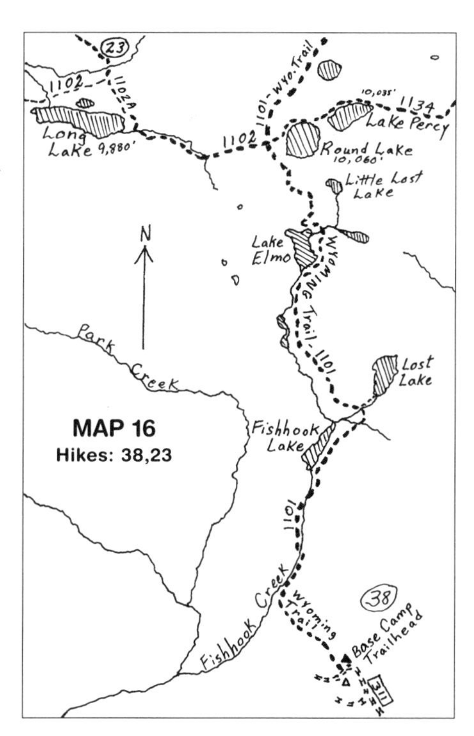

plenty of mosquitoes. Now, before you knock em', take a closer look. In Colorado, there are approximately 43 species of mosquitoes. Some species have a life cycle from egg to adult in only 3 to 4 days! Only the females are out for blood, as they need the protein to develop eggs. They lay eggs in stagnant water. Larvae hatch and live just below the surface of the water, breathing through a tube on their tail. Being at the bottom of the food chain, mosquitoes feed fish, frogs, salamanders, birds and other insects. Without them we would lose our yummy trout, beautiful birds and serenading frogs. Think about that next time you swat one!

The dark spruce/fir forests along the stretch of this trail to Lake Elmo provide excellent habitat for many different fungi. In a very moist summer a few years ago, over forty species of fungi were counted in this area. Even if you don't actually see the fruiting bodies – what we call mushrooms – there are still plenty of other fungi. Just pull up a bit of forest duff and find lacey white fuzzy strands of hyphae, fungus in vegetative state, hiding there. This covers the forest floor under the duff. Fungi can be saprophytes – recyclers of dead materials, mutualistic sympionts – fungi living together with other organisms in a mutually beneficial relationship, or parasites – fungi living on their host. (Also see hikes [22] and [23] for more Yampatika information on the area.)

Fishing:

Please practice Catch and Release.

- *Fishhook Lake: 9.5-acres; depth 5'; good for brookies 6-10" using flies or live bait.*
- *Lost Lake: 15-acres; depth 34'; great for fat brookies and rainbow 10-16" range; trees!*
- *Lake Elmo: 12.6-acres; depth 8'; great for fat brook 10-12" range; grassy, open shoreline.*
- *Round Lake: 16-acres; depth 40'; good for small brook.*
- *Percy: 17-acres; depth 23'; good for brook along eastern shore.*
- *iLong: 40-acres; depth 32', good for brook to 12" along north shore.*

Map: Trails Illustrated 118; Book map 16.

How to get there: Drive on U.S. 40 for 19-miles southeast of Steamboat Springs, up Rabbit Ears Pass, to the Dumont Lake sign. Turn left, north, at this sign, and drive about 1.5-miles to the old Rabbit Ears stone monument. Turn left here, onto FSR 311, and drive slowly for about 4.3-miles on a very bumpy, but usually car-accessible, dirt road, traversing steep slopes through very pretty terrain. Check with the Forest Service to see if the gate for this road is open, and what condition this road is in, especially if it's early in the season or after heavy rains – 879-1870. Eventually, the road levels off, and you'll reach the trailhead sign for Fishhook Lake, also called "Base Camp." This is also a section of the Wyoming Trail-1101, and part of the Continental Divide Trail. Park here.

The Hike: Immediately descend steeply down the remnants of an old jeep road, through the woods, for about a half-mile. Then, travel through a grassy valley meadow, soon crossing Fishhook Creek, a good place to stop for a rest. Hike through more woods, a clearing, and then begin to climb again back into the woods.

Drop down a bit and re-cross Fishhook Creek, and you will have arrived at the southeast end of Fishhook Lake. Find good campsites to the right of the outlet stream.

If continuing on to Lost Lake, about 0.2-mile away, travel along the east side of Fishhook Lake, through the woods, until you come out of the woods to a grassy clearing, which may be wet. Follow a sometimes-faint trail up a grassy slope to the right. Walk for a couple minutes until you see a trail leading into the woods ahead of you, and to the right. Walk about 150-yards on this trail, through a mature spruce and fir forest, until you come to a trail junction sign. Turn right and walk about 0.1-mile to Lost Lake. Look for an old hand-made sign: "If you love this place and its critters, leave it this way – please don't litter!" Fly fishermen may be challenged by trees, which grow near the lake.

Return to the junction and turn right, north, to travel on to the other lakes. The trails are all well marked from here. Or, turn left to return to Base Camp. Continuing north on 1101, you'll pass Lake Elmo, a shallow lake but good for fishing because it's fed by large springs. Little Lost Lake is to the right. Continuing north, reach the intersection with the Lake Percy Trail-1134. A left turn here takes you to Long Lake and Fish Creek Falls, and a turn right, to Round and Percy Lakes.

39. Windy Ridge Indian Quarry

As long as the moon shall rise - As long as the rivers shall flow
As long as the sun shall shine - As long as the grass shall grow
~ Terms of an Indian Treaty

Of Note: This is a fairly gentle hike along a ridge, and then up to the top of a small peak, to the remains of an old Indian rock quarry, once visited by many tribes, which used its orthoquartzite rocks for making tools and arrowheads. A breathtaking view from atop the peak awaits the visitor – so don't forget to take a camera. Avoid the ridge if lightning threatens.

Because this is an important site and has special meaning to Native American Indians, it is very important to treat this area with respect. Do not pick up or remove from the site any of the cultural remains. It is illegal to do so. Take only photos - leave only footprints, please.

Distance: About 2.5-miles, each way.

Hiking Time: 1.5-hours, each way.

Use caution if you decide to sit on the ledge to enjoy the stunning views. Note the trail on the ridge.

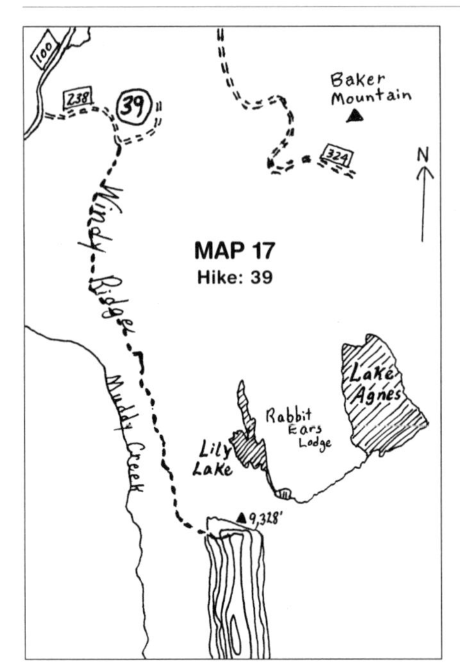

Elevation: Trailhead: 9,000'; Quarry Peak: 9,328'.

With Children: *This is an excellent family hike, with only the last section providing a very short challenge. It would be great fun to read about the area's Indian culture before making this hike, since the tribes considered this a place of special significance. Since hiking along this windy ridge in a cold rain can be a challenge, it's best to make this hike with children only in good weather. Take sunscreen and plenty of drinking water.*

Yampatika Notes: *This quarry produced a beautiful and-durable stone called orthoquartzite. It flaked well and didn't shatter upon impact, so it was a valued resource for the Utes and other Indian tribes collecting it. Look for sandstone at the site. Orthoquartzite started out as sandstone, then with intense heat and pressure, the chemical bonds were changed, and this tough rock, orthoquartzite, was formed.*

Map: Trails Illustrated 118; Book map 17.

How to get there: When you reach the Dumont Lake sign on the left, up on Rabbit Ears Pass, about 19 miles southeast of Steamboat on U.S. 40, continue driving on U.S. 40, past the sign, for 0.9-mile more, and turn right onto F.S. 100. Drive 1.2-miles on 100 until you see a four-wheel drive road on the left. This may or may not be marked. If you don't have a 4x4 vehicle, park here along the road. Walk up F.S. 238 for 0.4-mile, until you see what looks like a fork in the road. This is actually a loop, which circles left, around some campsites, and returns to 238. If you are driving a 4x4 vehicle, park here.

The Hike: From this loop, continue walking on F.S. 238 for just a few minutes. As soon as you notice that the road turns sharply at a 90-degree angle to the left, look carefully right for an unmarked path, which you might easily miss if you aren't paying attention. This path drops steeply down into a large open, sunken meadow. Follow it due south through woods and meadows until you come up onto Windy Ridge. Once on top of the ridge, pass through several woods. Notice a jeep road coming from the right, joining the trail you are on. Pay attention to this fork so that it doesn't confuse you on your return trip out.

At this point, the path on the ridge now becomes an old double track jeep road. Notice a high point outcrop ahead and to your left. The top of this outcrop is your destination. Choose your footing carefully to miss occasional unpleasant cow pies left behind by grazing cattle.

Enjoy the beautiful views and keep walking south, passing Lily Lake on your left. Come to a fork in the road. The left goes down to Lily Lake and Lake Agnes, so you will stay right, heading to the quarry.

Upon entering woods at the bottom of the outcrop, make a final few-minute climb, up through the woods to the top. Enjoy the outstanding views of Lake Agnes and the surrounding peaks. Be careful when climbing over the loose, sometimes slippery, quartz and rocks. Explore the top, noticing the remains of an archeological dig. It is a violation of Federal law to remove any artifacts. Be very careful if you venture out to sit on the over-hanging rocks, even if you are sure-footed.

40. Routt Divide Trail - 1108

Happily may I walk. May it be beautiful before me, behind me and below me.
May it be beautiful above me and all around me.
~ Navaho Song

Of Note: This is a long, 7.1-mile trail, with many alternating elevation gains and losses, and the whole trail makes a better horseback trip than day hike. However, the most interesting part of the trail can be hiked on a 7-mile round-trip section of it, accessed from the southern trailhead. The northern trailhead can be accessed on Forest Service roads with four-wheel drive vehicles, but the drive to the southern end is much more convenient and car accessible.

The Routt Divide Trail runs north and south along the Park Range, south of Rabbit Ears Pass, and along the east side of the Sarvis Creek Wilderness Area. The route is seldom used, so you'll enjoy lots of solitude. But the path itself is well established, wide and easy to follow. It travels mostly through a thick forest of spruce and firs, and it leads to a marvelous large boulder field. Take plenty of water along, since there are no good sources along the way.

How did this get here?

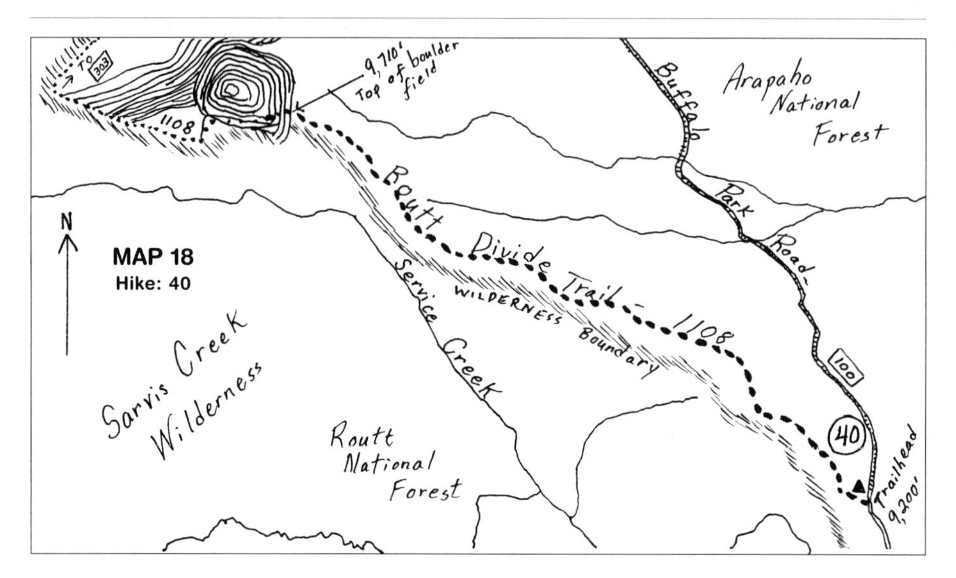

Distance: About 3.5 miles, one-way, to the boulder avalanche field.

Hiking Time: Approximately 1.5-hours, one-way.

Elevation: Southern trailhead: 9,200'; top of boulder field: 9,710'. You'll gain and lose the same 500' many times along the trail.

With Children: *Since this is a "dry" route following no streams nor leading to any lakes, and since it climbs up and down, this is not a good hike for young children. However, if you can turn the hike into a geology lesson, older, in-shape children would enjoy learning about the boulder field – and so would I, if anyone out there can explain it to me!*

Map: Trails Illustrated 118; Book map 18.

How to get there: Driving up Rabbit Ears Pass from Steamboat on U.S. 40, drive 9.5-miles past the Mt. Werner Exit sign. Turn right at FS100, the Buffalo Park Road, and drive 11 more miles until you see the trailhead sign on the right. Off-road parking is available here.

The Hike: Begin walking on a level path through some pleasant small meadows and aspens. The trail soon enters a thick forest of spruce and firs, and then begins a series of up and down gradual climbs. After hiking for about 20 minutes, notice the huge boulder in the middle of the forest on the right, which looks like just a few trees are holding it up. About 20-minutes later, look for two large gnarled elbow-shaped trunks on two pine trees on the left. Shortly after that, watch on your right for two huge round boulders. Sitting atop these boulders, a person can enjoy spectacular vistas, including an outstanding view of the Rabbit Ears. You can also look straight down – almost from the tops of some very tall trees, on the cliff side of the boulders – enjoying a bird's eye view of the world. Use extreme caution if you sit on these rocks. A fall for you or your K-9 from this spot would be deadly. There are numerous huge boulders scattered throughout the forest, and it's difficult to imagine how and when nature placed them there. If you are a geologist and you make this hike, please write and explain it to me.

Continue hiking for about another 45-minutes to an hour, and you'll arrive at the top of a huge boulder avalanche field on your right. Don't descend down the steep switchbacks unless you're investigating the boulders or you feel the need for more exercise, for you can happily enjoy the view from the top. Turn around and return from here.

Visiting a sheepherder on the Walton Peak hike.

41. Walton Peak

How hard it is to realize that every camp of men or beast has this glorious starry firmament for a roof! In such places, standing alone on the mountaintop, it is easy to realize that whatever special nests we make – leaves and moss like the marmots and birds, or tents or piled stone – we all dwell in a house of one room – the world with the firmament for its roof.
~ John Muir

Of Note: Walton Peak was named after William Walton, one of Steamboat Springs' founding fathers, who came from Missouri and lived on what is now Walton Creek for several summers in the late 1870's.

The gentle descent, and then the climb up to Walton Peak are filled with lovely meadows of wildflowers, numerous campsites, and spacious, stunning views off to the side. You may encounter a sheepherder and his flock of Wyoming sheep somewhere along the way, which live and graze here during the summer.

There are no water sources along most of this trail, so bring plenty for you and for K-9 companions.

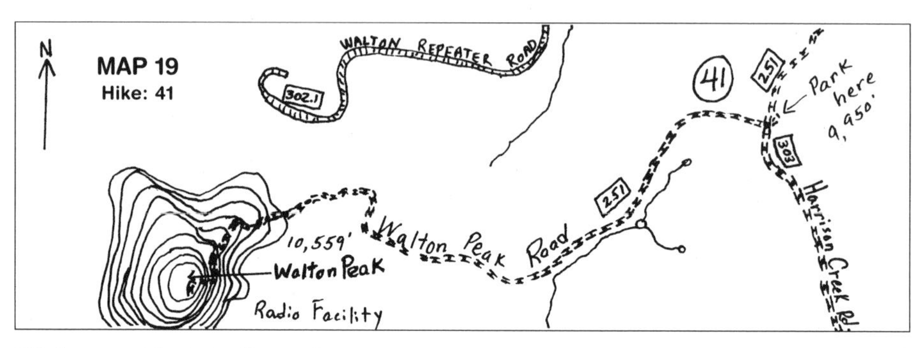

Distance: About 4-miles, each way.

Hiking Time: About 2-hours, one-way.

Elevation: Trailhead: 9,950'; Walton Peak: 10,559'.

With Children: *This route makes an excellent day hike for children, for whatever distance they can make it. The grade is gentle most of the way, and there are many scenic places where you can stop to smell the roses with them. You'll also find numerous outstanding photo opportunities for shots of the kids and family dog, with whole mountain ranges in the background. Since most of it is out in the open, take hats, sunscreen and lots of water.*

Map: Trails Illustrated 118; Book map 19.

How to get there: Drive up Rabbit Ears Pass from Steamboat Springs on U.S.40 for about 19-miles, until the Dumont Lake sign on the left. Turn onto the dirt road to the right, opposite the Dumont Lake side of the road. A sign says Harrison Creek #251. (See hike [36].) Another sign may say: Dead End Road – not maintained for public travel. Except for early in the summer season, the first two miles of this road can usually be driven on in a non-4-wheel-drive car. At 1.2-miles, you'll begin to see a series of nice family car campsites with overlooks. At 2-miles, you'll come to the junction with Buffalo Park Road #303. The sign may say 3-miles to Hwy. 40, but it's actually 2. Park here, since the road becomes much more difficult-to-impossible for non-4x4 vehicles after this point, especially following heavy rains.

The Hike: Continue on foot down 251, the Walton Peak Road, for four-miles to the peak. You will hike gently down a long hill for about 1.5-miles, through alternating trees and meadows. After this, you'll begin to climb gradually up, with the grade increasing in steepness. Switchbacks then lead to the top. Please stay away from the State Highway relay station. Take your camera to record the lovely, expansive views!

42. Sarvis (Service, Sarvice) Creek Trail - 1105
43. Silver Creek Trail - 1106

The clearest way into the Universe is through a forest wilderness.
~ John Muir

These two routes, in the northern part of the Gore Range, parallel each other, and together, they represent the entire twenty miles of trails in the Sarvis Creek Wilderness, which was created in 1993. The area is located about 13 miles southeast of Steamboat Springs, in the Routt National Forest. It is 47,140 acres in size, and elevations range from 7,000' to 10,700'.

The area's ecosystem is comprised mainly of riparian, lower elevation ubiquitous forests of spruce-fir and lodgepole pines. Backpackers enjoy much solitude and ever-changing terrain in this primitive area, and many combine the two trails for a three-day loop trip. Some day hikers shuttle cars at both ends, making it a long almost-11-mile day hike. Others simply walk in part way, and then back out, for a nice day hike.

The trails follow two long marvelous, meandering tributary creeks, Sarvis and Silver, both of which have their headwaters in the Buffalo Park section of the Park Range, and exit into what eventually becomes the Yampa River. As the water in these two creeks journeys toward Steamboat Springs, it passes through a continuous rolling timberland, blanketed by dense stands of lodgepole pines, Engelmann spruce, and subalpine fir, which emit delightfully refreshing forest scents. Here and there, the trees open up into boggy, grassy meadows or in rocky areas, impressive in their unusual formations. Elk, deer, mountain lions, bear, coyote, beaver, marmot, ptarmigan, hawks and eagles all thrive in the thick forests.

Unlike other Colorado wilderness areas, and even other trails in the southern section of the Gore Range, no sections of alpine tundra exist here, nor big, glamorous crystalline lakes or jagged trophy peaks. Yet a trip through these unique, sheltering, quiet forests will reward you in other very special ways.

Hiking along Sarvis Creek.

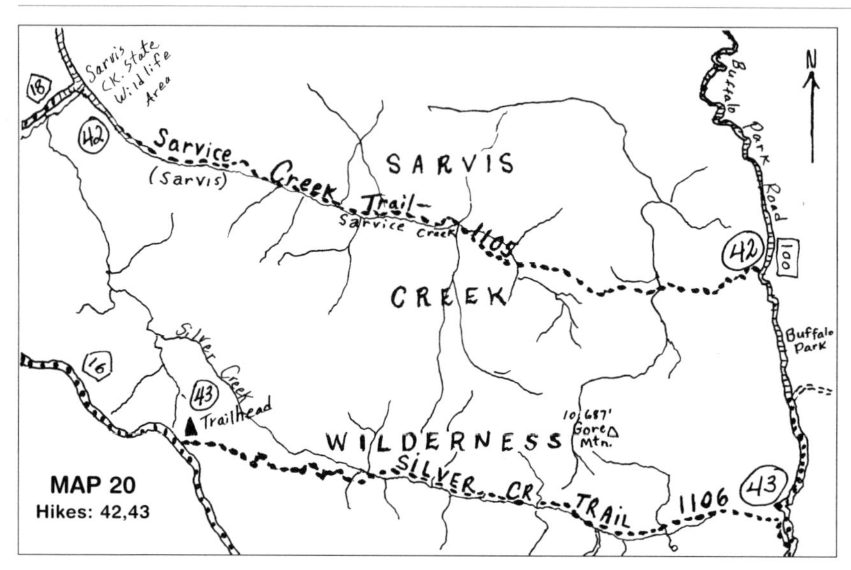

Stories differ as to how "Sarvis Creek" became the "Service Creek" on many maps and trail descriptions, but most locals blame it on an early-day mapmaker who named the creek 'Service' after the many serviceberry bushes, which still line its banks. The name Sarvis – often misspelled "Sarvice," to make matters even more confusing – comes from the Sarvis Timer company operations, which logged this area many years ago.

The eastern trailheads for both hikes are near Buffalo Park, so named because it had been used many years before as grazing range for buffalo.

The tree you saw, which grew large and strong, with its top touching the sky, visible to the whole earth, with beautiful leaves and abundant fruit, providing food for all, giving shelter to the beasts of the field, and having nesting places in its branches for the birds of the air – you, O King, are that tree!
~ Daniel 4:20-22

Of Note: 42. Sarvis (Service) Creek Trail - 1105

Day Hike: Travel west-to-east for the first 4.6-miles, to the remains of an old cabin. Use access #1 below. Although the first two miles from this direction will entail a 1,000-vertical-foot climb, the trail levels off to a much more gradual ascent up a gorgeous valley, along a most-inviting creek.

Backpack Trip: Hike east to west, so that you'll mostly be heading downhill. Use access #2 below to begin, and reverse hike description below.

Distance: Day hike: 4.6-miles, each way; Backpack Trip: About 12.2-miles, each way.

Hiking Time: Day hike: About 2.5-hours, each way; Backpack: 5-hours, one-way.

Elevation: West trailhead: 7,204'; East trailhead: 9,240'.

With Children:

Day Hike: Western Trailhead: Because of the initial long climb, this is not a good hike for very young children. However, older children used to hiking can easily make this day trip. Many years ago, when our youngest was nine, she described it as "the perfect kid's hike: lots of sandy beaches, pools for wading and fishing in, wildflowers, butterflies, deer and cabins to watch out for, and strawberries and raspberries to pick and eat along the way!"

Backpack Trip: This would make a wonderful muti-day, one-way, gentle backpack trip for families, but hike it from east to west, especially if you can have a car waiting for you at the western trailhead, so that you're heading mostly downhill. Because of terrain, finding a good campsite at least 100-feet away from the water may take a bit of time, so save some time for this chore.

Yampatika Notes: *In late spring, search for some unusual plants under the lush foliage by springs along the flat stretch before the bridge, looking for broad-lipped twayblade, a shy, greenish orchid with stunning little flowers. In the deep coniferous forest of this same section, look for a variety of pyrolas. These unobtrusive plants deserve a very close look at their magical flowers. Many have heavenly scents, as well.*

Fishing: *the lower western end of this sparkling trout stream is heavily fished, but still great fun; better Catch and Release "fishing grounds" for small brook trout are found along the upper, eastern end of the creek.*

Map: Trails Illustrated 118. Book map 20.

How to get there:

Access #1: West Portal: Drive out of Steamboat Springs towards Rabbit Ears Pass on U.S. 40 for 3.8-miles from 3rd St., until Hwy. 131. Turn right onto 131 and drive 4.4-miles until Routt 18. Turn left onto 18 and drive 3.45-miles until a Y. Turn left at the Y and drive 3.1-miles until the sign for "Sarvis Creek Trail #1105." Turn left here and drive 0.4-mile to the trailhead and parking area.

Access #2: East Portal: From Steamboat, follow State Hwy. 131 south to Yampa. From Yampa, drive 9.5-miles south to Hwy. 134. Follow 134 east for 11-miles to FSR 250. Follow 250 north for 9-miles to FSR 100. Drive on FSR 100 for 8.5-miles to the Sarvis Creek trailhead on the left, at the north end of Buffalo Park.

The Hike:

From the western trailhead, the path begins at the west end of the parking area, and immediately it begins to climb up through a spruce and aspen-covered hillside, which looks down on Service Creek Canyon, on the western side of the Gore Range. After this point, you'll not have easy access to the creek again for about the first two miles. About 0.25-mile into the hike, enter a large meadow, at the end of

Llamas crossing Sarvis Creek.

which you'll see some Rocky Mountain Douglas-fir trees, a species that thrives on the steep, cooler, slopes of this canyon. Continue to climb through mixed aspens, spruce and firs, until reaching 7,800', about 1.2-miles into the hike. After this, the trail levels off a bit for about the next mile, until you finally reach the large bridge, which crosses the water and puts you on the north side of the creek for the rest of the hike. This begins the prettiest part of the hike, with the trail following closely along the creek, and a surprise awaiting you at almost every turn. Enjoy rock formations, sandy picnic areas along the creek, a waterfalls and perfect campsites along both sides of the creek. Please remember to stay at least 100' away from the water and trail.

At about 2.6-miles into the trip, the creek is filled with large rocks, and the stream disappears underground for several hundred yards or so. Try to guess its course from the sounds.

After a couple hours of hiking, you'll begin to see the remains of old log chutes and splash dams. These were part of the Sarvis Creek Timber Company logging operations, which started up in 1913 and went broke in 1918 – and it's hard to believe that after 80 years, relics of some of these wooden structures still exist. The chutes were used to float logs from the upper part of the creek down to the Yampa River, where they were to be milled.

After 4.6-miles of hiking, you'll see the remains of a still-standing, yet dilapidated, old homesteader's cabin across the creek. Ford the creek on the rocks, explore the cabin, and then, if day hiking, turn around and return from there.

If continuing to the Buffalo Park end, continue walking through a series of small meadows. If you decide to camp here, since it's about the halfway point, please remember to stay at least 100' away from the creek and trail.

At about the 7.3-mile mark into the hike, the trail begins to head southeast, pulls away from the creek, and climbs steeply for about 500' in the next mile and a half, until it levels out again through stands of lodgepole pines. You'll soon reach an old jeep road and follow it for almost another mile to Buffalo Park and the intersection of FSR 100.

Interesting rock formations present themselves along both the Sarvis and Silver Creek trails.

You will go out in joy and be led forth in peace; the mountains and hills will burst into song before you, and all the trees of the field will clap their hands. Instead of the thornbush will grow the pine tree. And instead of briers, the myrtle will grow. This will be for the Lord's renown, for an everlasting sign, which will not be destroyed.
~ Isaiah 55:12-13

Of Note: 43. Silver Creek - 1106

Running parallel to, and only four-miles south of Sarvis Creek, Silver Creek and its trail, 1106, provide yet another easy access into an extremely primitive, heavily forested area. For our purposes of a day hike, we begin on the eastern end, up in Buffalo Park. Silver Creek feeds directly into Morrison Creek, a large tributary of the Yampa River. Hiking 1106 from this direction, from the headwaters down, you'll pass through spongy wet meadows and watch tiny ponds and streams quickly begin to merge, growing in size and strength, transforming into one real creek! Backpackers often hike the entire eleven-miles and then return on the Sarvis Creek Trail – or vice versa. Or they shuttle two cars at both ends and hike one way.

The silvery-white appearance of its rapids gave Silver Creek its name. Buffalo Park, on its eastern end, is a large alpine meadow that once was the summer home for grazing buffalo. And Morrison Creek was named after an old prospector who nearly lost his life trying to find a lost gold mine in the area.

Like 1105, its remote twin trail to the north, 1106 is definitely a place of great beauty and solitude, where you can enjoy the undisturbed hush of a deep fragrant forest, the cold waters of a percolating, bubbly trout stream, dramatic mammoth rock formations, and if you visit very quietly, many surprise serendipity animal sightings.

Distance: Day hike: About 3.5-miles, each way; backpack trip: 10.7-miles, one-way.

Hiking Time: Day hike: about 2-hours, one way; Backpack trip: about 5-hours, one-way.

Elevation: Eastern trailhead: 9,730'; Western trailhead: 7,960'.

With Children: *This is an easy day hike for children of all ages, although there is one stretch of eroded hillside where little ones will have to be helped to keep from slipping. Once you reach the creek, there are limitless places to rest and picnic, as well as excellent campsites for longer family backpack trips. Be sure to camp at least 100' away from streams and trails.*

Fishing: *Good for small brook trout. Please practice careful Catch and Release.*

Map: Trails Illustrated 119. Book map 20.

How to get there:

For shuttling cars: Access #1: West Portal: Go east on U.S. 40 for about 3.8-miles from 3rd Street, until Hwy. 131. Turn right onto 131 and drive for 6-miles south, just past Oak Creek, until Hwy. 14. Turn left onto 14, at the sign for "Stagecoach Reservoir." Continue on 14 until it junctions with Hwy. 16, just past the reservoir. Follow 16 for about 7-miles to the trailhead on the left for Silver Creek-1106. Park here.

Use this for day hike: Access #2: East Portal: Heading up Rabbit Ears Pass, U.S. 40, from Steamboat Springs, drive 9.5-miles past the Mt. Werner Exit. Turn right at FSR 100, Buffalo Park Road, and drive 16.9-miles to the trailhead and parking area on the right.

For shuttling cars: (consult a F.S. map): From the west portal, continue driving south on Hwy. 16, over Lynx Pass to Hwy. 134. Turn left onto 134 and drive to F.S. 250. Turn left and take 250 to F.S. 100. Turn left and follow 100 to the eastern portal on the left.

The Silver Creek Hike offers good family camping.

The Hike:

For day hike: From the parking area of the eastern portal, the trail immediately fords a stream. If the water is too high, you can avoid the wet crossing by walking around the stream on the road and cutting up to the trail. Walk along the old jeep road, through pinewoods for about 1.5-miles, enjoying pretty views of the Buffalo Park area off to the right. There are several old branching jeep roads going off in different directions, which might be a bit confusing, but just remain on the most distinct one.

After about 40-minutes of hiking, you will come to the beginnings of Silver Creek, which at this point is not much more than a ditch. Cross many side streams, and come upon several very interesting rock formations, avalanche remains and a chain of beaver ponds. The creek gradually widens, providing endless spots for fishing, picnicking and camping. After about 3.5-miles, you'll come to where the creek joins with its south fork, and this is where I suggest day hikers turn around.

For backpack or one-way shuttle: For those planning to hike the whole 11 miles, backpackers or day hikers who shuttled cars, continue along the north side of the rushing, tumbling creek. At about mile 7.4, cross Silver Creek itself, and then 1.4-miles later, enjoy unfolding views of the rapids and sheer rock cliffs. When the creek appears 700' below the trail, you'll begin to walk on fairly level ground, which winds its way through a lodgepole pine/Douglas-fir forest. Vegetation now begins to change as you approach the top of an 8,680' ridge, where you will have a raw, exciting view of Morrison Creek. Now descend for 0.8-mile down a dry, sage-covered hillside, away from the creek and among rock outcrops, scattered oak brush and ponderosa pine. Close the gate behind you, and continue downhill for about another 0.1 mile to the parking area.

44. Stagecoach Reservoir

44a. Elk Run Trail
44b. Wetlands Angler Trail

If fishing is like religion, then fly fishing is high church.
~ Tom Brokaw

Of Note: Three-mile long Stagecoach Reservoir is an 866-acre Colorado State Park situated in the lower elevations of the Yampa River Valley, south of Steamboat Springs. It sits in an arid flatland of rolling dry shrubs, sagebrush, and scrub oak, blending together with contrasting lush native grasslands and flowering plant vegetation. Shimmering aspens and forests of lodgepole pines dramatically sweep down to the reservoir from surrounding mountain ridges.

Two good naturalist hikes in the Upper Yampa River Valley can be taken at Stagecoach State Park. The first, Elk Run Trail, meanders in and out of good fishing coves for five miles around the southern shoreline of the reservoir, from the dam on the northeast end, to its inlet at the southwest end. The area attracts mule deer, badger, elk, raccoon, muskrat, squirrels and chipmonks. A large variety of songbirds and waterfowl, including the huge white pelican, can also be spotted while on the trail.

The second hike in this area, on the Wetlands Angler Trail, is a short half-mile roundtrip at the Stagecoach State Park Wetland Area, and it offers fantastic bird watching opportunities. It's located at the intersection of Routt 14 and 16, at the southwest corner of the reservoir.

A fee is required to enter the park. For more park information, call: 970-736-2436.

44a. Elk Run Trail.

You may begin the Elk Run Trail at either the southwest end or the northeast end of the large reservoir. Hiking trail signs will direct you. Most of this trail is wide and level, though other sections climb up and down a bit. Picnic tables are available at many points along the trail, where you may stop for lunch and a little fishing. Bring your birding book and binoculars – enjoy watching sage grouse, hawks, eagles, and various songbirds and waterfowl, including seagulls and the white pelican, one of the largest birds in North America. Watch pelican fly in formation and herd fish to shore.

Six interpretive stops will teach you about the three main ecotypes you will pass through, if you hike for the entire 5 miles. Enjoy views of the Service and Morrison Creek mountains to the east, the Flat Top Mountains to the southwest, and to the north, the cliff face of Blacktail Mountain. Your best chance to see large wildlife is early evening, in or near the woods on the northeast end of the tail. Note: future plans include eventual completion of the trail around the entire reservoir. Call the park if you wish to volunteer to help.

Distance: 5 miles, one way.

Hiking Time: About 2 hours, each way.

The Elk Run hiking trail.

Elevation: 7,212'.

With Children: *This is a very good nature hike to take with children of all ages. Obviously, few can make the whole 10 mile round trip, so it's best to just hike a section of it, and then return at a point appropriate for their ability, or shuttle two cars on either end. Since most of this hike is out in the open, remember to take plenty of water, hats, sunscreen, lip balm and bug repellant, and make certain children use it all. Take a picnic lunch and fishing gear, and stop for some fun along the way.*

Fishing: *Stagecoach Reservoir contains feisty Rainbows and Snake river cutthroat trout, Okanee Salmon, Pike and Splake, a cross between lake and brook trout. Almost any fishing method seems to work in the reservoir. For more information, call: 879-3922.*

Map: Trails Illustrated 118; Park map available at park entrance.

How to get there: From 3rd Street, drive 3.8 miles east out of Steamboat on U.S. 40; turn right, south, on Hwy. 131, and drive 5.5 miles to Routt 14. Turn left here and follow the sign to the reservoir. There is a fee to enter, and tickets are freely issued to vehicles which fail to display proof of payment.

44b. Wetlands Angler Trail

This trail is set up to blend in with the area's natural habitat, and it teaches people about wetland ecology and species. The highest concentration of wildlife in the park is found along this trail. A half-mile round trip on boardwalks through a riparian-type wetland area, called the Angler's Trail, takes hikers to a series of interpretive stops where details of the area's water fowl are taught. Wooden waterfowl viewing blinds allow nature lovers to spy on waterfowl. Two handicapped accessible fishing areas are available here as well. Take along your bird book and binoculars for this one.

Yampatika Notes: *A few of the birds you can see include common yellowthroat, yellow warbler, American coot, cinnamon teal, green-winged teal, red-winged blackbird, great blue heron, white-faced ibis, ring-necked duck, northern harrier, belted kingfisher, several species of swallow and sparrows, and white pelicans. This colony is generally of one-year-olds, not yet ready to breed. The first breeding colony of white pelicans in Colorado was east of Greeley in 1962. Only 15 colonies totaling about 35,000 birds remain in the world.*

Distance: 0.5 mile, roundtrip.

Hiking Time: variable, since this also involves study time.

Elevation: 7,250'.

With Children: *If you are visiting Stagecoach State Park, the Wetlands is a must for all ages of curious, nature-loving children.*

Map: Map kiosk at the trailhead.

How to get there: Follow the directions for [44a] above.

45. Morrison Divide Trail - 1174

The tree which moves some to tears of joy is in the eyes of others only a green thing that stands in the way.
Some see nature all ridicule and deformity...and some scarce see nature at all.
But to the eyes of the man of imagination, nature is imagination itself.
~ William Blake

Of Note: In 1878, Joe Morrison, a prospector, almost starved to death trying to find a lost gold mine on the creek, which was later named after him. Ute Indians in the area told James Crawford, Steamboat's founding father, that a "crazy man" had lost his bearings, and Crawford initiated a successful search for Morrison.

This Morrison Divide Trail has northern and southern trailheads. From the north, the trail climbs steeply up the east slope of the Green Ridge to Muddy Slide, a geologic landslip. The entire trail is about 13.3-miles long. Since it climbs about 2,000', it's best to make two separate day hikes out of the whole trail, each beginning from different trailheads. Or, hike the entire distance on an overnight backpack trip, leaving cars at both trailheads.

For a day hike, I suggest taking the northern route, about four miles up to the top of the Morrison Divide, to see the gigantic ravine on top of Green Ridge, a large muddy mountainside. Sweeping views of Rabbit Ears Pass, and even the ski runs of Mt. Werner, are also yours to feast on.

Dirt bikes are allowed on this trail, and if your ears object to the occasional loud motorbike engine noise, you should probably not make this hike on the weekend, when dirt bike traffic is heaviest. At this writing, I have not yet hiked the south portal section of this trail, but I provide information from the Forest Service for those of you who want to do so.

Distance: 4-miles, each way.

Hiking Time: 2.5-hours, each way.

Elevation: Trailhead: 8,209'; Muddy Pass: 10,184'

With Children: *If you're looking for a pretty place to backpack in for an overnight with children, yet not have to walk too far, this is a good hike for you and your family. After about an hour of hiking, you'll find several beautiful meadows and creeks, each inviting you to come on in and set up a camp. If you can spend two nights, and if the children are hardy souls, day hike from your base camp the next day to the special view on top, and then back, carrying your packs out on the third day.*

Yampatika Notes: *From a distance, Muddy Slide looks like a barren spot on Green Ridge. Up close, the power of destruction is quite apparent. Looking down into the slide, you'll notice mostly shales, sandstones and softer rocks. These have no solid rock layers down to where Muddy Creek exits underground, far down below. As spring rains and snow melt saturate the soft layers, massive sections slide on well-lubricated particles down from the hillside to be carried away on the fast-flowing waters. How many more years do you think this hillside will remain?*

Map: Trails Illustrated 119. Book map 21.

How to get there: Drive east on U.S. 40 for 3.8 miles from 3rd St. Turn right onto 131 and drive for 6 miles, just past Oak Creek. Turn left onto Routt 14 at the sign for Stagecoach Reservoir. Continue on 14 until it junctions with 16, just before the reservoir. Turn right onto 16 and follow it for about 12 miles, until you see the Morrison Divide North Trail sign-1174, on the right. Park here.

The Hike: This hike is a good climb. The last stretch is an effort, but before this tough part, the trail will cross somewhat gently through beautiful flowered meadows and forests of pine and aspen, with alternating up and down portions. Streams are plentiful and easy to cross, including Clear Creek and Muddy Creek, which takes its name from the cloudy water caused by the runoff from the gigantic slide above. There are numerous perfect camping sites on the lower section of this hike. Birds and wildflowers are plentiful, and the variety of terrain is a joyful surprise.

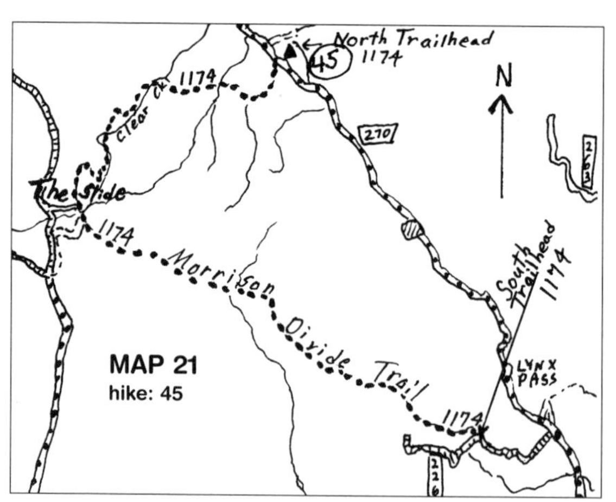

After you've hiked about an hour-and-a-half, begin to look for

Dudley and Sammy encounter a yak at the Morrison Divide Trailhead.

a right turn, marked by a rock cairn, off to the right, on a less-worn trail. You need to turn right here, off the more worn trail you're on, and it's very easy to miss if you aren't looking for it. Then, feast your eyes on the unique, curious geological oddity ahead of you!

From the U.S. Forest Service: *From the south trailhead, the trail begins adjacent to private land in the Morrison Creek Valley. Some confusion may exist at its location. The traveler should proceed southwest from the parking area, staying just below the tree line. The first mile remains in the sagebrush covered meadow. Continuing in a southwesterly direction, it climbs a small hill covered with lodgepole pine, and then descends to Muddy Creek (mile 1.1) Turning easterly, it again begins a gradual ascent to an elevation of 8,600'. But again it drops 120-feet to a crossing of Clear Creek (mile 2.0). The remaining part of the trail follows the Clear Creek drainages up the east slope of Green Ridge. Several switchbacks are required to make the climb.*

46. Tepee Creek Trail - 1173

They will set up their camps and pitch their tents among you...
~ Ezekiel 25:4

God has cared for these trees, saved them from drought, disease, avalanches, and a thousand straining, leveling tempests and floods; but He cannot save them from fools.
~ John Muir

Of Note: Many, many moons ago, this creek, near what is now the Lynx Pass area, was a very popular camping area for Ute Indians, and thus evolved the name, Tepee Creek. They used the area's straight and skinny tall trunks of the pine trees for constructing these tepees, or lodges, and thus evolved the name "lodgepole pine." Modern-day backpackers now carry and set up rip stop nylon tents with folding metal poles, but this area is definitely still an ideal place for easy "family tenting." The Indians knew a good thing when they saw it!

The trail makes many gradual, moderate up and down climbs, traveling through varied types of forests and meadows. It reminds me in many ways of the Sarvis Creek Trail, just to the north, although, because of timbering roads, this area is far less primitive or removed from civilization than is Sarvis Creek. Early on in the hike, you'll encounter one nasty area, the dregs of a timber cut, along with a wind-caused blowdown of trees on the edge of this cut, which has since been cleared from the trail.

Because this trail is part of the Gore Pass Mountain Bike Trail System, you may encounter cyclists along the way.

Distance: 4 miles, each way.

Hiking Time: About 2 hours, each way.

Elevation: 9,000'.

With Children: *Yes! This is a good, moderate trail for an easy family backpack trip. First, purchase and take with you a book about the Ute Indians at the Yampatika Nature Store at 10th and Lincoln. Then read it to the children around the campfire at night, as you try to imagine a tepee where your nylon tent now stands. Tepee Creek itself is a pretty mellow, kid-friendly stream. If packing in is a challenge for your group, you need only hike in a couple miles before finding excellent campsites along the creek.*

Yampatike Notes: *As you enter each stream crossing where there is mud along the edges, you may notice a moving mass of blue flower petals that suddenly flit away as you draw near. These small bright blue butterflies, called "the little blues," are sipping or sucking up minerals from the mud through their proboscis, a straw-like tongue that is curled up under their faces. These are mostly males that you see, since they need extra minerals during courtship.*

Fishing: *You'll be able to see and catch the brookies in the creek and beaver ponds along the way; fishing is also very good for rainbow trout in Rock Creek, the end destination for this hike.*

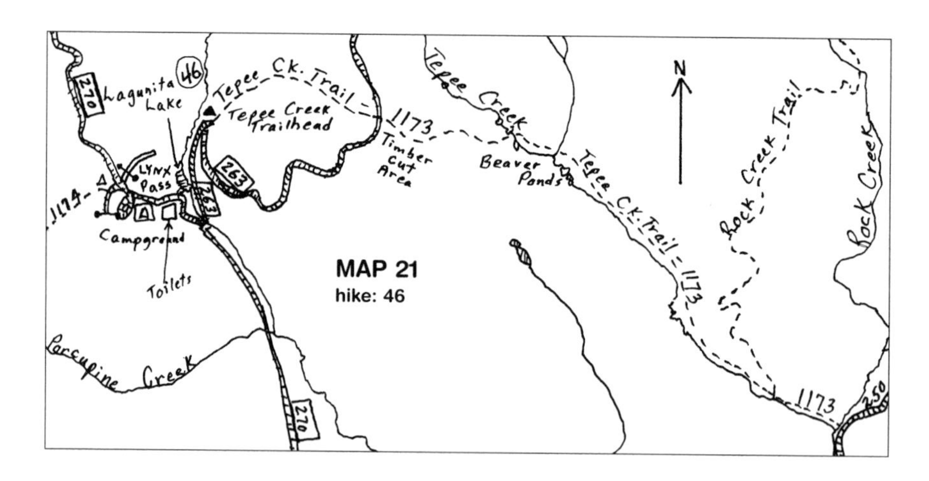

Map: Trails Illustrated 119. Book map 22.

How to get there: Drive east on U.S.40 for 3.8 miles from 3rd St., until Hwy. 131. Turn right, south, onto 131 and drive for 6 miles, just past Oak Creek. Turn left onto 14 at the sign for Stagecoach Reservoir. Continue on 14 until it junctions with 16, just before the reservoir. Turn right onto 16, Morrison Creek Road, and follow it for about 18 miles (16 becomes 270). Continue past the Lynx Pass Campground on the right and the outhouse on the left, and watch shortly thereafter for the sharp left-hand, north turn onto FSR 263; at this writing, the sign for 263 had been knocked down, but there is still a sign telling you to turn here for the Tepee Creek Trail. Follow 263 for about 0.25 mile, and you'll very soon see the trailhead sign on the left – exactly at the switchback in the road. Park here.

Good campsites abound along the gentle Tepee Creek.

The Hike: The trail climbs a bit for the first mile, as it follows a small stream. After it crosses FDR 263, you'll come to the unsightly timbered area mentioned above. You'll soon cross a fork of Tepee Creek, and then cross Tepee Creek itself, continuing for the remainder of the hike on the north side of the creek. Near the end of the hike, go past the intersection with the Rock Creek Trail, which goes left, north. Remain on the main trail, heading southeast. A bit further on, you'll reach the crossing of Rock Creek itself and see FSR 250. Turn around and return at this point. (Please note: anglers seeking to add additional mileage to a backpack trip in this area can turn north and find some good fishing along Rock Creek.)

47-49 Sheriff Reservoir

47. Black Mountain Creek Trail - 1117
48. Four Fun Lakes: Spring, Camel, Crater, Sand - 1123
49. Bunker Basin Trail - 1109

Elk country is home to all sorts of wildlife – from tiger salamanders to zebra Swallowtails to cutthroat trout. These creatures don't have antlers or horns or big brown eyes, but they are all vital strands in the web of life.
~Rocky Mountain Elk Foundation

Hiking along Sheriff Reservoir.

Of Note: Some of the drive to Sheriff Reservoir from Steamboat Springs is along a section of the Flat Tops Trail Scenic Byway. The route to the trailhead for these three hikes winds through a great variety of stunning terrain – fertile rangelands, farmlands, rolling hills, woodlands, canyons, high plateaus, meadows, valleys, and streamside riparian areas. If you're a photography buff, you'll want to stop often to capture scenes of picture-postcard working ranches and farms, surrounded by snow-covered Flat Tops Mountains in the background. The U.S. Forest Service slogan, "Land of Many Uses" is very apropos for this area, since on any given visit, you may encounter cattle ranchers, real cowboys, hunters, anglers, campers, picnicking tourists, outfitters, hikers, loggers and sheep herders, in no particular order!

In 1991, the U.S. Forest Service officially dedicated the Flat Tops Trail Scenic Byway, a distance of 82 miles, from Yampa, Colorado, to Meeker, Colorado. The Byway route was used many moons ago by the Ute Indians, and perhaps driving along this section of it will wet your appetite to someday explore the whole distance. Stop at the U.S. Forest Service office in the town of Yampa (300 Roselawn; 970-638-4516) to pick up a free copy of "The Flat Tops Trail Scenic Byway" to guide you on this lovely journey.

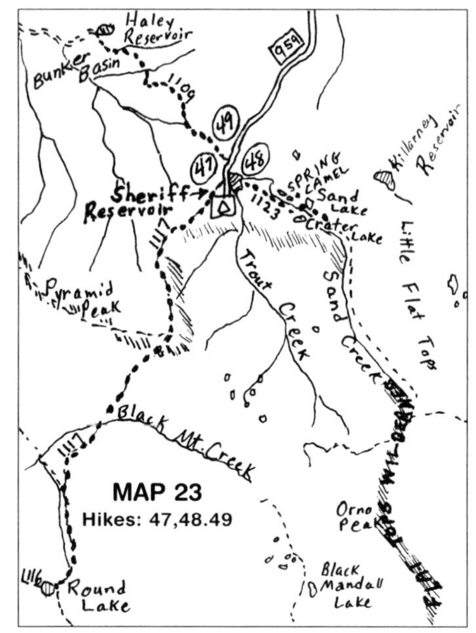

Three trails out of Sheriff Reservoir are covered in this book, and because of the driving involved to get there from Steamboat, you may want to plan an overnight car camping trip at or near this reservoir to allow you to take in two of the hikes, as well as enjoy the delightful reservoir itself, which serves as a supplemental municipal water supply for nearby Oak Creek.

How to get there: To Sheriff Reservoir: Drive out of Steamboat Springs towards Rabbit Ears Pass on U.S. 40 for 3.8-miles, from 3rd St. until State Hwy. 131. Turn right here, south, and drive about 25-miles to Yampa. Just as you arrive at Yampa, where 131 junctions with Main Street on the right, turn right onto County Road 17. The street sign names it as such. Travel north on 17 for 5 miles to County Road 132. Follow 132 west to Forest Highway 16, also called Rio Blanco 8, and follow this for about 9-miles to 959. Turn left at the Sheriff Reservoir sign, and drive for about 3-miles to the trailhead parking, at the north end of the reservoir, which sits at 9,520'.

47. Black Mountain Creek Trail - 1117

When an old bull elk dies in February, coyotes, ravens and magpies quickly clean up the meat.
Next spring, gophers gnaw on the bones for calcium and other minerals.
When one of the gophers dies, beetles eat its decomposing carcass.
And what's left over decays into the earth and is reborn as more nutritious grass.
- Rocky Mountain Elk Foundation

Of Note: This trail out of Sheriff Reservoir is an opportune place for spotting deer and elk, enjoying wildflowers in mid-to-late July, spectacular views, and a marvelous contrast in colors in the fall. It is 5.3-miles long, and it connects with #1119, which, with an additional 1.5-miles of hiking, will take you all the way to Round Lake, a beautiful little lake well worth a visit, if you have the time and energy to backpack in.

Don't make this hike unless your legs and lungs are in good shape, since it requires lots of climbing and stream-crossing. Interestingly enough, there doesn't seem to be any Black Mountain in the vicinity of this creek, so the origin of this creek's name is something to wonder about! Trail #1117 parallels some of the Flat Tops Wilderness boundary and heads toward the Pyramid Peak area, the first mile on an old logging road. After that, it travels 4.3 more miles through very primitive, lush meadows and open woodlands, until joining up with #1119.

River crossings can be very difficult to impossible in the early summer weeks along this route, so it's probably safer to hike this trail after mid-summer.

Distance: 5.3 miles to the junction with #1119; about 6.8-miles if going all the way to Round Lake.

Hiking Time: About 2.5 hours, each way, to the #1119 junction. Approximately another 1-hour if continuing on to Round Lake.

Elevation: Sheriff Reservoir: 9,780'; East of jct. with #1112: 11,100'; At jct. with #1119: 9,730'; Round Lake: 10,490'.

With Children: *This is not a good hike for children, with even the first part of it climbing more than 1,000'.*

Yampatike Notes: *The open meadows along this trail, particularly at lower elevations, are ablaze in late July and August with orange sneezeweed. The Comanche and other Native Americans inhaled the dried, powdered flowers to make them sneeze to clear out their sinuses. Sheepherders avoid taking their flocks through fields of this plant since it is highly poisonous. Watch for a myriad of other flowers in these meadows, including tall larkspur and little sunflower.*

Fishing: *Sheriff Reservoir is good for rainbow; fishing good for brook in Black Mountain Creek and Williams Fork along the trail; good-sized cutthroats waiting to challenge the angler at Round Lake.*

Map: U.S.G.S. Dunckley Pass and Trails Illustrated 122. Book map 23.

How to get there: Follow directions to Sheriff's Reservoir above.

The Hike: Please note the trailhead sign for #1117 on the right-hand side of the road, opposite the reservoir dam. Begin a long, two-hour climb southwest up from Sheriff Reservoir, through a lovely large meadow, gaining almost 1,000' above the reservoir, which, when looking east, you'll be able to see down far below you. At mile 1.4, you'll cross a shale outcrop. If the shale is wet from rain or snow, be especially careful crossing it. When the trail turns south, you'll be traversing the Windy Gap area, the ridge between two drainages named for the ever-present wind. Ascend less steeply now, as the trail begins to level out a bit – thank goodness! Soon it begins a gentle descent down through a timber forest. From this vantage point, you can look down into Bunker Basin to the west and to the Trout Creek drainage to the east. At mile 2.5, you'll cross into the Flat Tops Wilderness, which will be the highest point on this trail at 11,125'. You'll also have wonderful views of Sand Point at 11,132' to the east, of Dunckley Pass and the Dunckley Flat Tops to the north, as well as of the impressive Pyramid Peak to the west. At mile 3.0, the junction with #1112, you can take a one-mile side trek to Pyramid Peak, if you have the time, or better yet, save it for its own special hike.

Continue a gentle descent through many beautiful small stands of trees and open meadows, and look for deer and elk. Follow a small intermittent stream for about a mile through a low stream valley, and then cross the stream. You may have to get your feet wet, so keep the water-crossing shoes handy. The rest of the trail winds down along a ridge of spruce and firs, and then

Little Flat Top Mt. looms above Sand Lake.

begins to descend steeply, crossing Black Mountain Creek. You'll head downhill, across a steep, clear hillside and junction with trail #1119.

Head south if you plan to continue on to Round Lake. After about another 0.5-hour of hiking, you'll reach another fork in the trail. Take the trail right. Look carefully for this junction, and be aware that it may not be marked. You'll need water-crossing shoes to ford the East Fork Williams River, and early in the season, it may be too dangerous to do so. Look for the continuation of the trail on the other side, and then follow the trail, which bears uphill, right. The last 0.4-mile section of the trail up to this beautiful lake is almost straight up, but once you arrive, you'll be happy you made the effort. The round-shaped lake enjoys steep banks on its north side, and it is decorated with huge evergreen trees and a scenic background vista of the Devil's Causeway outcropping. Enjoy! Enjoy!

48. Four Fun Lakes: Spring, Camel, Crater, Sand - 1123

Where else would be a better place, to park yourself and slow the pace?
Perhaps to sit and check the map, or better yet, to take a nap.
~John Fielder, Colorado Wildflowers

Of Note: Here's a short, fun 1.2-mile hike to four small, delightful mountain lakes, each just a few minutes away from each other. Yet, because the trail ascends up the face of a broad low ridge, the hike is steep enough that you'll feel you've gotten some good exercise while you're at it. Early in the season, especially, the ground around the lakes can be swampy.

Distance: 1.2-miles, each way.

Hiking Time: About an hour each way, if you don't spend too much time at each lake.

Elevation: Sheriff Reservoir: 9,520'; Sand Lake: 10,192'; Camel Lake: 10,100'.

With Children: *Although quite steep in some places, this hike is still short enough for most youngsters to enjoy. Use the U.S.G.S. Dunckley Pass quad, and make a game out of your child first drawing his or her own map to the "Four Fun Lakes," and then follow their homemade map to the lakes. Have the children try to guess how each lake got its name; e.g., Crater Lake was named for the crater-like depression in which it was formed, etc.*

Yampatika Notes: *After crossing the dam of Sheriff Reservoir, make a detour to a small pond to the right as you begin to climb. An unusual plant, buckbean, can be found in the water. If you're lucky enough to find it in bloom, you'll be rewarded with frilly-edged cream-colored flowers. The three-parted leaves are visible in the water other times of the year, as well. It is found in scattered ponds in northern Colorado. Why it grows in some ponds and not in others is unknown. Please do not disturb these plants.*

Fishing: *Excellent, high-quality fishing exists at Sheriff Reservoir. Spring Lake supports few fish. Camel Lake, 2-acres in size and 5-feet deep, contains a few brook and cutthroat; Crater (4 acres, 10 feet deep) and Sand (2 acres, 12 feet deep) lakes prove more promising, both providing good habitat for cutthroat and brook. Fish habitat improvement projects are evident in this drainage. A pipeline supplying water from Sand Creek to Crater Lake, to prevent winterkill, was constructed in 1966. The water level at Sand Lake was also raised about this time, as well.*

Map: U.S.G.S. Dunckley Pass. Book map 23.

How to get there: Follow directions to Sheriff Reservoir above.

The Hike: As you arrive at Sheriff Reservoir, stop and park in the large turnout areas on either side of the road. You'll see the Forest Service kiosk on the right. The trail for Sand Lake begins across the road, on the left/east end of the dam. Walk over the spillway bridge and meet up with trail #1123, heading southeast through a thick spruce and fir woods. Cross Sand Creek, and then drop down some 200 feet in elevation. At 0.8- mile, arrive at Spring, and then, almost immediately afterwards, arrive at Camel Lake. About 1/3 of a mile later, arrive at a fork. First, follow the sign's direction to crystal-clear, emerald-colored Crater Lake, and then, retrace your steps back to the fork and hike for just a couple more minutes to Sand Lake. Little Flat Top Mountain looms high above this lake, and you'll probably want to capture it in a photo. Here's where you'll turn around and return the way you came.

For the more adventurous, this trail continues on for another five miles, crossing Little Flat Tops, and eventually ending up near Yamcolo Reservoir, just below Stillwater Reservoir.

49. Bunker Basin Trail - 1109

When people and mountain lions are hunting elk in October, the elk head for the north slopes of mountains and burrow into thick stands of dark timber. Lurking among the deadfall where pine martens live, the wary elk position themselves so that they can smell, hear and see any intruder long before they themselves are seen.
~ Rocky Mountain Elk Foundation

Of Note: If you want to photograph majestic elk close up, or just take pictures of gorgeous aspen groves and wildflowers, make this lovely hike with a telescopic lens camera. Travel quietly in the early morning hours through these huge aspen groves, and you'll probably see more elk than you can count.

The trail leads to a sun-swept open basin, and then to Haley Reservoir, a small irrigation reservoir, and it travels through some of the prettiest, most-awesome aspen groves I've ever been in. This is also a fabulous place to view aspen leaves in the fall – but wear a lot of orange if hiking during September's bow hunting season.

On an early morning, late-July hike on this trail, Dudley and Sammy llamas were absolutely intrigued at every elk encounter on the way in, when we were upwind of the animals. On the return, downwind from the big wapitis, the llamas had to stop every few yards to smell the elk scent and search with their eyes for these huge beautiful creatures. The 350-pound llamas seemed far more enchanted than alarmed by the five-feet-at-the-shoulder elk, which weigh 750-pounds or more.

Distance: 2.9-miles, each way.

Hiking Time: About 1.5-hours, each way.

Elevation: Sheriff Reservoir: 9,617'; Haley Reservoir: 8,788'. You'll hike downhill almost 1,000' on the way in, and uphill that much on the return.

With Children: *Before making this hike with children, visit Yampatika Nature Store at 10th and Lincoln, and purchase a children's book about elk, or borrow one from the library. The night before making the hike, car camp with the children at Sheriff Reservoir, and read the elk book to them around the campfire. Then, rise very early and take them on this hike–or at least on a part of it–through these amazing aspen groves, and you will all most likely get to see live elk.*

Also, borrow or buy a copy of my children's book, Stop Spitting At Your Brother! Life Lessons of a Rocky Mountain Llama, at the library, or from Yampatika or Off the Beaten Path Bookstore, and read Chapter 4 around the campfire as well, in which Dudley and Sammy have a very funny encounter with an elk in an aspen grove.

Fishing: *Excellent fishing at Sheriff Reservoir.*

Map: U.S.G.S. Dunckley Pass. Book map 23.

How to get there: Follow directions to Sheriff Reservoir above.

The Hike: As you arrive at the north shore of Sheriff Reservoir, stop and park in the large turnout areas on either side of the road. On the right-hand side, look for a large rock and a small sign for Haley Reservoir – Bunker Basin. The trail heads up through a beautiful lush meadow. At the top of the meadow, you'll see a sign on your left for Bunker Basin, and you'll enter a mixed stand of spruce and fir trees and begin to head in a northwesterly direction. After about 0.6 mile, you'll enter a series of pretty meadows known as "Sneezewood Park." (Somebody must have needed antihistamines here!) You'll travel through a series of dense aspen groves, where you'll most likely see elk. After about an hour into the hike, enter a large marshy meadow. This is Bunker Basin. The trail may seem to disappear at this point, but look for a pole and rock cairn directly north and a little to the left, and head for it. Easily cross a tributary of Bunker Creek and reach the pole and the once-again obvious trail. At the pole, trails go straight ahead, right and left. Continue straight ahead, north, at this point, until you see another pole-rock cairn. The trail now travels through some timber and parallels an irrigation ditch, which flows into Haley Reservoir, the southwest shore of which you'll reach after about ten more minutes of hiking. The six-acre reservoir was constructed in 1920 for irrigation purposes. A dirt road on the west end provides maintenance access and connects with Routt 16 near the town of Pyramid, along the Williams Fork River.

On your return, just after climbing up into the trees again from Bunker Basin, be sure to turn left at a junction with another trail going right, which you may not have noticed on your way in. Look for an old gray tree stump, which many years before had been chopped off with an ax, and head back that way. Also, watch carefully for the trail when you reach the meadow where you can once again see Sheriff Reservoir. If you aren't careful, you may end up off the trail and on an old logging road, which drops onto the main road, FSR 959, below the reservoir and your car, a bit out of your way.

During the fall rutt, mid-September through mid-October, elk descend from the higher elevations and gather in the large, grassy meadows like Bunker Basin. The average bull elk stands about five-feet at the shoulder and weighs 700 pounds, twice as much as the average llama.

50. Allen Basin Trail - 1181

Creeps and idiots cannot conceal themselves for long on a fishing trip.
~ *John Gierach*

There he stands, draped in more equipment than a telephone lineman, trying to outwit an organism with a brain no bigger than a breadcrumb, and getting licked in the process!
~ *Paul O'Neil*

Of Note: Allen Basin was named after a pioneer homesteader who filed a claim on the water in the early 1880's, but he never proved up on the claim. Area ranchers built the reservoir, 100 surface acres in size, to increase their supply of irrigation water.

The drive to this trailhead is a long one for just a short two-mile hike, but the Routt County 15 portion of the drive is worth the trip alone. It travels through scenic Colorado ranch country, with photo-inspiring views of the Flat Top Mountains in the background. The short hike is moderate, pleasant and offers lovely views, solitude and good fishing. The trailhead for this hike is very close to another resource, Crosho Lake, which is also worthy of a visit. Trail #1181 provides the only public access to Allen Basin Reservoir.

Distance: 0.9-mile, each way.

Hiking Time: About 0.5-hour, each way.

Elevation: Trailhead: 8,070'; Allen Basin: 8,080'.

With Children: *There are a few steep sections on this hike, but most children will be able to make it, since it's less than a two-mile roundtrip.*

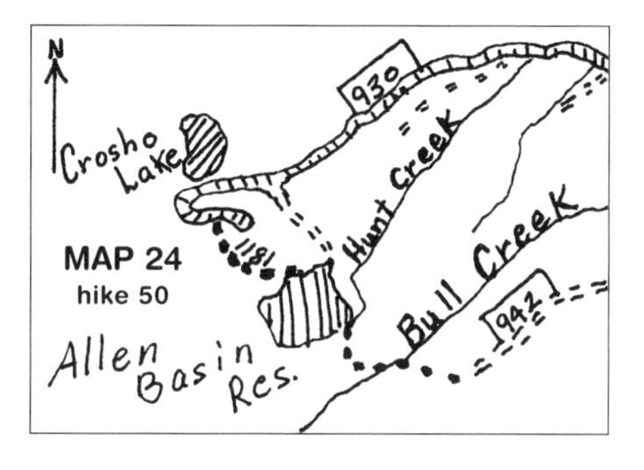

Fishing: *Rainbow, brook and cutthroat are plentiful in the 14-16" range. The required hike in takes the pressure off the resource. Flies and lures only.Nearby Crosho Lake is one of only two lakes in the area which has grayling, and the bag limit on grayling is two 16" or longer. It also contains brook and rainbows. Flies work best at Crosho Lake.*

Map: Book map 24. Use Forest Service map for drive to trailhead.

How to get there: From 3rd St., drive west on U.S.40 out of Steamboat for 3.8-miles until Rt. 131; turn right onto CO131, and drive south for 21 miles, and then look for Routt 15 on the right, just as you are leaving the town of Phippsburg. Follow 15 for 9.3-miles, enjoying the scenery as you go. At every junction, remain on 15. The last three miles narrows and climbs, and you'll now see signs calling it FSR 930. Travel past the sign for #1181 on the left for a wee bit to first check out Crosho Lake. There are a number of good, primitive car campsites at the lake. When you're ready to hike, return to the sign for #1181, now turning right, and drive about a half-mile until the trailhead. Park here, and pick up the trail at the sign.

The Hike: The narrow footpath leads into an aspen grove and soon meets a wider old jeep road; turn left onto the road. The wider trail now heads gradually down, through forests of pine and aspen. Keep in mind that the trip back may take longer because you'll be returning uphill. There's an easy stream crossing, which is also a good water source if you have a filter. At one point, you'll see the large reservoir down to the left, over a stock fence, but the trail will enter more woods for a while, and eventually bring you down to the water's edge. Enjoy some good views along the way. Coming back, watch carefully for the metal trail marker on the right, which takes you off the road and back onto the narrow trail through the woods, returning you to your car.

If you hike in this area during the fall rutt season, the strange noises you'll no doubt hear will be the bugling of lovesick bulls, which compete with each other for the elk cows.

Spitting

AMC

Looking down at Stillwater Reservoir.

51-58 Flat Top Wilderness Hikes

In the wilderness, prepare the way of the Lord; make straight in the desert a highway for our God. Every valley shall be lifted up, and every mountain and hill be made low; the uneven ground shall become level, and the rough places a plain. Then the glory of the Lord shall be revealed, and all people shall see it together.
~ Isaiah 40:1-8

In all of nature, there is something of the marvelous. ~ Aristotle

Of Note: Mention "the Flat Tops" to Steamboat Springs residents, and they will point to a distant flat-topped mountain range, which almost appears to have had its top sliced off, about thirty miles to the southwest. Then they will probably proceed to tell you all about their scary hike over the infamous Devil's Causeway. But more than 160 miles of trails cross the Flat Top Wilderness, encompassing 235,000 acres of scenic terrain, located on the White River Plateau. To do it justice, I would need to write a whole book just on hikes in the Flat Tops Wilderness. But, for the purpose of this book, I cover just the most easily accessed eight Flat Tops hikes, if you're coming from Steamboat. Hike [47] also heads into the Flat Tops, but it has a different access point than do the other eight hikes described in this section.

The area's Ute Indians used to call this landscape "the Shining Mountains," and its vast wilderness and high plateau has a fascinating geological history, making the mountain range unique to Colorado. Here and there, an occasional 1,000-foot peak rises up above this level plateau, but no tall-spired "fourteeners," and few steep-sided peaks challenge the visitor. Rather, the Flat Top range is a massive plateau of rock, which Mother Nature lifted upward and then planed level, leaving above-timberline flat mesas and abrupt drop-offs at the cliff edges.

Millions of years ago, molten lava erupted from beneath the land and flowed for miles across this terrain, and the process began. About 52 million years ago, these glorious mountains were uplifted, molded and sculpted. More volcanic activity followed this uplift, capping the tops, and then ice-age glaciers formed and crawled along, slowly gouging out small jewel-like lakes, deep, U-shaped valleys, and high-cliff amphitheaters.

Today in the Flat Tops Mountains, a maze of more than one hundred miles of icy streams and eighty sparkling high mountain lakes beckon day hikers, anglers, horseback riders, backpackers and hunters. Elevations are high, between 10,000 and 12,000-feet, as trails cross over cliffs

Crossing the Stillwater dam.

and expansive alpine tundra, as well as through lush, rolling wildflower-bedecked subalpine meadows. The whole area provides excellent habitat for a myriad of species – including trout, elk, deer, black bear, fox, coyote, bobcat, pine marten, mink, beaver, snowshoe hare, marmot and pica. Occasionally, mountain lions, bighorn sheep and moose are spotted. Birders, too, find this area a nirvana.

Tree species change with the elevation – from oak, aspen and conifers, to lodgepole pine, Engelmann spruce and subalpine fir. Treeline begins around 11,000', with the spruce and firs at this level changing into the familiar flag trees – stunted, gnarled "Krummholtz" – "twisted wood." Above timberline, alpine tundra appears, hosting the traditional delicate, tiny alpine plants, which tenaciously hug the ground for survival and enjoy their brief time in the sun, before the early winter snows begin to bury them again in early fall.

The first two hikes presented here, to Harper Reservoir and to Heart Lake, are not within the wilderness area, but since their trailheads are close to the access points for the others, they are grouped with the Flat Tops hikes. The other six hikes all begin at points between Yamcolo and Stillwater Reservoirs, and all of these do lie within the wilderness boundary.

Steamboat residents especially enjoy hiking this section of the Flat Tops Mountains in late September, when even more breathtaking beauty returns to the area's prodigious aspen forests, creating whole quilts of shimmering golden-sloped hillsides, topped by snow-covered mesas and cliffs.

Stop in at the U.S. Forest Service office in Yampa, (300 Roselawn, 970-638-4516) to pick up a free brochure, "Flat Tops Wilderness," which provides a good map and a more in-depth description of this area. An excerpt from the brochure offers:

"The Flat Tops are a concentration of flat-topped headlands dominated by the White River Plateau, a flattened dome of geological strata capped with lava. The plateau is most prominent at the Chinese Wall and the Devil's Causeway, a narrow ridge between the drainage of the East Fork of the Williams Fork River and the North Fork of the White River.

Wide canyons, eroded by centuries of wind and water, reach far into the plateau, forming great amphitheaters ringed by rock escarpments. Above the cliffs is a gently rolling grassland dotted with islands of timber. Elevation – approximately 10,000 feet."

Most locals refer to the following set of Flat Top hikes as the "Stillwater hikes" because they originate at or close to the Stillwater Reservoir, headwaters of the Yampa River. Before the reservoir was built in 1939-41, a narrow gorge at that location held the water flow of several streams, and they formed an area of still water. Thus came the name, "Stillwater" Reservoir, one of FDR's Great Depression public works projects. To this day, the reservoir provides irrigation water to area ranches.

The scenic drive from Steamboat Springs to the Stillwater section of the Flat Tops takes you through the old-west town of Yampa, Colorado, "Gateway to the Flat Tops." While in Yampa, stop at the Montgomery Merchandise – a delightful, old-fashioned general merchandise store on Main Street where, it's like the slogan for Lake Wobegon's "Ralph's Pretty Good Grocery Store," 'If we don't have it, you probably don't need it.' Then, visit the historic Antlers Café and Bar for a delicious lunch or dinner. Built in 1902, the Antlers was once an overnight stage stop between Steamboat and Wolcott, and for a time, the largest hotel in Routt County.

Because of the enormous amounts of water in this wilderness area, especially early in season, be prepared for annoying flies and mosquitoes.

51. Harper Reservoir

Set up road signs; put up guideposts. Take note of the highway, the road that you take. ~ *Jeremiah 31:21*

Of Note: I don't generally enjoy hiking on roads, even rustic, gravely ones, but this short hike is an exception to my rule. Unless it is muddy, you can actually drive a car to this destination, but the walk in is quite pleasant, unique and worth the effort. The first part of the hike climbs a little, but after that, it's a pretty gradual walk in to a scenic reservoir. During the week, this hike offers quite a bit of solitude, as well. This is also a good birding hike.

Families can base camp at lovely Gardner Reservoir, and then day hike from there to Harper, enjoying two reservoirs for the price of one, so to say. This is a wonderful hike to make in late September. It also provides some excellent opportunities to shoot photos of large scenic park areas. And Stillwater Reservoir is "just up the road a bit" from this trailhead.

Distance: Just over two-miles, each way.

Hiking Time: About 45 minutes, each way.

Elevation: Gardner Reservoir: 9,630'; Harper Reservoir: 9,820'.

With Children: *This is a gradual climb on a gentle, wide road, so most children can easily make this hike, though on a hot day, be certain to take lots of water, since most of it will be in the open. Families can also enjoy car camping, picnicking, and easy mountain biking at Gardner Reservoir.*

Yampatika Notes: *From Gardner Reservoir, look toward Big Flat Top Mountain. Those exposed glacially carved cliffs show the layers of many volcanic eruptions, beginning around 24-million year ago until around 7.5-million years ago. Steam and lava oozed through fissures in the earth created by the White River Uplift, which began about 40-million years ago. Layer after layer of volcanic materials were laid down over the millions of years to harden into what we see today.*

Fishing*: Gardner, rated fair for rainbow and brown, sometimes has winterkill; brook trout generally exist in Harper, although it may dry up in a drought year.*

Map: Trails Illustrated 122. Book map 25.

How to get there: Driving east out of Steamboat, turn right, south, on Hwy. 131. The total driving mileage from CO131 to the trailhead is 38.3 miles, if you want to measure it. Upon entering the town of Yampa, stay right, on Main Street, and at the Antler's Inn, turn right onto CO7, which eventually becomes F.S. 900. At mile 36.4 from Hwy. 131, you'll see the sign for Gardner and Harper Reservoirs on the left. Turn here onto 910, and drive 1.3-miles to Gardner Reservoir. Park here.

The Hike: Continue hiking on 910, turning south on the east side of Gardner Reservoir. Stay left at the first fork – right takes you to a good camping site and a toilet at Gardner. Hike on 910 until it forks with 915. Continue south on 915, passing through forested areas and wide-open, lovely meadows. At the intersection of 915 and 915-1A, look to your right and notice a huge, perfectly oval-shaped grove of aspen trees – just as if a gardener had planned it that way. Turn left, east, onto 915-1A, and follow this road for a few minutes to Harper Reservoir. Note the nice view of 12,172' Dome Peak looking southwest of the reservoir.

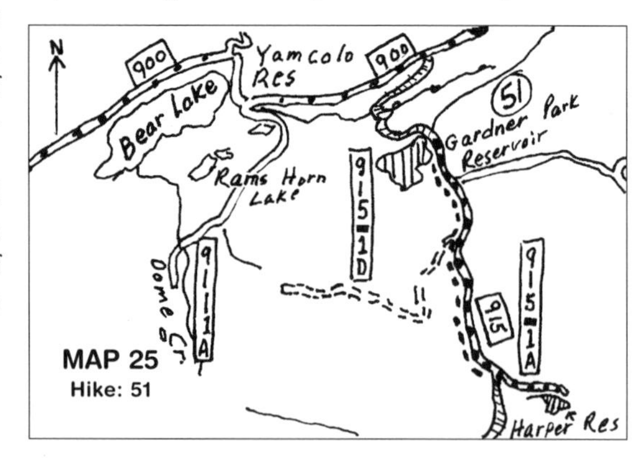

MAP 25
Hike: 51

A well-done scenic handicapped accessible interpretive trail, which is located on the southeast side of Gardner Reservoir, runs through the forest adjacent to the reservoir.

Sammy at Harper Reservoir, with Dome Peak in the background.

52. Heart Lake - 1110

Create in me a pure heart, O God and renew a steadfast spirit within me.
~ Psalm 51:10

Of Note: If you enjoy taking impressive photos, here's a hike for you! To avoid the crowds and ATV's, try to hike this trail during the middle of the week, when it's not heavily used. Don't be tempted to shoot all your photos at the first impressive sight, for there will be more along the way.

The 13-mile roundtrip hike up to Heart Lake is too long for most people to make in a day. The trail climbs up and down long stretches of moderate steepness. But even if you can only make it part way for a day hike, it's well worth the effort. You'll alternate hiking through glorious stands of aspens, open lush meadows and parks, and cooling, thick forests of spruce and fir. This trail is also a marvelous place to enjoy listening to bird sounds, encounter elk and deer, and to observe and study the different life stages of the aspen tree – here contrasting dramatically from whole enormous stands of very young to huge stands of tall, mature aspens.

If you can backpack in, with or without llamas, there are a zillion good campsites before and at the lake itself. Stream crossings are numerous, but almost all easy.

This should be on your list of top spots to go for fall colors, although be aware that the trail is also popular with hunters in the hunting season.

Distance: 6.5-miles, each way.

Hiking Time: About 3-hours each way, at a steady pace.

Elevation: Stillwater Reservoir: 9,347'; Heart Lake: 9,947'; gain and lose this same 600' many times along the route.

With Children: *Even if you have to turn around after two or three miles, this is a worthwhile trip for children, especially if you can put them into the wonderful photographs you'll want to take. Take a tree book along, for this is a perfect kid's hike for tree study—especially for aspens.*

Fishing*: Heart Lake: 24-acres in size and 18' deep; large rainbows!*

Map: Trails Illustrated 122. Book map 26.

How to get there: Drive out of Steamboat Springs toward Rabbit Ears Pass on U.S.40 for 3.8-miles from 3rd Street. Turn right, south, on Hwy. 131, and drive about 25-miles to the town of Yampa, staying right on Main Street as you approach the town. Drive through town, and at the Antler's Inn, turn right onto CO7, which eventually becomes F.S. 900. Drive southwest for ten miles, just before the Yamcolo Reservoir, to the Heart Lake Trailhead sign on the right. Turn right, north, just after the sign, and stay on this gravel road to the parking area, a wee bit past the camping sites and latrine.

The Hike: Begin a rather steep descent to a bridge, which crosses the fast-flowing Bear River. Then cross another footbridge over an irrigation ditch coming from Coal Creek, and begin a two-mile climb through stands of aspen, to the hike's high point at 10,045'. At about mile two, you'll cross the first of several gorgeous open meadows, Moore Park, named after Herb Moore, who settled here in 1890. The trees now change from aspens to forests of fir and spruce. At mile 3.5, cross Moody Creek, and the trees return back to aspens. Go through a section of the forest, noticing the dregs of an old timber sale. At mile 4.3, you'll pass through a break in an old fence, and at about mile 5.0, arrive at Bull Park Reservoir. Pass on the west side of this reservoir and head steeply west, up the hill, on the very visible old wagon road tracks which lead to Heart Lake.

Gorgeous scenery awaits you along - 1110.

Before heading up, however, if you have the time, you can follow the trail north for about 10 minutes to check out McChivvis Reservoir. Once there, climb up the hill overlooking the reservoir to get a spectacular view of the valley below. Camp overnight up on this spot, if you want to simultaneously see a vast array of God-made stars above you and man-made lights down below you, emanating from the town of Yampa, off in the distance.

From Bull Park, it's a moderately steep mile-and-a-half ascent up to Heart Lake, through a cool, very dense forest of spruce and fir. The pretty 24-acre lake sits at 9,947', and campsites are plentiful. Explore the remains of old lodging facilities that existed here during the 1930's. The natural-made lake was converted to an irrigation reservoir in 1910 with the raising of its water level.

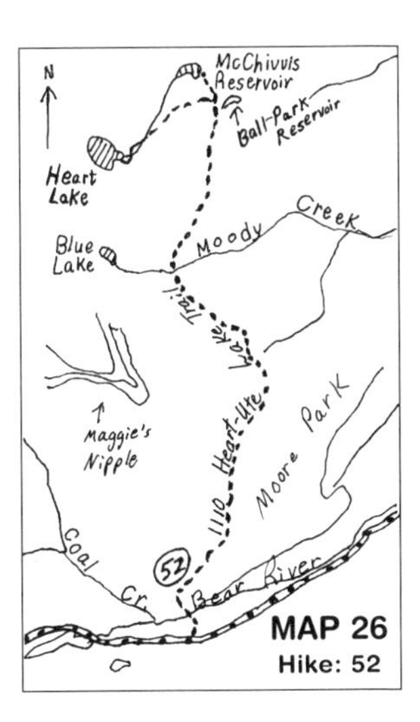

53. Mandall Lakes and Pass - 1121

Sing to the Lord with thanksgiving; make music to our God on the harp. He covers the sky with clouds; he supplies the earth with rain and makes grass grow on the hills. He provides food for the cattle and for the young ravens when they call. His pleasure is not in the strength of the horse, nor his delight in the legs of a man; the Lord delights in those who fear him, who put their hope in his unfailing love.
~ Psalm 121:7-8

Of Note: There are actually five named Mandall lakes and several small, unnamed lakes along this trail. Black Mandall is the largest and most frequently visited, and due north of it, you can climb to the top of almost 12,000' Mandall Pass to enjoy eye-opening views. The trek to the top of the pass and the return to the trailhead can be made by robust hikers in a day, but the lakes offer good fishing and comfortable respites from the dog-eat-dog world, if you can backpack in for an overnight or two. Coming and going, you will be treated to outstanding views of the Flat Top peaks on this hike. In early July, colorful flower-dappled alpine meadows delight visitors.

If you aren't fond of flies and mosquitoes, it's better to make this trip late in the season, when the insects have dissipated. Take water-crossing shoes to help navigate possible tricky stream crossings.

Distance: About 4-miles to the lake; another mile from there to the Pass.

Hiking Time: About 3-hours, each way, to the top of Mandall Pass.

Elevation: Trailhead: 9,840'; Black Mandall Lake: 10,770'; Mandall Pass: 11,980'.

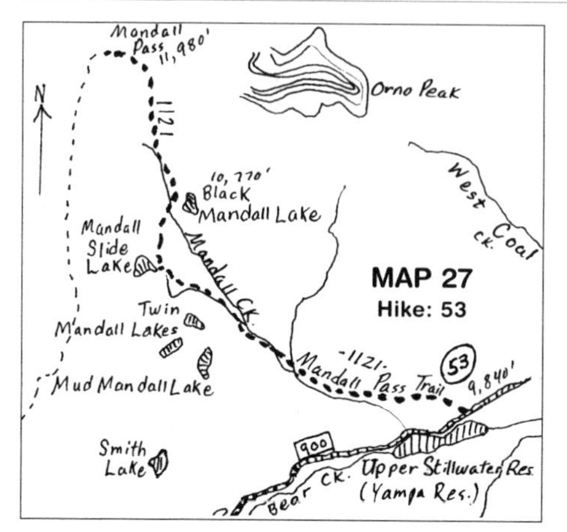

With Children: *This is too long a day hike for most children, but if you divide it into a three-day family backpack trip, most strong-legged youngsters will have fun here, late in season, when the bugs are long gone. Children may need some help with stream crossings.*

Yampatika Notes: *From an airplane, the Mandall Lakes look like a string of pearls. In this glacially formed valley, huge blocks of melting ice remained in large depressions, as the main bulk of the glacier retreated. The ice eventually melted, leaving behind a beautiful-colored kettle lake. The brilliant blues of glacially formed lakes come from the extremely fine sediments floating in the water left by the glacier.*

Fishing: *Bear Lake: 47-acres in size – built in the 1960's as a conservation and recreation reservoir: brook, cutthroat and heavily stocked with catchable rainbows – fish west and south ends of lake; Mud Mandall Lake: 2-acres in size, 3' deep, brook, cutthroat and rainbows; Twin Mandall Lakes: lower: 5 acres in size, 5' deep, brook and rainbows – upper: 8-acres in size, 15' deep, brook and rainbows; Slide Mandall Lake: Cutthroats; Black Mandall Lake: 9-acres, brook and rainbows.*

Map: Trails Illustrated 122. Book map 27.

How to get there: Drive out of Steamboat Springs towards Rabbit Ears Pass on U.S.40 for 3.8-miles from 3rd St. Turn right, south, onto Hwy. 131 and drive about 25-miles south to the town of Yampa, staying right on Main Street, as you approach the town. Drive through town, and at the Antler's Inn, turn right onto CO 7, which eventually becomes F.S. 900. Drive 12.7-miles and arrive at the Bear Lake Campground. Park across the road from the Mandall Lakes trailhead sign. [Please note: On some maps, Bear Lake may also be called Upper Stillwater Reservoir or Yampa Reservoir].

Black Mandall Lake.

View from Mandall Pass.

The Hike: The first mile to the wilderness boundary traverses gently through woods of tall aspens, on the north side of Mandall Creek. After about twenty minutes of hiking, you'll see and hear Mandall Creek. Notice fallen dead timber lying in between the green live trees on the hill-side. At mile 1.5, cross the creek—there are logs, but you may need your water-crossing shoes. The stream now switches to your right. After about 45 minutes of gradual climbing, the trail levels off in a meadow, and then into a subalpine Englemann spruce/fir forest. Wide meadows alternate with the trees. Soon, cross the stream again, and now hike for a ways between two streams, one on your right and one on your left. After reaching a beaver pond on your left, at mile 2.6, come to a trail which takes you back to four Mandall Lakes – Mud, Twin and Slide. This trail is not officially maintained. Look northeast to see Orno Peak, 12,133' high and about two-miles away.

After investigating these lakes, return to the main trail, climb up through more woods, passing over a man-made footbridge spanning a boggy area, and soon come to a fork in the trail and a sign. At mile 3.2, follow the trail to the right to get to Black Mandall Lake, about another quarter-mile from this point. Or, to climb Mandall Pass, take the trail to the left. From here, you'll leave the headwaters of the Mandall Creek drainage and begin a steep, rocky ascent up to the top of the pass. Notice several small, unnamed lakes and dark-green, sun-splashed meadows down below you.

At mile 4.0, in just a half-mile, the trail will gain 450' in elevation. Expect to find snow at this point, even in mid-summer. At mile five, arrive at the top – 11,960' high, and enjoy studying the sweeping Flat Tops amphitheater cliffs to your right, the serene beauty of 12,027' Orno Peak to your left, and the fragile alpine tundra treasure, directly underneath your feet!

54. Smith Lake - 1194

Flowers are there for our souls to enjoy. These souls would have no rainbows if our eyes had no tears. ~ Sioux Indian Proverb

Of Note: Smith Creek and Lake are named after Tom Smith, a fur trapper who lived in the surrounding area around 1880. Smith supposedly crawled into a grizzly bear's den, killed the animal and sold its fat for 10 cents a pound, an early-day version of, "I Can't Believe It's Not Butter!"

This is a friendly, easy hike up to a charming lake, which you should take if you're camping in the area and you don't have much time to make one of the longer hikes. The trail will give you a good taste of what the area has to offer. In just over half a mile, you'll gain only about 267 feet, so even visiting relatives from rolling Kansas can probably join you on this one. With just a little investment of time, you'll be treated to impressive views, and if in season, masses of colorful wildflowers in hilly alpine meadows.

You'll enter the official Flat Tops Wilderness just below the south shore of the lake. Following the North Elk River, the trail is well established and easy to follow. Be prepared to cross several creeks and streams. Early in season, be prepared for pesky insects! Camping is not allowed within 0.25-mile of Smith Lake.

A visit to charming Smith Lake.

Distance: About 0.7-mile, each way.

Hiking Time: About 20 minutes, one-way.

Elevation: From Cold Springs Campground: gains 277' to Smith Lake: 10,500'.

With Children: *A very nice hike for children. They may need help crossing streams. Take a picnic lunch and fishing equipment, and make a fun day of it.*

Fishing: *Smith Lake: 11 acres in size and 12' deep; good for brook and cutthroat trout.*

Map: Trails Illustrated 122. Book map 28.

How to get there: Drive out of Steamboat Springs toward Rabbit Ears Pass on U.S.40 for 3.8-miles from 3rd Street. Turn right, south, on Hwy. 131, and drive about 25-miles south to the town of Yampa, remaining right on Main Street as you approach the town. Drive through town, and at the Antler's Inn, turn right onto CO 7, which eventually becomes F.S. 900. Drive for 16 miles, until you see the sign for Smith Lake and the Cold Springs Campground on the right. The trailhead begins at this campground behind site number 4.

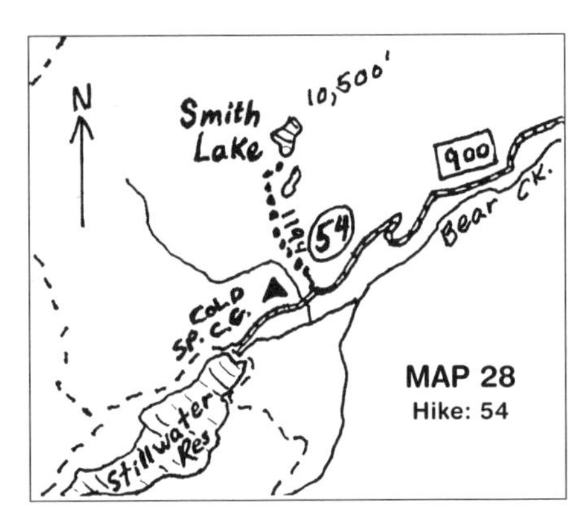

The Hike: The trail climbs steeply in the very beginning, but never fear – it will level off after just a few minutes and remain gentle for the rest of the way. It quickly crosses Cold Spring Creek, named so because its temperatures during the summer average 35-degrees – just above freezing.

After entering a small patch of spruce and fir, the trail turns north. About a half-mile into the hike, go right at a fork, pass two ponds – one on your right and one on your left—and very quickly arrive at the lake.

55. Hooper and Keener Lakes - 1122 & 1160

Climb the mountains and get their good tidings. Nature's peace will flow into you as sunshine flows into trees; the winds will blow their own freshness into you, and the storms their energy, while cares will drop off like autumn leaves.
~ John Muir "The Wilderness World of John Muir"

Of Note: The trail to Hooper and Keener Lakes takes you south from Stillwater Reservoir, up through thick aspen and fir forests and meadows lush with wildflowers, to a timberline saddle at 11,190', and then down to these two delightful alpine lakes, which offer good fishing and camping. Outstanding views present themselves along the whole way up, and even more impressive ones are encountered once up in the saddle. The trail begins in the Routt National Forest and ends in the White River National Forest.

Like most of the Flat Top lakes, Hooper and Keener were carved out by icy glaciers, which grew along the plateau's rim. Raw basalt cliffs, which stand above the lakes, cap the top of the high plateaus like outcrop fortresses.

One of the largest forest fires ever in the State of Colorado once burned within one mile of these two lakes, in June 1980, when more than 10,000 acres were charred.

Distance: 3-miles, each way.

On the way to Hooper and Keener Lakes.

Hiking Time: 2-hours, each way.

Elevation: Trailhead: 10,280'; Saddle: 11,190'; Hooper Lake: 10,864'; Keener Lake: 10,780'.

***With Children**: Most older, in-shape children will enjoy this day hike to the top of the saddle, and then down to the two lakes. Because of the initial ascent up switchbacks, this would be a difficult backpack trip for most children.*

***Yampatika Notes:** Standing in the saddle with Big Flat Top Mountain rolling dramatically to the northeast and Ship Rock looming to the west might make you feel like you're in another world. The trees here are dwarfed and bizarre. This miniature forest is the "krummholz," German for "crooked wood." Winds constantly prune them to grow horizontally into dense, protective thickets eking out an existence at their upper limits. They provide great protection for ptarmigan and other animals.*

***Fishing:** Stillwater Reservoir: good supply of rainbow, brook and occasional cutthroat in the 10-14" range; best fishing near the boat ramp on the northwestern end; Hooper Lake: 22 acres in size, 10' deep – good for plump rainbows; Keener Lake: 12 acres in size, 30'deep – good for rainbows.*

Map: Trails Illustrated 122; Book map 29.

How to get there: Drive out of Steamboat Springs toward Rabbit Ears Pass on U.S.40 for 3.8 miles from 3rd St. Turn right (south) onto Hwy. 131 and drive about 25 miles south to the town of Yampa, remaining right on Main Street as you approach the town. Drive through the town, and at the Antler's Inn, turn right onto Co. Rd. 7, which eventually becomes FSR 900. Drive 17 miles on FSR 900 to Stillwater Reservoir. Don't be confused when you pass two other reser-

Standing above Keener Lake.

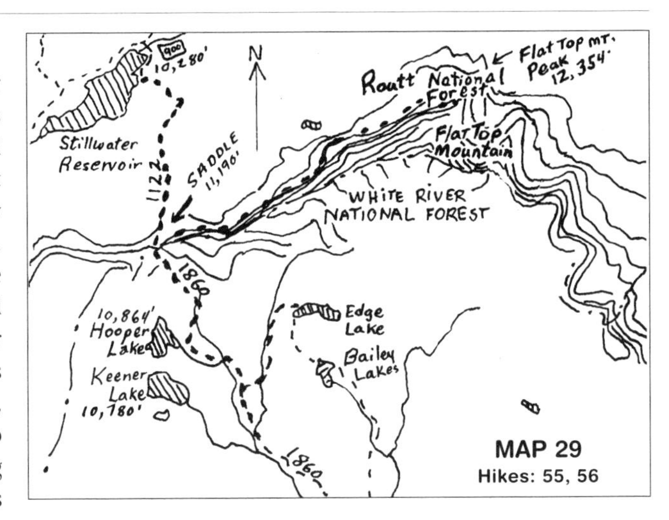

voirs, Yamcolo and Bear Lake (also known as Upper Stillwater). FSR 900 dead-ends at Stillwater, so you'll know it when you get there. Don't panic if you see hoards of cars parked here. The trailheads for several popular trails begin out of Stillwater, and many cars also belong to people fishing and picnicking at this large reservoir.

The Hike: Follow the road across the crest of the dam. Once across the dam, look for a small sign, sign the registry, and then pick up the North Derby Trail-1122 south. Head into the woods and cross a large open park. Then begin a moderate climb up through stands of spruce and fir. At mile 0.8, after reaching 10,445', the trail reaches the boundary of the Flat Tops Wilderness. It heads downhill for a short while, bending right and passing some small ponds. It then turns left and climbs again along a small stream, heading up toward the pass.

At mile 1.5, enter a section of forest which burned in 1980, in a fire caused by a careless smoker. Continuing in a southerly direction, at mile 1.8, cross a small stream and then begin making a very steep climb up a rock outcrop on a series of switchbacks. Pause every now and then to catch your breath and enjoy the views, as you finally come to the top of the saddle at mile 2.1, altitude 11,190'. This high spot is the divide for two river drainages – the Yampa and the Colorado, and it also is the boundary line between the Routt and White River National Forests, as well as the beginning of the Hooper Lake Trail-1860. Let your eyes soak in the superb views, and then continue south, down the saddle on #1860. [Please note: if you are hiking to the top of Big Flat Top Mountain, hike # [56], you will turn east at this point.]

The remainder of the hike is an easy mile down to the lakes, mostly through gently sloping, soggy meadows, where the trail sometimes seems to disappear. After passing part of an old tree trunk, which looks like a big gray wishbone, watch carefully for the faint side trail to the right, which leads to Hooper Lake. The best campsites are on the eastern and northern sides of the Lake. You must camp at least 0.25-mile away from the two lakes.

Continuing on from Hooper to Keener, rejoin the main trail, which passes the lower end of Hooper. A few hundred yards past Hooper, watch for a right turn to Keener. A gorgeous long waterfall cascades into Keener Lake.

After Keener, if you have the time and inclination, continue on #1860 for another half-mile down along the North Fork of Derby Creek, to a pretty meadow and a side trail, which travels north-northwest to nearby Edge and Bailey Lakes.

John Duffey and friends on the alpine tundra of Flat Top Mountain.

56. Flat Top Mountain via 1122

The rocks they try so hard to keep, the plants from going very deep
But here the smallest bit of earth, is just enough to prove their worth.
~ John Fielder - Colorado Wildflowers

Of Note: In the parking area at Stillwater Reservoir, before making this hike, take out your map and identify Flat Top Mountain. You should be able to trace with your eyes the entire route you're going to go up that day – a unique feature of this hike.

This is a high altitude trek, climbing up 2,064', the second-half of it up on a high-above-timberline mesa. At 12,354', this peak represents the highest point in all of the Flat Tops. Take plenty of water with you, since there's none along the second half of this challenging hike, and at this altitude, out in the open, your body will require more fluids than usual. Be certain to leave your plans with friends, since you may very well have the peak of Flat Top Mountain all to yourself.

The first half of this hike follows the same route up to a saddle as is described in the previous hike to Hooper and Keener Lakes. See hike [55]. It's a climb up through woods and meadows, and it increases in steepness just before you reach the saddle, where the two hikes part company – one turning east, for an additional 2.1 miles to the top of Flat Top Mountain – and the other continuing south, to the lakes.

Along the way, you'll enjoy impressive views of the Stillwater valley below, and once on top of Flat Top Mountain, the panoramic views will be unsurpassed – Steamboat Springs to the northeast, the Elkhead Mountains to the northwest, southwest to the Grand Mesa, and southeast to the Sawatch and Gore ranges. Look about six miles to the northwest to see 12,133' Orno Peak. If the day is clear, you'll be able to see for more than 100 miles.

Make this hike as early in the morning as you can to avoid the threat of afternoon thunderstorms. Don't remain on the peak if storm clouds form. Like all peaks, this is certainly a place to show lightning all due respect.

Distance: 4.3 miles, each way.

Hiking Time: about 2.5 hours, each way.

Elevation: Trailhead: 10,280'; Peak: 12,354'.

With Children: *Older, in-shape children should be able to make this climb. To insure their success, be sure to take along sunscreen, hats, high-energy snacks, good raingear and lots for them to drink.*

Yampatike Notes: *Atop Flat Top Mountain, you are walking on a carpet of life. Above timberline, around 10,500', is the vast alpine tundra.*

It is a place of extremes – intense sunlight, heavy, persistent winds, cold temperatures, and a very short growing season – about thirty-days long. Many of the plants found in the alpine zone seem to thrive on this abuse. But they don't thrive on footsteps, so please walk lightly and remain on existing trails wherever possible, or rock hop. A misplaced step can damage a moss campion only as big as a dinner plate, but as old as 100 years.

Map: Trails Illustrated 122. Book map 29.

How to get there: See driving instructions in hike [55].

The Hike: Follow the instructions in hike [55] up to the saddle, the halfway point for this hike [56]. From there, turn left, east, and follow a user trail up a steep section to get atop the ridge. Although from the saddle, facing northeast, you can see the Big Flat Top Mountain off in the distance to the right, you can't see the summit from this point. You may be tempted to aim right for the peak, but don't. Stay hiking left. The trail will dissipate from time to time on the open alpine tundra, so always try to stay left, following the rim of the ridge.

At a little more than three miles into the trip, the trail heads up and over an 11,685' knob of the ridge, and then it dips down into a low saddle. Rock cairns will help you continue northeast along this tundra-covered mesa, as the established trail becomes pretty much nonexistent. Watch for a tall rock cairn that marks the summit. Look for ptarmigan birds, which are common on the tundra, as well as tiny blue belly flowers and periwinkles, and a bronze U.S.G.S. marker. Add some rocks to the cairn and sign the CMC Registry. Breathe in the staggering vistas, and let them speak to your spirit.

57. The Devil's Causeway - East Fork - 1119

Again, the devil took him to a very high mountain and showed him all the kingdoms of the world and their splendor. "All this I will give you," he said, "if you will bow down and worship me." Jesus said to him, "Away from me, Satan! For it is written: 'Worship the Lord your God, and serve Him only.'" Then the devil left him, and angels came and attended him. ~ *Matthew 4:8-11*

Of Note: This steep hike is "a rush," and one of my all-time favorites. It takes the in-shape adventurous up and across one of the most exciting landmarks in northern Colorado. But I have to say that, like others who will admit it, I am one who crosses over the Devil's Causeway – a short, four-foot wide passageway over a volcanic cliff – crouched apelike to the ground, using my arms and hands as much as my feet, while my children walk upright over this uneven, rocky gangplank, showing no fear of the 1,500-foot drops on either side, down to the valley far below. As far as I'm concerned, this is a very good time for believing hikers to pray for "attending angels!"

This is not a good hike for people with weak knees or lungs, or those suffering from acrophobia, although you don't have to actually cross the causeway itself to still tremendously enjoy the hike – as I did on my first visit. Unless something is wrong with your camera, it's very difficult to take a bad photo up here. In season, glorious, brilliantly-colored wildflowers abound, and the stunning views will delight you. Take your wildflower book, topographical map and compass along to help you identify and appreciate all that you see.

As always, start early in the day, and avoid the top if lightning threatens.
This is a very popular hike, accommodating over 5,000 visitors a year.

The shortest way back to your car is to return the way you came. But an enjoyable alternative, which will add 4.5-miles to the hike, involves continuing south across the plateau. Since I haven't personally hiked this section, I asked my friend, Renny Daly, who has, to write it up for the book. He did such a good detailed job of writing up the whole hike, I include it here under "The Hike," heading, with my thanks to him.

Two ways to cross – upright, like Claire and Jesse (see far left) ...or as we "older folks" do it – here Renny and Jain – crab like on all fours!

Distance: 6-miles roundtrip, if return is the same; 10.5-miles total if you continue south after crossing the Causeway.

Hiking time: About 3 to 4 hours roundtrip, if return is the same; about 6 to 7-hours total if you continue south after crossing the Causeway.

Elevation: Trailhead: 10,280'; Causeway: 11,600'.

With Children: *Although it's definitely a tough climb, older, in-shape children will love this hike! Years ago, when our youngest was about ten years old, I couldn't watch, as friends led her safely and fearlessly upright over the Causeway.*

Yampatika Notes: *Imagine during the Pleistocene Ice Age, two glaciers back to back carving ever closer until the only thing separating them is a thin wall of volcanic basalt called an arête. Aren't we lucky? On the walk up, notice the "silver forest" or "ghost forest," masses of standing dead trees. On June 19, 1939, hurricane force winds blew down 10-acres of spruce-fir forests on the White River Plateau. The resulting epidemic of bark beetles ranked as one of the most destructive in history, except for an epidemic in Alaska. By 1949, over 3.5-billion board feet of Engelmann spruce had been killed. Only after temperatures of –56 degrees F in 1951 killed most of the over-wintering beetles was the epidemic controlled.*

Map: Trails Illustrated 122. Book map 30.

How to get there: Please follow driving instructions in hike [55] to Stillwater Reservoir.

The Hike: Begin the hike along Trail 1119, the East Fork Trail, which skirts the northern side of the reservoir. About mid-reservoir, Trail 1120 (Bear River Trail) exits to the left. The East Fork Trail turns right (northwest) at this point and begins its ascent. There is a sign-in register at this route junction. The East fork Trail climbs gently, passing above and to the right of Little Causeway Lake about 1.75 miles from the trailhead. The walking is pleasant, but somewhat buggy. Views are sporadic, but several opportunities exist to look back down to Stillwater Reservoir, and across it to Flat Top Mountain. About two miles from the trailhead, the trail emerges from the woods, presenting an unobstructed view of the ridge containing the Devil's Causeway, the saddle to its north, and the high ground to the north of the saddle. In another quarter mile, the trail commences a series of long and steeper switchbacks. Hikers, with good reason, are cautioned by a sign to stay on the trail and not take shortcuts between the switchbacks. At about 2.7 miles, the trail reaches the top of the couloirs. At this point, the trail up the final ascent to Devil's Causeway departs left. The East Fork Trail continues straight ahead. There are excellent views west to the Lost Lakes Peaks.

The final ascent is steep, in nearly a straight line, and contains numerous log steps or bracing points. Upon reaching the top, just to the west (right) of the highest ground, the Devil's Causeway looms just ahead. Approximately 25 yards long, it starts about 10 feet wide and narrows to about four feet in width towards the southern end. At that point, the rocks are uneven, and some climbing up and down of about a foot and a half is necessary. Even the strongest of heart would be well advised to proceed cautiously at this point. The trail then becomes more level, and slightly wider, and in about ten more feet, reaches the open plateau at the southern

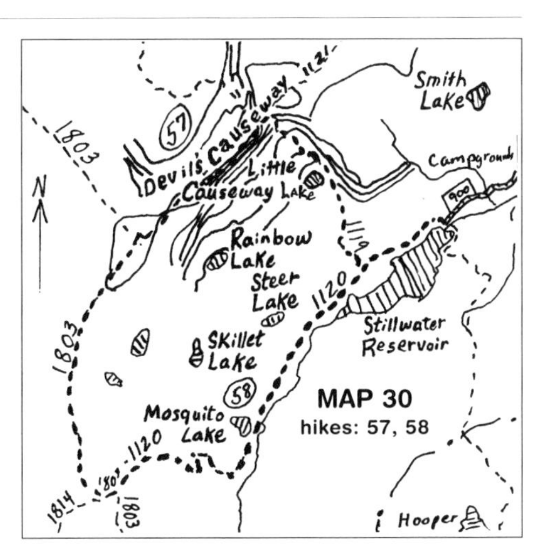

end of the Causeway. There are abundant places to sit, enjoy the views, which are spectacular, and generally permit the heart to return to normal rhythm. You are now about 3-miles from the trailhead. Be careful with the fragile alpine vegetation. Walk lightly, rock hop and sit on rocks if you can when making rest stops.

The shortest way back to the car is back across the Causeway and down as you came. But an enjoyable alternative, about four and a half miles longer, involves continuing south across the plateau. To the Causeway, the trail is very clearly defined, making navigation a simple matter. South of the Causeway, however, matters become somewhat trickier. The trail follows, for the most part, a bare strip recessed about six inches into the ground. Only about a foot wide, and narrower in places, it can be difficult to walk in. A series of cairns, typically ten or fifteen yards away from this trail, confirm that you are on track.

About a mile after the Causeway, the Devil's Causeway Trail blends into the Chinese Wall Trail-1803. This intersection is apparently unmarked and ill defined. None of those in our party saw it. Indeed, there appears to be but the one trail we were on, heading southwest as expected. The trail skirts higher ground to the left, and is nearly flat. Wildflowers abound during the prime season.

About two and three-quarters miles after leaving the Causeway, the trail suddenly, and somewhat mysteriously, peters out. Perhaps an opportunity existed to bear right onto another path, but none in our group saw it. When the trail ended, however, a cairn was readily visible about fifty yards to our right (west). It was a simple matter to walk over to the cairn, and near it another trail headed off in the correct direction (nearly south). Within a half-mile, and about 3.2 miles after leaving the Causeway, the well-marked junction of trails 1803 and 1814 (Stillwater Trail) is reached. There is a large cairn and signposts. While the sign suggests that it is possible to continue straight on Trail 1803, no trail was apparent, no cairns were seen, and the maps indicated to the contrary. In any event, the route back to Stillwater Reservoir required a left turn at the junction, heading east on Trail 1814. In approximately one-quarter mile, another trail junction is reached. Proceed straight ahead as Trail 1814 becomes Trail 1120 (Bear River Trail).

In a short distance, the Bear River Trail commences its descent down the couloirs to the southwest of Stillwater Reservoir. The trail is well marked, but as late as mid-July may pass through several snowfields in the couloirs. Melting snow may cause running water along parts of the trail, though it should be possible to keep dry feet with careful walking. The runoff gives rise to fast running water and at least one waterfall visible during the descent. About a mile after you join the Bear River Trail, it reenters the vegetation – at first scrub pine and then the forest in earnest. While somewhat steep, the path is not difficult. About a half mile after entering the forest, the trail reaches gentler terrain near the bottom of the valley and passes just to the right of Mosquito Lake. The exit stream is crossed without difficulty under normal conditions, and the trail continues gently down the valley to the reservoir. Several streams flow down to the Bear River, which is always to your right. Several of these streams are crossed on bridges of varying sophistication. Nearly three and a half miles after joining the Bear River Trail, it ends at the trail junction where you registered, midway along the northwest side of the reservoir. To finish, backtrack the last three-quarters of a mile along trial 1119, following the northwest shoreline.

58. Mosquito Lake - Bear River Trail - 1120

Keep a green tree in your heart, and perhaps a singing bird will come.
~ Chinese Proverb

Of Note: Here's an excellent destination for a family backpack trip. The hike is short, scenic, a gentle climb and, except on weekends, usually uncrowded. The lake itself is a delight, surrounded impressively by several of the Flat Top Mountains. This also makes an easy, yet very worthwhile day hike, or a good place to set up a base camp while you check out several other destinations in the area.

Listen and watch for yellow-bellied marmots, also known as "Whistle Pigs," on the hillside early on in the hike. Enjoy walking above and beyond the north shore of Stillwater Reservoir and along the Bear River, a major tributary of the Yampa River, which eventually flows through the middle of downtown Steamboat Springs. Hike through several delightful forests of spruce and fir, and if you continue on for just another mile past Mosquito Lake, you'll reach a high-point of 11,400' and enjoy unsurpassed spectacular views of the glorious Flat Top Mountains. As the name implies, it will be quite buggy here early in the season – but then, most places are.

Distance: 2 miles to the lake; one additional mile to the scenic high point.

Hiking Time: About 45 minutes to the lake; 30 additional minutes to the high point.

Elevation: Trailhead: 10,280; Mosquito Lake: 10,620'; high point: 11,412'.

With Children: *Finally, a great place to hike with children of all ages! The lake is easy to get to, and there's much to enjoy along the way. Good campsites above the lake make this an excellent family backpack destination.*

Yampatika Notes: *As you enter the open, rocky areas high above Mosquito Lake, keep your eyes peeled for a small, fast falcon cruising the skies. The peregrine falcon has made a fine recovery in the Flat Tops. This stunning bird has long tapered wings, a long broad tail, dark crown on its head, with dark sideburns – like Elvis! They nest in cliff ledges and will let you know if you're too near their nest by sounding a high pitched "ki-ki-ki-ki-ki" alarm call. Respect this and leave the area so that you won't stress out the parent birds. Watch carefully to see a peregrine falcon dive to catch another bird in mid-air!*

Fishing: *Mosquito Lake: 10 acres in size, 6' deep; good for brook trout.*

Sunset at Mosquito Lake, where Dudley and Sammy make a Push-Me-Pull-You."

Map: Trails Illustrated 122. Book map 30.

How to get there: Please follow driving instructions to Stillwater Reservoir trailhead in hike [55].

The Hike: Both trails #1119 (East Fork) and 1120 (Bear River), which begin on the west end of the parking area, are common for the first 0.8 mile of this hike. The trail parallels the north shore of the reservoir, about 50' above it and in the open, until it junctions with #1119 after the first mile. At this point, the trail heads west, through a series of spruce and fir forests, following the Bear River southwest, until it crosses the drainage of Rainbow Lake. Before you know it, you'll easily arrive at Mosquito Lake. Look for good campsites in the woods on the north end of the lake. If camping here, check out the lovely huge meadow behind – north of – the campsites. If you walk very quietly here in the early morning, you may see a herd of elk, as I once did.

If you wish to climb up a bit further for some spectacular views, continue on the main trail past Mosquito Lake for about a half mile. After this, the trail now turns west, leaving the Bear River, and begins a gradual switchback ascent up the divide separating the Routt from the White River National Forest, climbing up a glacially-carved wall that extends south from the Devil's Causeway. At mile 3.0, you'll reach the high point of 11,400'. Take your camera to capture some of the majestic landscape.

If you aren't ready yet to return to Stillwater, a look at the topo map will show you many other options for additional hiking, including completing this trail all the way to the famous Trappers Lake, which, in the early 1900's, inspired the beginning of the preservation movement in America. Forest Service brochures explain in depth how Trappers Lake, and thus the Flat Tops itself, played a key initial role in the establishment of the National Wilderness Preservation System. Pick up a brochure at the Forest Service office in Yampa, 300 Roselawn.

59. California Park to Sugar Loaf Mountain - 1144

It was a great, wild country. In the creek bottoms, there were a good many ranches, but we only occasionally passed by these on our way to our hunting grounds in the wilderness along the edge of the snow line. The mountains crowded close together in the chain, peak and tableland...
~ President Teddy Roosevelt – A Colorado Bear Hunt

Of Note: The Bear's Ears section of the Routt National Forest is a huge hunter's paradise, so for safety reasons, you should only make this hike in mid-June through mid-August, before hunting season, when you'll also get to enjoy solitude, wildflowers, and exceptional wildlife viewing. Begin this hike early in the day to avoid the hot sun in the initial dry, open area of the hike.

The whole Bears Ears trail is a very long forty-four mile loop around Black Mountain, and much of it is accessed from Craig, beyond this hiking guide's boundaries. However, the hike presented here is accessed north of Hayden, and getting there will take you into the huge 8,000-acre California Park area, known for its big game hunting. You can view this vast park from atop various area peaks such as Sand Mountain, but this hike will allow you to get down into the Park for a little taste of what the Bear's Ears section has to offer.

The hike covers only a tiny portion of the loop, on its southeast end, from California Park, almost to the base of Sugar Loaf Mountain, with a return on the same route. Just a couple miles west of California Park, this trail passes through one of the largest aspen stands in the whole state of Colorado. It is also prime habitat for more than 300 species of wildlife, including elk, mule deer and numerous varieties of migratory birds. The park is home to Colorado's largest population of Greater Sandhill Cranes.

Friends and I were lucky enough to make this hike on a September 19th, right during

Returning from Sugarloaf Mountain through California Park.

the break between bow and rifle hunting seasons, co-incidentally when the area was also bathed in fall's glorious shimmering splashes of golden-red quaking aspen. The fifty-mile drive to get there takes you miles through lonesome arid ranch lands, with their vast, open pastures, a great contrast to the lush terrain and mountain landscape which you'll then encounter on the hike itself. Because of the long driving distance each way to the trailhead and back, and because of the remoteness of the area, make certain to fill up your gas tank before leaving Steamboat, be well-prepared with all the essentials for a day hike, including a car cell phone, if you have one, don't hike alone, and be sure to leave your detailed itinerary with friends or family members.

This hike also offers what I consider one of the prettiest examples of life in and around several superbly built beaver ponds. God willing, I intend to make this hike again some day, when I have lots of time, a good lunch, a camera, and a book about beavers. I will sit quietly for a couple hours at these beautiful ponds, reading and observing how the industrious dam-building mammals modify a riparian ecosystem to their own liking.

If you would like to explore more of this vast Bear's Ears area, check out www.Colorado-go-west.com, or call 1-800-864-4405 and ask them to send you a Black Mountain 100-Mile Self-guided Tour brochure.

Distance: About 5-miles, each way.

Hiking Time: About 2-hours, each way.

Elevation: Trailhead: 8,000'; intersection with F.S.116: 8,930'.

With Children: *This hike would be a marvelous place to take in-shape children to study beavers. The ponds mentioned above are reached after about an hour of walking, much of it on a very gradual uphill. Make this hike early in the day with children, so that they aren't initially walking out in the open in the hot sun. To increase your child's enjoyment of this trail, before leaving Steamboat, stop by Yampatika Nature Store at 10th and Lincoln to pick up a children's book*

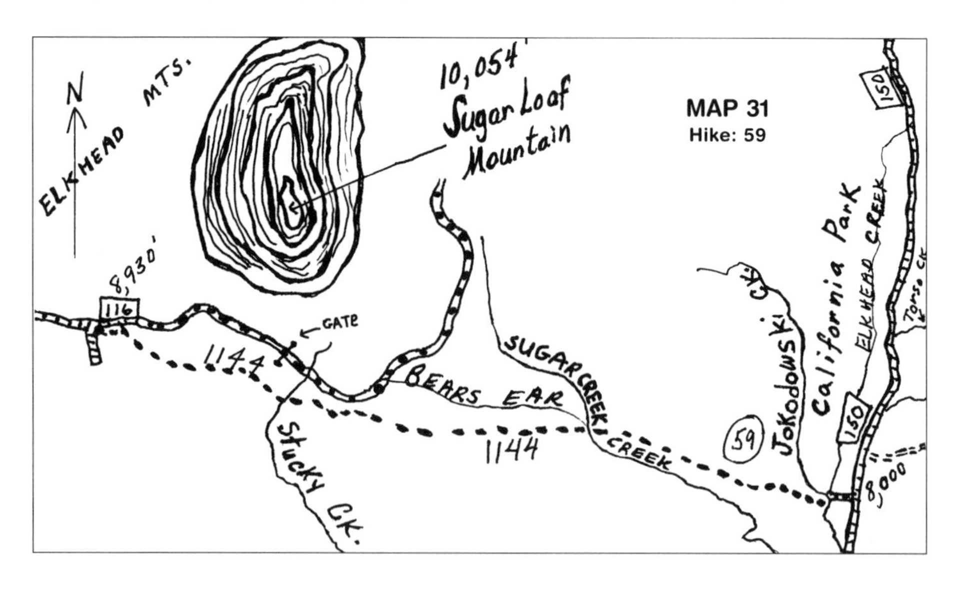

about beavers, as well as a myriad of other wonderful nature study items. Let them also take along a disposable camera, a notebook, sketchpad, and so on, for recording their "Mr. Beaver" observations.

Yampatika Notes: *The Elkhead Mountains are a group of volcanic mountains active between 12 and 10 million years ago. At the beginning of this volcanically active time, what is now Colorado was covered in sedimentary rock of sandstone, limestone and others. As the volcanism occurred, many sedimentary layers were uplifted and tilted. Look for sandstone and limestone layers throughout the Elkhead Mountains, with the cones of once volcanic Sugarloaf, Bears Ears, Black Mountain and others rising above.*

Fishing: *Try your luck for brookies in the many beaver ponds along the way.*

Map: U.S.G.S. Bears Ears Peaks; book map 31.

How to get there: The total mileage from Steamboat to the trailhead is 50.3-miles. Heading west out of downtown Steamboat on U.S.40, Lincoln, from 13th St., drive 24.7-miles, halfway through the little town of Hayden. At mile 25.6, turn right, north, onto County Rd. 80 and travel northeast; at mile 44.2, County Rd. 80 now becomes FDR 150; at mile 46.2, enter California Park, and at mile 50.3, watch for the trailhead sign on the left for 1144. Turn left and drive about 200 yards to the trailhead.

The Hike: The first part of this trail takes you out through a large open pastureland. Begin your hike early to avoid the hot sun in this open area. You'll hike west, right toward Sugar Loaf Mountain, which looks like a flattened loaf of bread. Early on, cross two streams, Elkhead Creek and Circle Creek, and then the trail forks. Since this is open rangeland, there are game and pasture animal paths, so watch for poles to guide you on the correct trail, which are numerous and easy to see. Cross Jokadowski Creek, and look for another pole up to the right. Arrive at the top of a hill, and notice a sign from 1983 telling you that this trail is "maintained by funding from the Roundup Riders of the Rockies." If you're old enough to remember it, allow yourself to sing a few lines from Frankie Lane's, "Ghost Riders In the Sky," at this point.

After about 45-minutes of hiking, begin to walk up an aspen-covered hillside; after crossing Sugar Creek, the trail heads up to the right. About 1.25-hours into the hike from the trailhead, arrive at the wonderful beaver ponds mentioned above, and then, about 45-minutes after that, cross the West Fork of Stucky Creek and soon arrive at FDR 116. Just before this point, however, watch off to the right for a nice established campsite, which affords a good close-up view of Sugar Loaf Mountain.

You'll reach a logging road, which extends south from FDR 116. Trail 1144 continues on the road's other side, but for a day hike, this is a good place to turn around and return to California Park. As usual, you'll probably notice and appreciate the awe-inspiring views on the way back down much more than you did on the way up.

60. Pearl Lake

The birds of the air nest by the waters; they sing among the branches.
He waters the mountains from his upper chambers. The earth is satisfied by the fruit of his work.
~ Psalm 105:12-13

Of Note: When our children were very young, Pearl Lake was one of our favorite places to car camp – we'd hike around the lake's undisturbed shoreline during the day to fish and study nature, and then camp overnight, studying the stars above the lake.

Pearl Lake is a Colorado State Park, and it's quite a beautiful, serene gem, much more primitive and pristine than the average state park. The 41-car campsites are well designed and placed so that many of them sit just above the lake itself. The "official" hike takes you from the day picnic area, south, to the right, around the southwest end of the lake to the dam at the southern end. It's only about three-fourths of a mile long, and you can spend a whole afternoon hiking your way along the wakeless water shoreline with children, stopping to fish, observe and explore.

The park brochure offers, "Many kinds of waterfowl nest near the lakes and the marshes that surround them. Elk, deer, bear, coyote, fox, beaver, chipmunks and other small mammals make their home in the area."

During the drier part of the hiking season, it is also possible to hike the whole distance around the lake, and it takes about a bit over an hour to do so. However, if you do circle the lake, some of the time you may be crossing on private land, so observe and respect any signs. Also, part of the time, you'll be hiking through willows or boggy areas, where the trail will disappear, so be prepared for a little wet bushwhacking.

If you want to car camp at Pearl Lake, for reservations call 1-800-678-CAMP or 970-879-3922; website: www.coloradoparks.org. To spend just the day at this park, if you don't already have an annual Colorado State Parks pass, you'll need to stop at the self-service pay station at the park's entrance, pay a fee and display the sticker on your car. Citations are freely given for those who fail to do so.

Distance: About 1.5-miles, round trip.

Pearl Lake is truly a gem!

Hiking Time: On the hiking trail, if you don't stop for anything, it's about 45-minutes round-trip; with children, however, it can be as long as their curiosity and energy hold out.

Elevation: 8,087' at the lake.

With Children: *Definitely! See "Of Note" above. Before leaving Steamboat, stop by the wonderful Yampatika Nature Store at 10th and Lincoln and pick up some books and nature study items to take with you to enjoy on this trip.*

Fishing: *Pearl Lake offers a Gold Medal cutthroat trout population; restricted to flies and lures; also good for brook, Snake River cutthroat, brown trout and grayling. Please practice Catch and Release fly-fishing.*

Map: Trails Illustrated 116; see also map in park brochure.

How to get there: Drive west out of Steamboat for 1.3-miles past 13th St. on U.S. 40, Lincoln, to the Airport/Clark turnoff, Routt 129. Turn right, north, here and stay on 129 for 23-miles. Look for the Pearl Lake sign on the right. Turn right and drive two more miles to the entrance, where the mountains and surrounding majestic peaks will suddenly seem to reach out and greet you.

The Hike: The official trail begins to the right, at the day use picnic area. Look for the sign. Unless you're going to try to venture around the whole lake, return on the same route.

61. Steamboat Lake - Tombstone Nature Trail
62. Steamboat Lake - Willow Creek to Marina

The voice of the Lord is over the waters; the God of Glory thunders,
the Lord thunders over the mighty waters.
~ Psalm 29:3-4

Of Note: Steamboat Lake State Park is mostly water, with 1,058-acres of surface water and 447-acres of land. It sits in a broad scenic valley surrounded by majestic mountain views of Hahns Peak, Sand Mountain, and the soaring peaks of the Continental Divide's Park Range. This park offers 198 campsites, 35 picnic sites, a marina, interpretive programs and an amphitheater.

Constructed in 1968, the outstanding man-made lake was created to capture the water from several nearby creeks into a water storage area. Today, however, its primary purpose is for recreational uses.

There are two Steamboat Lake hikes covered in this book, one a short 0.75-mile, quick-'n-easy self-guided tour on a nature trail, and the other, from the main highway back to the delightful Steamboat Marina.

Steamboat school children hiking around Steamboat Lake.

Distance:

61. Tombstone Nature Trail: 0.75-mile, round-trip.
62. Steamboat Marina via Willow Creek/Sunrise Vista Trail: 1.6-miles, each way, from the Visitor's Center; 1.0-mile each way from Hwy. 129.

Hiking Time:

61. About 30-minutes, roundtrip.
62. About 45-minutes each way, if from Visitor's Center; about 30-minutes if from Hwy. 129.

Elevation: Steamboat Lake: 8,060'; hikes gain and lose little elevation.

With Children:

61. Yes! Easy and delightful. Make sure you pick up a brochure first.

62. Yes! After hiking to the Marina, on a hot day, the children can take a refreshing swim. So, besides the usual water, sunscreen, bug spray, etc., also carry bathing suits, towels, fishing poles and money for boat rental, lunch or treats at the Marina.

Yampatika Notes: *When walking around Steamboat Lake, listen in the spring for a low-pitched "karoo karoo karoo." Look in open meadows or marshy areas for a large, up to four-feet tall gray heron-like bird with a dark red patch on its forehead. Young birds develop the red patch after their second year.*

About forty pairs of Sandhill Cranes nest in Northwest Colorado, and they can be spotted in this area. This breeding population was considered "endangered," but it has recently been down-listed by the Colorado Division of Wildlife to "threatened." During migration, Sandhills form large flocks, but they will be seen as pairs in the summer. Their courtship dance is a beautiful series of graceful jumps and bows, with much vocalization. Nests are large mounds of vegetation on the ground or in shallow water, with one-to-three eggs. Generally, only one colt, young bird, will survive.

Fishing: *Try the lake's many coves for good-sized rainbow trout. Fishing supplies can be purchased at the Marina.*

Map: Trails Illustrated 116; also, use Park map.

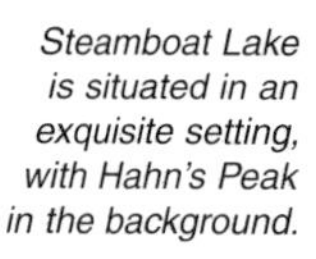

Steamboat Lake is situated in an exquisite setting, with Hahn's Peak in the background.

How to get there: Drive west of Steamboat for 1.3-miles past 13th St. on U.S.40, Lincoln, to the Airport/Clark turnoff, Routt 129. Turn right here and stay on 129 for about 27 miles until you see Steamboat Lake on your left. Just before your arrival there, however, at miles 26.4 on your right, stop into Village Treasures for a bite to eat, for some homemade fudge or for a fun souvenir. While there, you can also check out the wonderful old town of Hahns Peak, founded in 1870. For many early years, this was the Routt County seat. Then, to continue on to the lake, get back on 129 and 0.6-mile further, turn left into the Visitor's Center, if you are parking there.

For more information or reservations to camp at Steamboat Lake: 1-800-678-CAMP or 970-879-3922). www.coloradoparks.org

The Hike:

61. This is an easy 0.75-mile level loop hike near the lake's northeastern shore, at Placer Cove. A brochure teaches you all about the lake, nearby Hahns Peak and about the lake's construction. Views and a vast array of wildflowers await you on early July hikes. Park behind the Visitor's Center, where you may also purchase a park pass and pick up the free brochure. Follow the map to the Nature Trail, and hike the loop clockwise, beginning left. Citations are issued freely for people who fail to display the pass on their windshields.

62. This is an easy mile-and-a-half hike around part of the lake to a most delightful marina. This is a good choice if you want to combine a little hiking with some fishing, boating, swimming or picnicking beside a very big lake located in a spectacular setting.

You can begin this hike from two points:

Access 1. Purchase and display on your vehicle a day pass at either the Visitor's Center or at a self-pay station. Park near the Visitor's Center off Highway 129 and begin the hike at the trailhead sign near the day parking area behind and to the left of the center.

Access 2. Unless otherwise posted, you may park your vehicle near a cattle gate off Hwy. 129 outside the park and enter it through this gate on foot. The gate and trail are obvious from the highway. Parking along the country road and walking into the park does not require a pass, but if you do so, park your vehicle well off the road, and use caution if crossing the highway. This spot is located 0.6-mile northwest past the Visitor's Center. Remember to close the cattle gate behind you. Starting here shortens the hike by 0.6-mile, but the part you'll miss is just a section that runs very closely to, and parallel with Hwy. 129, through a cow-pie pasture.

This hike will take you on a gentle grade down through meadows and woods, along the lake, and to the delightful Steamboat Lake Marina, where you can go for a swim off a small beach, rent a paddle boat or canoe, fish and purchase groceries, fishing equipment, delicious deli sandwiches, cold drinks and even a copy of my children's book, Stop Spitting At Your Brother!, which entertains animal lovers of all ages with stories about Steamboat's very own real-life llamas, Dudley and Sammy. (Marina: 970-879-7019.) If you're camped at Steamboat Lake, it makes a great camp read for the whole family.

To make the hike, simply follow the Willow Creek Trail from behind and to the left of the Visitor's Center for 1.3-miles – or 0.7-mile if from Hwy. 129 – until reaching the Sunrise Vista Campground. From there, look for the sign for the Sunrise Vista Trail, and follow it for another 0.25-mile to the Marina. When the Marina first comes into sight from the trail, stop and take a photo of the pretty scene.

The Tombstone Nature Trail is one hike you can do even in the winter, wearing snowshoes.

63. Prospector Trail - 1156

Forests are the "lungs" of our land, purifying the air and giving fresh strength to our people.
~ Franklin D. Roosevelt

There are thoughts that moan from the soul of the pine,and thoughts in a flower bell curled.
And the thoughts that are blown with the scent of the fern are as new and as old as the world.
~ Sam Walter Foss

Of Note: This fairly steep trail is used mostly by dirt bike and mountain bike riders, who combine it with the Nipple Peak trail for a long loop. But a two-hour climb on a section of this trail will take a hiker up to the top of a ridge to enjoy an impressive panoramic stretch of mountains, which look down into Slater Park and the Bear's Ears countryside.

Having personally hiked this trail when autumn was putting on her glorious aspen show, I can definitely recommend it for taking some great photos of the shimmering, fluttering golden-colored leaves, with the scenic, bald-headed Hahn's Peak in the background. Stay alert for bike traffic.

The steep hike up 1156 will reward you with some great views.

Distance: About 3.5-miles, each way.

Hiking Time: About 2-hours, one-way.

Elevation: Trailhead: 8,500'; Ridge: 9,400'.

With Children: *Most children would find the climbing required toward the end of this hike to be a bit tortuous, especially since the route follows no water sources. However, in lieu of being "grounded," assigning this hike to a teenage rule breaker might be a better way to make amends – especially if they have to hike it with good old mom or dad!*

Map: U.S.G.S. Hahn's Peak, Meaden Peak; Book map 32.

How to get there: Drive west out of Steamboat for 1.3-miles after 13th St. on U.S. 40, Lincoln, until the Airport/Clark turnoff, Routt Co. 129. Turn right – north – here onto 129, and drive for 28.8-miles, just past the second entrance for Hahn's Peak Lake, until FDR 488 on the left. Turn left onto 488 and drive 1.25-miles until you see a rough spur road on the left. At the time of this writing, the trailhead sign had been knocked down, so it may be unmarked. Turn left here, onto this dead-end road, and drive 0.1-mile until the trailhead parking area.

The Hike: Follow the trail into a cool, refreshing, old-growth forest and enjoy the mix of trees and the smell of pine. The trail ascends gradually through alternating dense forests and sun-splashed, open, high mountainside meadows, affording the hiker the joy of encountering changing landscapes and many beaver ponds. The stream crossings are easy, with most having wooden footbridges placed over them to facilitate dirt bikers.

After about an hour, the trail intersects and crosses FDR 487, which comes from Hahn's Peak Lake. Unless you're out of energy, don't be tempted to stop here and turn around. The best is yet to come!

Cross the road and continue to hike smartly uphill for another half hour, climbing through a more wooded area, up to the divide between the Hahn's Peak drainage and Slater Park drainage. Soon, you'll reach the ridge top, where you can enjoy the sweeping view mentioned above. It's definitely worth the effort to make it up to this point.

The Prospector trail continues for two- miles west along Lopez Creek, where it connects with 1147. About three miles after the Prospector/Nipple Peak intersection, you would reach the

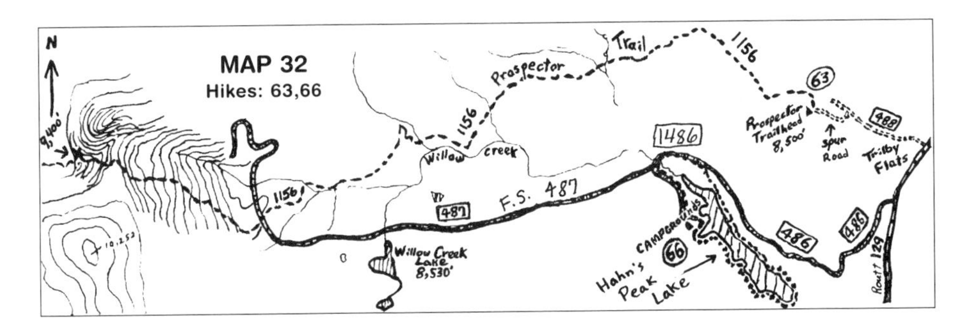

Slater Park Trailhead. But for our purpose of a day hike, we turn around after reaching the above-noted ridge, returning the way we came. You'll enjoy some unfolding views on the return, which you may have missed hiking uphill. It's amazing to me how that so often happens.

64. Prospector Extension - Northwest
65. Prospector Extension - East

Do not judge your neighbor until you walk two moons in his moccasins.
~ Cheyenne Indian Proverb

We can never have enough of nature. We must be refreshed by the site of inexhaustible vigor, vast and titanic features...the wilderness with its living and decaying trees, the thunder cloud and the rain.
~ Thoreau

Of Note: These two short hikes are taken on different sections of a newly-built extension to the Prospector Trail-1156, hike [63]. They begin at the same place but, divided by Routt 129, one heads northwest and the other east. The two sections of this extension were built by young people from the Community Youth Corps, primarily to extend the mileage for mountain and dirt bike riders, so be ready to share the trails with them. For hikers, these sections represent two short easy-access trips that you can enjoy if you're staying in the Steamboat Lake area and you want a nearby place to visit some pretty aspen groves and spruce forests. Both would be good paths to use for a meadow picnic or to identify wildflowers in season. Since they're only new sections of an already existing trail, neither of these hikes has an official trailhead nor Forest Service sanctioned parking area. And hikers, as well as mountain and dirt bikers, need to use care if crossing Routt 129 to continue east on this Prospector Trail extension.

Follow directions on page 177 if you'd rather park safely at the official Prospector Trailhead and reverse hike [64].

The return trip will offer you this pretty view of Hahn's Peak

The Prospector Extension East offers the hiker a lovely walk through the forest.

Distance:
64. Northwest: 2-mile loop, total.
65. East: 1.2-miles, each way.

Hiking Time:
64. About 1.5-hours, total.
65. About 45-minutes, each way.

Elevation:
64. Trailhead: 8,500'; Prospector Trailhead: 8,600'.
65. Trailhead: 8,500'; Turn around point: 9,000'.

With Children: *Both hikes are short enough to be appropriate for young children, and easy enough to return to the trailhead if they wilt along the way.*

Nature Note: *If you study an aspen leaf, you'll notice that its stem is flat and perpendicular to the plane of its surface. This is what causes it to shimmer or quake in the wind. During late September, when quaking aspen leaves turn yellow and red, the leaves reflect sunshine and imitate pieces of gold sparkling in the trees.* *(See page 4.)*

Map: Book map 33; U.S.G.S. Hahn's Peak; Trails Illustrated 116.

How to get there: Drive west out of town on U.S. 40, Lincoln, for 1.3-miles after 13th St., until the Airport/Clark turnoff, Routt 129. Turn right, north, here and drive for almost 28-miles, past Steamboat Lake State Park, until coming to FDR 486 on the left, which is also the east-side entrance for Hahn's Peak Lake. Turn left onto 468 and immediately find a place to park on the side of the road, out of the way. You'll see one path heading northwest and another across 129 heading east. Or, see driving instructions on page 177 to official parking area.

The Hike:

64. This extension section heads northwest and takes you from FDR 468 on a loop hike, first up to the main Prospector trailhead, and then returning on the parallel FDR 488. For a number of times, you'll gain and lose about 300' on a very moderate climb up through pretty aspen and spruce trees. You can venture off the trail a couple times to investigate beaver ponds, and you'll have access to a stream off the trail on the return trip. You'll enjoy a wonderful view of Hahn's Peak on your return trip, worth a photo. This hike also provides a good place for wildlife viewing in the early mornings. When you return, before reaching Hwy. 129, cut across the Trilby Flats meadow and head toward your car, rather than walking on 129.

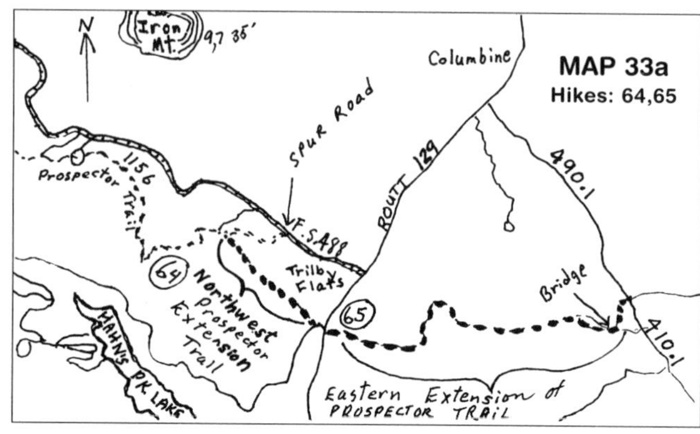

65. This extension section heads east, as it climbs gradually for about 1.2-miles, gaining about 500', with just a couple steep sections. It's yet another place to get off the highway a bit to enjoy the gorgeous mix of aspen, fir and pine trees and meadows, and during season, the wildflowers. After about a half-hour of walking, you'll cross Independence Creek on a constructed wooden bridge, and about ten minutes later, come to the trail's end, as it junctions with FDR 490 and 410. Return the way you came.

66. Hahn's Peak Lake Trail - 1191

Those who contemplate the beauty of the earth find resources of strength that will endure as long as life lasts.
~ Rachel Carson

Of Note: When our children were very young, Hahn's Peak Lake was one of our all-time favorite places to go for a full day of fun. We would take along an inflatable raft and row around in it, exploring every nook and cranny in the lake; then we would hike around the lake, exploring it from the land, as well. Now in my beginning senior years, this beautiful man-made lake remains a delight for me.

An easy-drive destination for picnicking and relaxing with friends, it's the perfect place to take visiting grandparents and relatives for the day, even if they are only able to make a portion of the hike, or no hike at all. Most everyone can generally catch fish here. A Forest Service day use fee or pass is required. Pleasant for-fee car campsites are also available at the west end.

Distance: 3.25-miles, if you circle the whole lake.

Hiking Time: About 1.5-hours for the full circle.

Elevation: A level 8,400'.

With Children: *A must for families with young children who would like to take a short, easy hike and spend some time playing or fishing close to the water.*

Fishing*: Stocked yearly, the lake is good for 10-12" trout; good shoreline. Please practice catch and release fly-fishing.*

Map: Trails Illustrated 116; U.S.G.S. Hahn's Peak; Book map 32.

How to get there: Drive west out of town on U.S.40, Lincoln, for 1.3-miles after 13th St., until the Airport/Clark turnoff, Routt 129. Turn right – north – here, and drive for almost 28-miles, passing Steamboat Lake State Park. There are two accesses: for the east side entrance, drive past Hahn's Peak Village for about 2-miles to FDR 485 on the left. For the west side access, continue about 1-mile past the east side entrance, to FDR 486. Turn left here and drive about two more miles to the west side day use parking area, which will be marked as such.

The Hike: There is a trail going around the entire lake, half official and half user-made, and you can get on it at any point. But I recommend the following options:

1. If you have time and energy for only a portion of this hike, begin it at the sign near the outhouse and day use parking area on the west side of the lake, hiking southeast through the forest. After you reach the picnic tables on the opposite side of the lake, which sit above the dam on the southeast end, turn around and return the same way you came. This will be about a 1.5-miles hike total. This section is the official Forest Service trail.
2. To make the whole trip around the lake, begin as in option one, but after the dam, continue hiking northwest on a user trail, around the lake. After the dam, be careful not to confuse the main user trail with the fisherman user trail down very close to the water, which offers more difficult footing. Going the upper route, the trail eventually climbs up onto the dirt road, FDR 485, where you will have to turn left and hike the final mile on the road back to the parking area. This option is about a 3.25-mile hike total.

Hike around Hahn's Peak Lake and enjoy all the area has to offer.

The firetower on Hahn's Peak from the top ...

67. Hahn's Peak Summit - 1158

I am an eagle, I live in high country, in rocky cathedrals that reach to the sky.
I am a hawk and there's blood on my feathers, but time is still turning and soon they'll be dry.
And all those who see me, and all who believe in me, share in the freedom I feel when I fly.
~ John Denver – The Eagle and the Hawk

Of Note: This is one of my favorite hikes in the book, mainly because of the awesome on-top-of-the-world feeling I have when I stand on the peak, looking out at some of the amazing beauty God has so generously bestowed on us.

Named after Joseph Hahn, an immigrant gold prospector from Germany who settled here in the 1860's, this symmetrical bald-headed cone is one of the area's best-known landmarks. Hahn died in 1867 on the banks of Muddy Creek after a dishonest partner took the gold and then failed to return from Denver with necessary winter supplies. Historic remains of old mine tailings, cabins and mine shafts, representing the dreams and despairs of old prospectors, can still be seen on the mountainside.

The much-photographed fire tower crowning the peak, which looks like a dot from far below, was constructed in 1912 and reconstructed in 1942. It has not been officially used since the early 1950's, and it is listed on the Colorado Inventory of Historical Places.

You should not make this climb if any storm clouds are building in the area. If you are already on top of the 10,839' summit and bad weather threatens, head down quickly. Never seek shelter from lightning in the fire tower.

The last short stretch up to the peak is a difficult climb over loose rock scree, so wear hiking boots with good ankle support – and knee supports, if your knees like to complain. Carefully choosing your footing on the way back down this section may prove more challenging than the trip up.

Take along plenty of water for this moderate-to-steep climb, since you'll find yourself getting thirsty, especially on sunny days, and there is no good water source along the route, for either you or your canine. Begin the hike early in the morning to avoid afternoon storms. Take sunscreen and hats, your camera and plenty of film, for you'll enjoy spectacular 360-degree panoramic vistas of Wyoming, eleven miles to the north, and of the surrounding ridges and valleys of the Routt National Forest.

Take your binoculars to enjoy both the views and the soaring eagles and hawks enjoying the thermals created when winds hit the side of the mountain and are pushed upward in strong rushes of air.

Distance: 1.7-miles, each way.

Hiking Time: About 1.5- hours, one-way, up.

Elevation: Trailhead: 9,200'; Summit: 10,839'; gain 1,639'.

...and from the bottom.

With Children: *Some of the hike on trail 1158 is a bit too steep for most young children, unless they are especially strong. Older, in-shape children will enjoy standing in the fire tower, taking photos with their own disposable cameras.*

Yampatika Notes: *At the top of Hahn's Peak, you'll be standing at a point where once, about ten to twelve million years ago, a very deep volcano existed. Ash and lava would have been spewing out its top and flowing past you. Then over the centuries, the volcano eroded, and this "neck" – the main artery, which was made of harder rock – was left. Gold and silver were mined from Hahn's peak from the 1860's to about 1912, when the county seat was moved from the town of Hahn's Peak to Steamboat Springs.*

Map: Trails Illustrated 116; Book map 33.

How to get there: Drive west out of Steamboat for 1.3-miles after 13th on U.S.40, Lincoln, until the Airport/Clark turnoff, Routt 129.

Turn right and drive for 29-miles to the old settlement of Columbine. When you reach the Columbine General Store on the left – which is generally open for business – turn right onto FDR 490. Travel slowly by car on this very rough but passable dirt road. At mile 0.9, at the junction with 410, remain left on 490 for another 0.4-mile. At the intersection of 490 and 418, go left onto 418. Drive for 0.1-mile until the parking area.

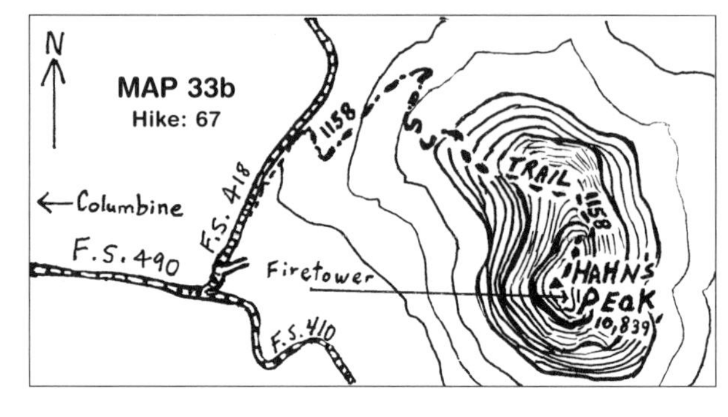

The Hike: Notice two jeep roads. Take the one uphill and to the right. You may have to share this road section of the hike with dirt bike users. The road alternates between steep and more moderate climbing. The good mixture of trees along this route will provide an ideal place to enjoy the fall colors. After a short time, notice the little town of Columbine, down to the left. Soon come to the trail marker for #1158, turn right here, and head up the narrow, rocky trail.

The trail now switchbacks up to the top, with wonderful views all along the way. After about a half hour's hike up, you'll see Steamboat Lake down to your right, and then get your first view of the fire tower up above. At this point, notice on your left a small grove of very, very determined stunted growth aspens, which have somehow managed to push their way up through the rocks. Don't be surprised to see parked ATV's just below the scree path. There is a 4x4 road up the other side of the mountain, which ends here.

After climbing the last quarter mile to the summit, enjoy, enjoy, and then, after returning to Hwy. 129, Columbine, turn right onto 129 and drive just a wee bit to the little gift shop, now on the left, where, among other neat items, you can purchase a cold soda and a shirt that proclaims, "I climbed Hahn's Peak!" The little log building once served as the area's schoolhouse.

Aspen trees near Columbine.

US
2168

68. Manzanares Trail - 1204

True accomplishment is when you use your strength to help someone else along the way, rather than to get to the top first yourself.
~ Author Unknown

Of Note: This is a tough hike, and to be honest, it's not among my favorites for solitude because quite a few dirt bikers and horseback riders also use it. Plus, it's steep and doesn't have easy access to water. At this writing, the access has been rerouted to avoid private property in Big Red Park, so it's now a bit longer hike than it was in my first guidebook. Given all that, however, the steep route does offer day hikers two good things: access to glorious Continental Divide views, and a thorough workout if you're trying to strengthen and challenge legs and lungs. Strong backpackers can also use it to access the pretty Manzanares Lakes on the other side of the Divide. Like most sub-alpine zone areas, these woods provide habitat for red squirrels, ermine, chipmunks, weasels, mule deer, elk and an occasional black bear.

Distance: About 4-miles, each way, to the Divide.

Hiking Time: About 3-hours up, less coming back down.

Elevation: Trailhead: 8,600'; 10,000' atop the Divide.

With Children: *This is not a good kids' hike. Take them on the Hare Trail instead [69].*

Map: Trails Illustrated 116; Book map 34.

How to get there: Travel west through town on U.S.40, Lincoln, for 1.3-miles from 13th St., until the Airport/Clark turnoff, Routt 129. Turn right here – north – and travel 29.8-miles on 129 to FSR 550. Turn right here and travel 3.7-miles until FSR 500. Continue for two miles and turn right onto FSR 505. After 0.5-mile, turn right into the trailhead parking area. Walk about one-quarter-mile further on the main road, looking for the trailhead sign on the left.

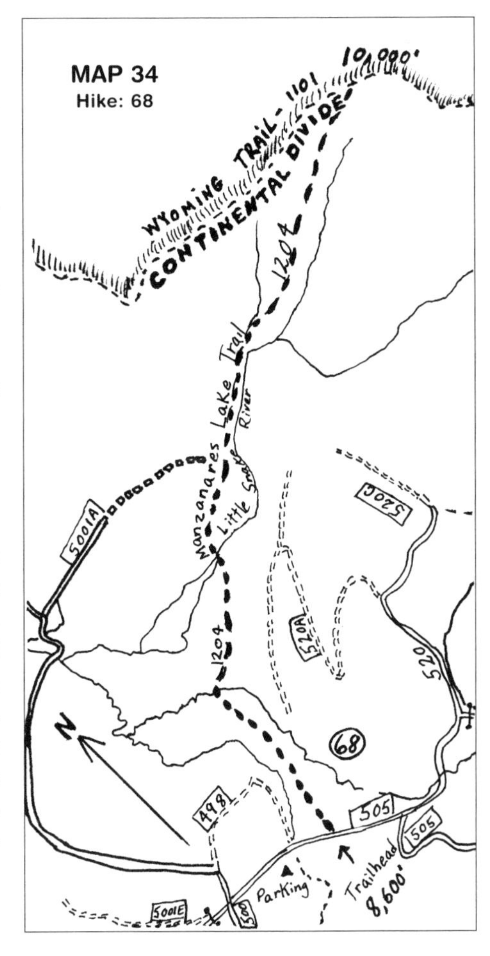

Looking down on Manzanares Lake from 1101.

The Hike: The trail heads north, paralleling the Silver City Creek, until it junctions with the old access trailhead in Big Red Park. Hike through the beautiful wide park meadow. When you come to a trail junction, take the trail to the left. Continue through the huge meadow, fording a stream – you may get wet feet. Head into the woods and begin to climb steeply through very tall aspens and firs. Cross several small streams, and continue traveling smartly uphill through lodgepole pines for about one and a half hours, until you finally reach the top of the Divide, where the trail will meet the Wyoming Trail-1101. The Mt. Zirkel Wilderness boundary begins at the top of the ridge. Turn right on 1101 and walk for a couple minutes until you see a clearing on a ridge to the left. Hike up here for some marvelous vista views. Notice the sign up to your left: "Continental Divide and West Fork Trail." To the right of this sign, going down the ridge, is the continuation of trail-1204, which takes backpackers down steeply to the Manzanares Lakes, clearly visible down below. This is also a good route for backpackers to link up with the West Fork of the Encampment River Trail, hike [70].

69. The Hare Trail - 1199

I think wilderness can give us a little hint about life on the other side.
The birds, lakes, trees, streams and mountains will tell us something about our Creator,
if we will just take the time to be still and listen to them with our hearts, ears and eyes.
~ Diane White-Crane

Of Note: This is one of my all-time favorite day hike trails! In only 3.25-miles, it takes a day hiker up to the Continental Divide, with its vast openness and spectacular views. It's pretty along the entire distance, and you'll forget that you're climbing 1,040', as the trail travels along a picturesque and very accessible creek for almost the whole way.

Most of the tough climbing is done on the first half, and then it levels off, taking you gently all the rest of the way up to the Divide. Dirt bikes are allowed on this trail, but if you hold your ears and step off the trail, they will soon roar off, leaving you once again in solitude. Numerous, perfect campsites exist along the entire second half of the trip, for those wishing to base camp just below the Divide.

On different camping trips in this area, my campsite has been visited by camp robber gray jays, elk, a bear and lots of howling coyotes – fortunately, not all on the same night!

Distance: About 3.25-miles, each way.

Hiking Time: About 2-hours, each way.

Elevation: Trailhead: 9,100' ; atop the Divide 10,100'.

With Children: *In spite of the initial climbing on the first half of this hike, this is an excellent hike for children to make – through a cooling woods, along a friendly, easy-to-reach, inviting creek. A little older child should have no trouble reaching the top, if they're in shape. About an hour into the hike, you'll come upon an old boulder avalanche field on the left, just waiting for children to come scramble over and explore.*

This is a perfect family backpack trip, with almost limitless places to camp all along the second half of the hike. And there are several campsites at the trailhead, should you wish to base camp there.

Author's Nature Note: *About a foot-long, the dark gray jay bird has a short bill, a long tail, and fluffy light underside feathers. Its collar and forehead are whitish, with a darker crown on its head. It comes by its nickname, "camp robber" naturally, since it will brazenly hang around in the trees when you're eating, waiting to quickly swoop down to help itself to any morsel you choose not to guard. My wonderful old German Shepherd dog, Annie, used to get frustrated trying to guard her leftover dog food at meal times from the pesky jays. Once while we were camped along the Hare Trail, to our great amusement, she even tried to bury her dog food bowl with dirt to protect her unfinished dinner from these delightful feathered thieves. If you're patient and hold food out to them, they will often take it gently right out of your hand.*

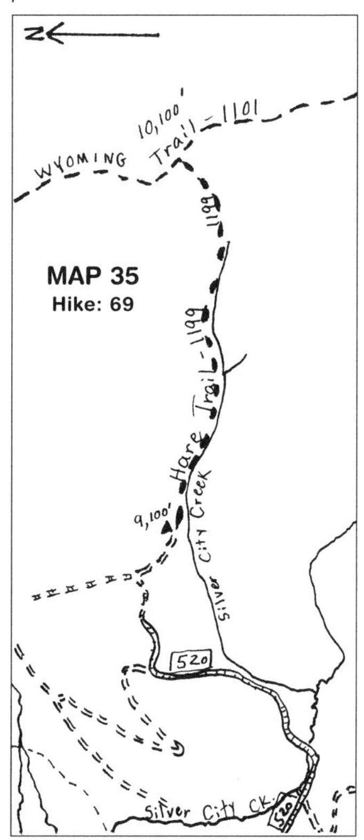

Map: Trails Illustrated 116; Book map 35.

How to get there: Drive west out of town on U.S.40, Lincoln, for 1.3-miles past 13th St. Turn right – north – at the Airport/Clark turnoff – Routt 129. Drive for 29.8-miles on 129 until you reach FSR 550. Turn right here and drive 3.7 miles until F.S.500. Turn right here and travel 2.5 miles until F.S.505. Turn right here. At 0.9 mile, 505 now becomes 520, and you will then stay on 520 for 2.8-more miles until you come to the base camp parking area.

The Hare Trail takes you gently up to outstanding vista views.

The Hike: From the base camp, look for and follow an old jeep road southeast for about 0.1-mile until you see a sign directing you left off the road. Turn left here, following this sign, "Hare Trail-1199." The narrow trail now takes you somewhat steeply up through lodgepole pines. After about 20 minutes of hiking, you'll hear and see the Middle Fork of the Little Snake River off to your right.

The terrain starts to level off after about 35-minutes into the hike, where you'll soon see the avalanche field mentioned above, and then eventually, many wonderful meadows and campsites on both sides of the creek.

After about 1.5-hours into the hike, the trail pulls left, away from the creek and passes through a level, marshy area. It soon arrives at the top of the Continental Divide and the Wyoming Trail-1100. When you reach this point, turn right and walk south for yet another half-mile for the best views.

For safety reasons, only well-equipped, experienced hikers should hike beyond this point on the Divide, since harsh weather and hard-to-follow trails can easily overwhelm wilderness neophytes.

70. Encampment River Loop - 1153 & 1152

Though in a wilderness, a man is never alone. ~ Sir Thomas Brown

Every river is a world of its own, unique in pattern and personality.
Each mile on a river will take you further from home than a hundred miles on a road.
~ Bob Marshall

Of Note: This is a wonderful, long, gentle fifteen-mile loop hike to use for a two-to-several-days long backpack trip, in a sparkling setting. The Encampment River and its many rippling forks and tributaries along the way are pristine and inviting. Gorgeous, high mountain meadows, abundant wildflowers and woods are outstanding, and ideal campsites seem to be everywhere you look.

Early-day Indian tribes spent their summers camped along this river in the area's broad meadows, living off the abundant wildlife, and thus evolved the name, "Encampment River." Like the Indians of yore, present-day backpackers will also find this area to be a campers' paradise. If you hike quietly, you will spot many mule deer, and perhaps elk along the way.

To get to the Encampment Trailhead, you'll drive about 59-miles north of Steamboat Springs, crossing over the Continental Divide into Wyoming, up and around the Hog Park Reservoir, and then south again, just over the line, into Colorado. You can also access the hike from the eastern side of the Mt. Zirkel Wilderness via Walden.

Taking this hike is a great way to explore and enjoy the northern-most section of the Mt. Zirkel Wilderness. After driving north past the town of Columbine, the roads become dirt and gavel, but they are very well maintained, and the hike is well worth the time and effort required to get there. Car campsites at the trailhead are plentiful, should you wish to arrive the night before, facilitating an early start in the morning.

Hog Park itself is situated in both Colorado and Wyoming. In 1877, John Farwell, an early-day settler for whom Farwell Mountain is named, constructed the Laramie Trail through Hog Park, which provided the first wagon access from Hahn's Peak to Laramie, Wyoming. In the late 1800's and early 1900's, each spring hardy loggers called "tie hacks" cut and floated about a half-million cross ties down the Encampment River's floodwaters to Ft. Steele, Wyoming, where they were used for railroad construction. Commissary Park, near the present-day trailhead, acted as a supply depot for the tie hacks. It now serves as a great place to base camp.

The first half of the loop hike travels south along the West Fork of the Encampment River to the lovely West Fork Lake. The second half of the loop returns the hiker north/northwest back to the trailhead of origin via the Main Fork of the Encampment River, as it flows downhill toward Wyoming. If you are a strong hiker and your time in the area allows only a day hike, I recommend hiking the first half to West Fork Lake, and then returning via the same route. This makes a fourteen-mile round-trip hike, but much of it will be on a very moderate, seemingly almost-level grade. Making the whole loop in one day can be done, but you need to be much younger and stronger than I am to do so!

Because of the many river, stream and soggy meadow crossings, be sure to take along your bug repellant, water-crossing shoes and extra socks, especially if early in the season or during a wet summer. Early in the season, usually mid-May through mid-July, crossings can be dangerous, especially in years with above-average snowfall. So use good judgment, and don't risk it if crossing look too difficult. If you have the time and energy to add on extra mileage, this route also provides easy access to side-trip destinations – among them west to Manzanares Lake, south to the Encampment Meadows, Gem Lake and Lake Diana, east to Seven Lakes, and east to Stump Park. The Mt. Zirkel Wilderness boundary in this area was recently expanded, so be certain to use a current updated Trails Illustrated map to avoid confusion when you encounter old wilderness boundary signs, which in some spots are still left in place. The trailhead itself has also recently been moved, improved and renamed, so don't be confused by descriptions in older hiking guides. As always, please leave no trace of your visit to this lovely area.

Distance: Encampment Trailhead to West Fork Lake: 7-miles, one way; West Fork Lake to Encampment Trailhead via Main Fork Trail: 9-miles, one way; Total loop: 15-miles.

The Adler family camping at West Fork Lake.

Hiking Time: About 3.5-hours from trailhead to West Fork Lake; about 4.5-hours from West Fork Lake to trailhead via Main Fork Trail.

Elevation: Trailhead: 8,374'; West Fork Lake: 9,305'.

Map: Trails Illustrated 116; Book map 36.

With Children: *Five Stars! This is the perfect route for a family backpack trip, even if you can only complete the first half of it – an extremely gentle climb through meadows and woods up to a lovely mountain lake. The second half descends very gradually through old-growth forests of dark, pine scented Englemann spruce and sub-alpine firs, changing to lodgepole pines. The lake, as well as the sparkling Encampment River itself, with its many forks and tributaries, provides families with a seemingly unlimited number of wonderful places for exploration, nature study, picnicking, resting and camping. The almost-surreal meadows, forests, wildflowers, wildlife viewing and good fishing make this route well worth several days of a family's vacation time.*

Author's Nature Note: *If you hike quietly along this trail, you'll probably spot large-eared mule deer all over the place! They will no doubt spot you, too, and leap away rapidly. Bucks have multi-branched antlers, with the number of antler forks being determined by the animal's diet and age. The brown mule deer has a white rump, chin, throat and tail with black on its tip. The animal's color turns grayish in the wintertime. Mule deer seem especially intrigued by llamas, and their curiosity often prompts them to come bravely into our campsite to spy on the tethered llamas. Perhaps, since both have very big ears, similar feet, and the same diets, these two animals are related – at least in spirit?*

Fishing: *West Fork Lake: good for 8-12" brook; Encampment River and tributaries good for brook and brown trout.*

How to get there: Access from Steamboat Springs: Drive west out of town on U.S.40 , Lincoln, for 1.3-miles after 13th St., until the Airport/Clark turnoff, Routt 129. Turn right here

– north – and drive for 30.4-miles to the intersection with FSR 550; turn right onto 550 and drive for 24.1-miles to a stop sign; at this stop sign, turn right onto Rt. 496 and drive 4.1-miles; then turn right at the intersection onto 821 and drive 0.4-mile until you see the sign on the left saying “Encampment Trail Head.” Turn left here, which is 821A, and drive 0.3-mile to the parking area and the trailhead, the sign for which will be found to the left of the outhouse. Don’t be confused if you see a sign on 496 pointing to Commissary Park and the Encampment River Trail on the left – that trailhead takes you north along the river into Wyoming, not south along the river, into Colorado, where you want to go.

Access from Walden: Drive north out of Walden via Hwy. 125 to Cowdrey; turn left – west – onto Jackson County 6 and drive for 19-miles, at which point Hwy. 6 becomes FSR 80. Drive on 80 for 16-miles, turning left at the sign for the Encampment Trailhead, FSR 821, which appears as soon as the road crosses the Encampment River. Then make another left onto 821A and drive 0.3-mile to the trailhead parking area. Look for the actual trailhead sign to the left of the outhouse.

The Hike: Follow the trailhead path immediately down to a meadow area, turning right onto what was once a very popular jeep road. Depending on the time of the year, keep your water-crossing shoes handy for possible use at river and stream crossings and boggy sections of meadows. Quickly come to the first of three West Fork River crossings. After about a half-hour hike from the trailhead, arrive at a fork and two signs – one educating hikers about the Mt. Zirkel Wilderness, and the other directing you left to the Encampment Meadows and right to the West Fork Lake. Take the fork to the right. For about a mile, climb up at a very slight grade through alternating forests of fir and spruce and superb meadows. The road gradually levels out and becomes a narrower trail. Cross the West Fork River a second time, and then enter the impressively beautiful West Fork Meadows. Look to the east of these meadows to see Black Mountain. This loop hike will eventually circle the whole of that mountain. After the meadow, enter a forest, and then, about a quarter-mile further, come upon a trail marker pointing the way west – right – uphill to Manzanares Lake. Remain on the main trail. About 1.5-miles after that, you’ll

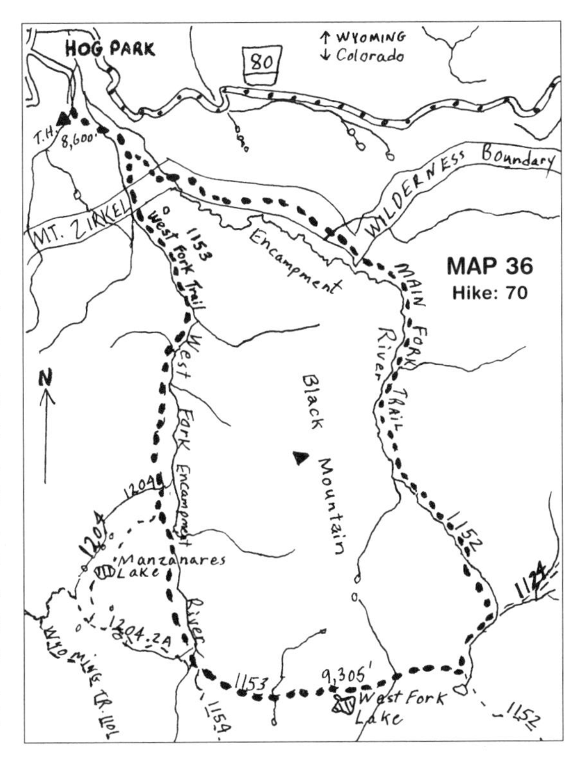

come upon yet another marker for Manzanares Lake. Looking at your map, you'll see how these two side trails connect to form a 2.5-mile loop hike to Manzanares Lake, for those who desire to add on an extra side trip to the itinerary. For the purpose of this hike, however, we travel past these two trail signs, remaining on the West Fork Trail.

After a total of about 7-miles, arrive at the glistening West Fork Lake, 9,305' high and thirteen-acres in size. A number of former campsites at the lake are being re-vegetated and are off limits to camping. Please respect this effort, and try to camp further away from the lake, where sites haven't been overused and abused.

Because this picturesque lake is a popular destination for horseback riders, it receives many day visitors. Unfortunately, some seem to leave litter and toilet paper behind in the campsites. Should you discover any of their trash, please burn or pack it out, if you can, and send an unkind telepathic message to the thoughtless person who left it there.

This loop hike eventually circles the whole of Black Mountain, here seen in the distance at the start of the hike.

After your visit to West Fork Lake, continue the loop by getting back on the West Fork Trail on the lake's north side, and hike east for another mile through open stands of verdant lodgepole pines, over the broad saddle to the intersection with the Main Fork Trail-1152. If you have the time and energy for a side trip, turn right and head south to Encampment Meadows, Gem Lake and Lake Diana. However, for the purpose of this hike, turn left and head north. After about a half-mile, 1152 intersects trail 1124, the Beaver Creek-Stump Park Trail, which heads off to the right – east. Unless you're making a side-trip here, continue heading north on 1152. At this writing, there is only a pole with no sign on it, but both trails are well defined.

Gradually descend down through old mature spruce and fir forests. Every now and then, you'll be able to catch a panoramic view of Black Mountain through clearings in the trees on your left. As the trail parallels the cascading river downhill, hikers can follow its growth from a gentle, meandering brook to a boulder-strewn rushing stream. The meadows, too, grow in size. Cross the river for a second time, and then eventually enter the Center Stock Driveway Trail – you'll see the old yellow signs on the trees. Stay on this wide driveway until the final crossing of the river, where you'll see a very old Mt. Zirkel Wilderness sign. Cross the river, and follow several rock cairns on the other side south for just a few yards, until they eventually lead you in a semi-circle, north again, quickly taking you back to the well-used trail. After about another half-hour of hiking, you'll once again reach the original junction and the sign that points two directions – to West Fork Lake-Encampment Meadow and to Hog Park. Follow the north-pointing arrow, back toward Hog Park, about another half-hour hike, returning you from whence you first began. You'll soon spot the outhouse up on your left, and then you'll reach the sign directing you up to the Encampment Trailhead parking lot where your car awaits you.

71. Nipple Peak Trail - 1147

Be my rock of refuge, to which I can always go. ~ Psalm 71:3

This country is geology by day and astronomy by night.
~ John Boynton Priestley

Of Note: Especially if you happen to be camping at Steamboat Lake, or if you're in the mood to "go climb a peak," or just get away from the crowds, this is a good place for you to go. You can also use this trail as the access for bushwhacking up City Mountain or Nipple Peak, if you have the correct topographical maps and the know-how to use them. Or, in late September, use the established trail to view the changing aspen colors without bumping into many people.

Distance: Two to four miles, depending on destination.

Hiking Time: One to three hours, depending on destination.

Elevation: Trailhead: 8,119'; picnic spot with children: 8,600'; top of City Mountain: 9,557; top of Nipple Peak: 10,324'.

With Children: *Older, in-shape children would enjoy climbing the peaks with you. But if you have younger children, you and they would enjoy hiking for about 45-minutes, after which you'll come to a pretty picnic area, which has a picnic table and a fire circle for a hot dog/marshmallow roast. All this sits next to a busy little stream, just waiting for a child's exploration.*

Yampatika Notes: *This volcanic plug was originally called "Maggie's Nipple" after Maggie Baggs, the common-law wife of George Baggs, as in Baggs, Wyoming. The couple received the first deed in Routt County and homesteaded in the 1870's. She was renowned for mistreating the ranch*

Stop at the pretty picnic area on 1147, along a stream, and have a hot dog roast.

hands at the Double Eleven Ranch. When a cowhand named the peak Maggie's Nippple on a roundup, Maggie horse whipped him in public.

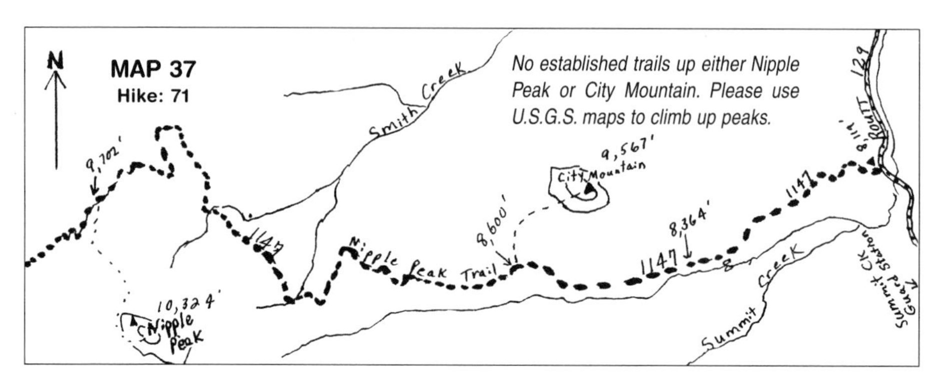

Map: Trails Illustrated 116 covers only a portion; and it takes sections of three U.S.G.S. maps to cover the whole trail: S. Elkhorn Mt., Shield Mt., and Meaden Peak; the map in this book gives a good overview of the entire hike.

How to get there: Drive west out of Steamboat for 1.3-miles past 13th St. on U.S.40, to the Airport/Clark turnoff, Routt 129. Turn right here and stay on 129 for 32.2-miles, driving past Clark, Steamboat Lake, Hahn's Peak and Columbine. At mile 32, you will pass the Summit Creek Forest Service Guard Station. Drive 0.2-mile more, and you'll come to a road sign on the left, F.S. 47. Park here on the side of the road.

The Hike: Start up the old jeep road, which climbs gently through a woods of aspen, spruce and pine. You may be met by the baaing of many grazing sheep, which will stretch their necks out to stare at you, and then take off in alarm, with their bells a-ringing.

After about 40-minutes of hiking, the trail meets and follows a small stream. A few minutes later, you'll come to the nice picnic area described in "With Children" above. There's a sign here saying, "Nipple Peak Trail-1147, Slater Park." Hike for a short time, and you'll come to where the trail intersects with remnants of an old mining road on the right. A sign on the trail to the left says 1147, and this trail now narrows from the jeep road 047 to the pack trail 1147.

If you want to hike up to the top of City Mountain, turn right, north, on this old mining road. It quickly ends, and you can easily see City Mountain ahead of you. If you know what you're doing, use your compass and map to bushwhack up to the top for a super view.

If you want to climb Nipple Peak, continue on the trail to the left, 1147. After hiking about another mile, you'll arrive at a hillcrest, where you'll spot Nipple Peak to your left. Here, using map and compass, you can leave the trail to bushwhack to the top of Nipple Peak. Note the one big rock on top, providing just enough room for a person to sit on and enjoy this bird's eye view of the world.

72. Bow Hunter Trail - 496.1A

Hold fast to your belief in Eternal Life. Death is not the end, but the doorway into Heaven.
~ Billy Graham

Going to the woods is going home, for I suppose we came from the woods originally.
~ John Muir

Of Special Note: On Wednesday, September 1, 1999, my husband and I hiked this trail for the first time, scouting it out for possible inclusion in this guidebook. By chance, we passed a camp of bow hunters from Texas and Louisiana, and after chatting with them a bit about the area, we continued on our way up the trail. Upon our return, the hunters invited us to stop at their camp for hot coffee, cookies, and some friendly conversation, with me giving them a hard time about hunting poor Bambi's mother, and they giving us a friendly hard time about our only wanting to "hunt" with our camera. A few hours after we left them, a member of their hunting party got lost in the area near Shield Mountain, due east of this trail. Three-and-a-half-days later, after an extensive, massive search effort, rescue dogs found his body. Tragically, he had lost his bearings and walked off a steep cliff in the dark, trying to return to camp and his buddies. His name was Kris, and it's to his memory that I name this lovely hike the "Bow Hunter Trail," and that I ask you – lost or not – never to bushwhack in the dark.

Of Note: The Bow Hunter trail travels over some rugged terrain. If you take this hike, please have your compass and the U.S.G.S. Shield Mountain map along with you, as well as your emergency survival kit (see front section of this book), and remain on the main trail.

This area provides a wonderful opportunity to observe a very unique mixture of trees. The moist habitat is perfect for Colorado Blue Spruce, which are generally found thinly scattered among other trees. The difference is that here, there seems to be an unusual profusion of these lovely blue trees, and they all look like perfectly formed Christmas trees. Some are bluer than others, but all show the deep blue color in their new growth. This blue contrasts beautifully with the whitish trunks and apple green leaves of the area's thick aspens, which, because of the optimal soil and moisture conditions, grow very tall and robust. In the fall, the color contrast becomes even more stunning.

Enjoy a close-up view of Shield Mountain at the end of the hike.

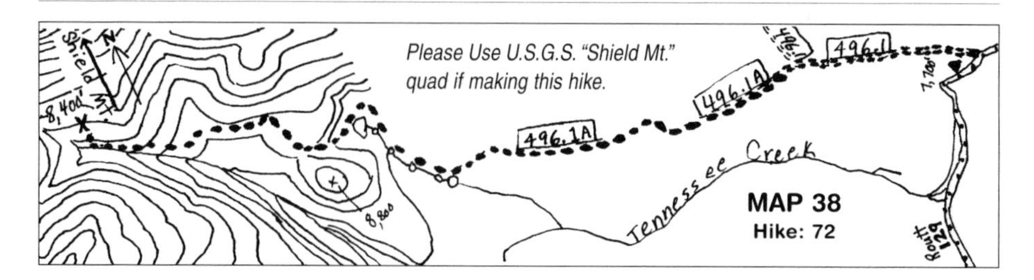

Distance: About 2.5-miles, each way.

Hiking Time: About 1.5-hours, one-way up.

Elevation: Trailhead: 7,702'; Ridge: 8,400'.

With Children: *Most older, in-shape children would enjoy making this hike through gorgeous stands of aspens and spruce trees, up to a pretty view.*

Yampatika Notes: *At the higher elevations on nearby Shield Mountain, Douglas-fir trees take to the warmer slopes, not able to handle the colder temperatures of the north-facing slopes. The dry, hot and windy exposures create bonsai trees with massive trunks and thick bark. A far cry from the massive Douglas-fir of the Pacific Coast, these populations are now recognized as two distinct varieties: Douglas-fir and Rocky Mountain Douglas-fir. At lower elevations in the valley, this tree is found in several extensive forests on north-facing slopes, where they thrive on ample moisture.*

Map: Not on Trails Illustrated; U.S.G.S. Shield Mountain; Book map 38.

How to get there: Drive west out of Steamboat on U.S.40, Lincoln, for 1.3-miles past 13th St. until the Airport/Clark turnoff, Routt 129. Turn right, north, and drive 38.8-miles on 129. After spotting marker "38" on the right-hand-side of the road, the trailhead sign for this hike will be 0.8-mile further, on the left. Park here on the side of the road, and walk up the jeep road.

The Hike: Begin walking west on the jeep road. After about a half-mile, the jeep road turns right. At this intersection, look for a trail marker sign on the left – 496A1 – and begin hiking west/southwest on that path.

The trail climbs gradually through numerous aspen groves, intermixed beautifully and uniquely with contrasting green/blue Colorado Blue Spruce and firs. The aspen groves vary in sizes – from stunted growth – to new growth – to gigantic old growth trees. Come late September, these aspen trees will decorate the skyline with shimmering golden colors and provide the trail with a rich tannin-scented, crunchy, groundcover.

You'll soon reach a series of three old beaver ponds on the left. Shortly after the third pond, look for an outcropping mini-sand dune, a magical treat placed there by Mother Nature. Shortly afterwards, about two-thirds of the way into the hike, the trail parallels a small stream on the left, probably the safest water supply along the route for filtering water, given the existence of grazing cattle in the area.

The trail now heads steeply up through a grove of very large aspens and spruce. Since this trail was created by fall hunters who don't seem to have time for switchbacks, be prepared to work your leg muscles for about 0.5-mile – almost straight up this section. When the trail levels out, you'll have about another ten minutes of walking slightly downhill until you come to a clearing with a pretty view of Shield Mountain. We use this as the turnaround for the hike. Even though many game and hunter trails seem to go off this trail in many different directions, hikers should always remain on the main trail, taking careful note of the route being followed, since it's easy to get turned around in this primitive area.

For as high as the heavens are above the earth, so great is his love for those who fear him;
As far as the east is from the west, so far has he removed our transgressions from us.
~ Psalm 103:11-12

GROUSE

73. Sand Mountain - 1175

No. 35: Plant a tree on your birthday; No. 181: Wear out, don't rust out.
No. 199: Park at the back of the lot at shopping centers. The walk is good exercise.
No. 245: Never cut what can be untied; No. 267: Lie on your back and look at the stars.
From "Life's Little Instruction Book" ~ H. Jackson Brown, Jr.

Of Note: The hike to the top of Sand Mountain is definitely one of my favorites. If you have a small, high-clearance 4x4-drive vehicle and the road's not muddy, you can actually drive to within one-mile of the top, but for the rest of us who don't, we need to park a couple miles below this point, and hike the three miles total up to the top.

Claire holds up the rock cairn. Notice Steamboat Lake down to the right.

The breathtaking, unsurpassed 360-degree views on top include east to Hahn's Peak across the valley, and of Mt. Zirkel, Big and Little Agnes, the Sawtooth Range and Steamboat Lake to the east and southeast. Views to the west include California Park, Hayden, Craig, and even – on a clear day – all the way to Utah. To the north, you'll see the Medicine Bow Range in Wyoming, and south, you'll get to peek at Sleeping Giant's "other side."

The first two miles climb gently on a jeep road, slowly gaining good altitude. Finally, the trail switchbacks steeply up the last mile, through an unusually lush, mature pine and fir forest, the floor of which is completely carpeted in a delicate green kinnikinnik ground cover. During wildflower season, along the way expect to see whole meadows in full, glorious bloom, including entire fields of tall, ambrosial-looking purple larkspur.

The chert rock materials which you see at the top make up portions of Sand Mountain's strata. Area Ute Indians once used similar rocks as these for making tools.

Begin the hike early in the day to avoid afternoon storms, and leave the peak if lightning threatens. Take plenty of water, film and sunscreen.

For this writer, the magnificent, eye-opening views remind me of Psalm 48:1-2: *Great is the Lord, and most worthy of praise, in the city of our God, his holy mountain. It is beautiful in its loftiness, the joy of the whole earth.*

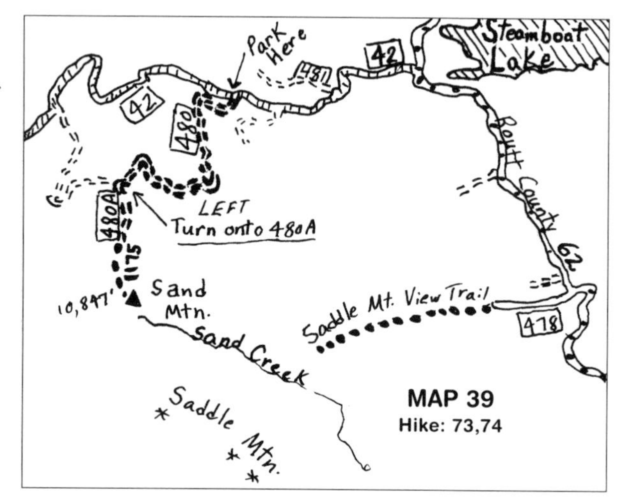

Distance: From the intersection of FDR 42 and 480, about 3-miles, each way.

Hiking Time: About 2-hours, one-way up.

Elevation: Parking area: 8.600'; Official Trailhead: 9,020'; Peak: 10,847'.

With Children: *If you have a 4x4 vehicle and can drive to within one mile – to the official trailhead for 1175 – with some help, even young children can generally make the short one-mile, steep switchback hike. If you have to hike the whole roundtrip six miles, only older, in-shape children can last long enough to get all the way to the top and back. But they will love it if they do!*

Author's Nature Note: *The profusion of delicate kinnikinnik groundcover carpeting the forest floor on the last section of this hike seems especially enchanting. This creeping shrub is most often found in open coniferous forests. It has glossy leaves that remain green all year, urn-shaped flowers and shiny, quarter-inch-in-diameter green berries that ripen into a dark red color, often remaining on the shrub's branches for several seasons. Petite scalloped pink flowers bloom and hang from the thin branches, remaining mostly hidden under the leaves.*

Map: Not yet on Trails Illustrated; U.S.G.S. Meaden Peak; Book map 39.

How to get there: Drive west out of Steamboat on U.S.40 until the Airport/Clark turnoff, 1.3-miles from 13th St. Turn right here, north, and drive for 26-miles, just past Steamboat Lake to CR 62. Turn left here onto CR62 and drive just over three miles to CR42. Turn right onto 42 and drive for 0.6-mile to the Forest Service gate and boundary, and then continue from here on CR42 for about 5.2-more miles, until it junctions with FDR 480. Parking is available on the right, just before this junction, and if you go past it, you can easily back up to it from the junction.

The Hike: After walking about 1.3-miles on 480 from the parking area, hike on 480A, straight ahead, since 480 now drops rapidly downhill to the left. Follow 480A about another 0.5-mile to the Forest Service trailhead sign for trail 1175. The trail forks about 100-yards past the trailhead, so take the single track to the left. After some steep switchbacks through the entrancing forest, arrive at the very top to revel in the awesome views.

Note the small Forest Service communications tower, three U.S. Coast and Geodetic Survey markers – critical for use in establishing the accuracy of topographical mapping in the area – and two very tall rock cairns, one of which you may have seen and wondered about on your way up.

Watch for numerous soaring ravens and hawks off the western side – diving, riding, and floating on the thermals created when the winds hit the side of the mountain and are pushed upward in strong rushes of air. Breathe in the views, and then lie on your back, look at the clouds and let them put you at peace with the world.

74. Saddle Mountain View Hike

He stretches out the heavens like a canopy, and spreads them out like a tent to live in...
~ Isaiah 40:22

The greatest wonder is that we can see these trees and not wonder more.
~ Ralph Waldo Emerson

Of Note: This is a short, moderate-to-steep, delightful little hike, which takes you through very pretty trees up to a ridge, where you will be treated to a wonderful close-up view of Saddle and Sand Mountains to the west, as well as good views on the return trip of a section of the western side of the Mt. Zirkel Wilderness. You can access this hike from RC62, either beginning at the Clark Store or from its other end at Steamboat Lake. This is also a good hike to make early in the season, when the higher-up trails are still covered with snow.

There are no water sources along this hike for filtering, so take enough water along. Although this trail is on Forest Service property, it's not an officially numbered or maintained trail; however, it is well used and well defined. Take along your binoculars for spotting elk and your camera for some nice photos. On my last hike to the top of this ridge, during bow hunting season, I found a hunter stretched out on the ground. There was no answer when I greeted him, and I feared the worst. But then he opened his eyes and, somewhat embarrassed, he told me he'd just been taking a nap. Seems that since elk nap at mid-day, so, too, do hunters!

Distance: About 1.5-miles, each way.

Hiking Time: About 45-minutes up; a little less coming back down.

Elevation: 8,100'; Ridge top: 9,100'.

With Children: *In-shape children of all ages will enjoy this hike. Even though it's a wee bit of a climb, it's short enough for most youngsters to eventually reach the top. The aspen woods along the trail are lovely and inviting for all ages.*

Author's Nature Notes: *The trees along this trail would be a good place to look for and identify birds that live in aspen forests. Bring a bird book and your binoculars and watch for: mountain bluebirds, black-capped chickadees, northern mountain flickers (woodpeckers), cordilleran flycatchers, Cooper's hawks, broad-tailed hummingbirds, dark-eyed juncos, red-breasted nuthatches, white-breasted northern pygmy owls, American robins, Williamson's sapsuckers, tree swallows, violet-greens, warbling vireos, orange-crowned warblers, western wood-pewees, hairy woodpeckers and house wrens.*

Nice view from the ridge.

Map: This is not an official trail, so the Forest Service map shows the road to the parking area, but no trail; Trails Illustrated maps (116 & 117) show the area but no trail; Book map 39.

How to get there: Drive west out of Steamboat on U.S.40, Lincoln, for about 1.3-miles past 13th St. to the Airport/Clark turnoff, Routt 129. Turn right, north, here and drive 17-miles to the wonderful Clark Store.

Like the fictional Ralph's Pretty Good Grocery Store in Lake Wobegon, Minnesota, the Clark Store could have the same motto: "If we don't have it, you probably don't need it!" Definitely try their ice cream cones.

After your Clark Store visit, drive on RC62, an immediate left after the Clark Store, and drive for 5.3-miles. Turn left onto FDR 478; drive 0.7-mile back to the parking area for this hike.

If you're coming from Steamboat Lake, driving northwest on 129, the other end of RC62 begins just past Steamboat Lake. Turn left and drive 6.4-miles on 62 until FDR 478; turn right onto 478 and drive 0.7-mile back to the parking area for this hike.

The Hike: The trail climbs first gradually, and then toward the last third of it, more steeply uphill, through lovely, cooling woods of mixed aspens and evergreens. The trail is well defined. Arrive at a clearing at the top of the ridge and look out at the glorious view of Saddle Mountain to the left and Sand Mountain to the right. You'll immediately see why it's called Saddle

Mountain. Let this view of Sand Mountain inspire you to hike to its top on another day, for even more spectacular views. See hike [73].

Hunters have continued this trail downhill from the ridge, but I suggest leaving that part of this trail to the hunters. Return the way you came.

75. Greenville Mine Road

It always amazes me that I find it less work to hike 20-miles on a pretty trail than to work out for 20-minutes on my Nordic Track.
~ Diane White-Crane

Of Note: This is a friendly, easy hike to make earlier in the season, before the trails in the higher country are free of snow. The initial car-accessible road to the trailhead, FDR 440, follows Greenville Creek, and then the hike, thereafter, takes you eventually along charming Big Creek, where ideal campsites are plentiful.

Most of the hike travels through a gentle, wide valley – a part of which parallels noisy, bubbly Big Creek. The turn-around point for this hike is also a good destination to see first-hand some of the damage done to the Routt National Forest during the 1997 Blowdown. Dirt bikers, ATV enthusiasts and horseback riders also use this trail, so you may not find a lot of solitude back here, but it's a delightful hike, nevertheless.

In the late 1880's, George Franz operated the Greenville Mine in the area, which produced some silver, lead, gold and copper. In the 1940's, the mine became much more productive, reluctantly surrendering more than 1,500 tons of zinc and silver ore.

Distance: About 2.5-miles, each way.

Hiking Time: About 1.5-hours, each way.

Elevation: Trailhead: 8,400'; Gain and lose about 500'.

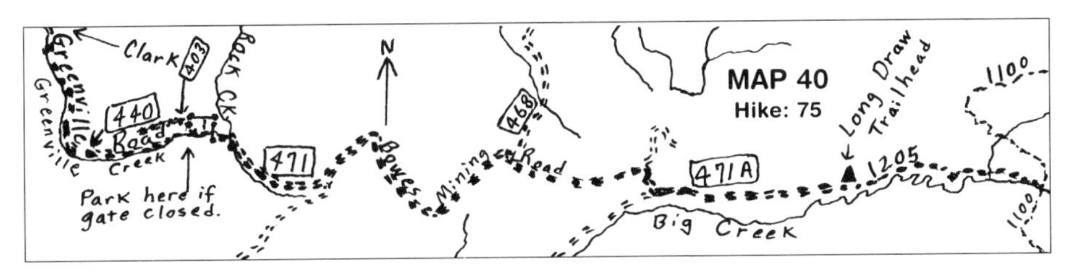

With Children: *Except for one steep section, this is a fairly level,kid-friendly hike. If you don't mind sharing some of the area with 4x4 vehicles, there are plenty of good campsites for a pleasant family backpack trip.*

While hiking on this trail, Dudley and Sammy befriend aliens from another planet.

Map: Trails Illustrated 117; Book map 40.

How to get there: Drive west out of town on U.S.40 for 1.3- miles past 13th St., until the Airport/Clark turnoff, Routt 129. Turn right, north, here, and drive for about 17-miles, until you see the "Welcome to Clark" sign on the right, just before the Clark Store. Turn right here onto FDR 440. Drive through a grove of huge aspens, a good place to see fall colors. There's a gate at 3.9-miles, and if it's open, you may continue to drive on what is now FDR 471, the Bowes Mining Road, for an additional 1.6-miles, where it junctures with FDR 468. Park here.

The Hike: Begin to hike straight ahead, still on 471. Emerge from the trees to a good view of the valley below. In the valley, the trail splits right and left. Go left onto 471A, and hike on level ground along Big Creek. The road eventually becomes the Long Draw Trail-1205, and it now alternates in and out of thick forests and open mountain meadows.

When you reach the Mt. Zirkel Wilderness boundary sign, look up to see some of the '97 Blowdown damage mentioned above. This is the turnaround point for this hike. If you have the energy, you can continue to the junction with 1100, the Swamp Park Trail, which was cleared in the fall of 2000. This is a great place to witness the results of this amazing wind phenomenon:

"He let loose the east wind from the heavens and led forth the south wind by his power." ~ *Psalm 78:26.*

76. Coulton Creek Trail - 1188

Holy Mother Earth, the trees and all nature are witnesses of your thoughts and deeds.
~ Winnebago Indian Proverb

Of Note: This trail offers much solitude and early-season access, since it's lower in elevation than most area trails. The first part of the hike presents you with beautiful views of the Elk River Valley, through which Seedhouse Road travels. The middle section offers wonderful opportunities to enjoy wildflower-bedecked meadows in early July and brilliant, golden aspen groves in late September. Wear orange if hiking during bow hunting season! The end of the hike takes you to the foot of Farwell Mountain, and if you get a very early start, and you have map and compass know-how and lots of energy left, you can bushwhack up to the top of Farwell Mountain.

The trail doesn't follow Coulton Creek until after about the first two miles. In the early summer, the creek flows very strongly, but after mid-summer, it tames to a very modest stream. So, take plenty of water along, since this is a relatively dry hike. If you hike quietly, you're likely to see many deer.

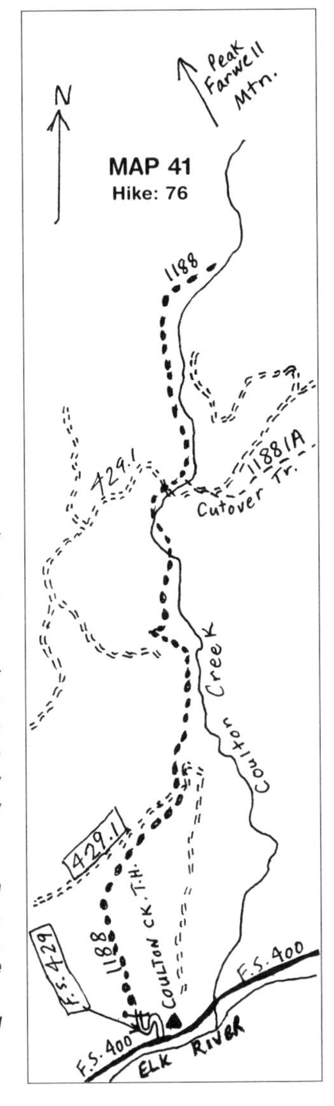

Distance: About 5.5 miles, each way.

Hiking Time: About 2.5 hours, one-way.

Elevation: Trailhead: 7,600'; Trail's end: 8,600'.

With Children: *This is not a good hike for small children, since the first half climbs and climbs, and there is no creek along this part of the hike for the children to explore. However, older children who don't mind a modest climb will enjoy all the hike has to offer.*

Yampatika Notes: *You'll hike through a beautiful aspen grove on the lower section of this trail, in season, full of summer wildflowers. The aspen tree is our main deciduous tree of the forests here. The rich soil produced from decaying leaves, and the cool shades produced in the spring create some stunning wildflower displays. Look for little sunflower, tall larkspur, cow parsnip, sweet anise, lovage, meadowrue, showy daisy, wooly daisy, sticky geranium, columbine and lousewort.*

Author's Notes: *The lush vegetation of the aspen grove floor provides rich habitat for many mammals, including elk, mule deer, bats, black bears, chipmunks, cottontails, coyotes, ermine, ground squirrels, marmots, lynx, deer mice, gophers, porcupines, shrews, skunks, voles, weasels, snowshoe hares, and if near water, beavers.*

From time to time, in these aspen groves, you can see black clawing scars on large aspen tree trunks, where black bear once climbed seeking new buds and foliage, or even to steal from bird's nests. The aspen grove's snowshoe hare turns from brown to white in the winter, and his large snowshoe-like feet help him escape in deep snow from larger prey animals, which sink into the snow. (See below.)

Map: Trails Illustrated 116; Book map 41.

How to get there: Drive west out of town on U.S.40 for 1.3-miles after 13th St., until the Airport/Clark turnoff, Routt 129. Turn right, north, here and drive for about 18-miles, until just past Clark, to the Seedhouse Road, FDR 400. Turn right here, and drive for 4.5-miles. Look for a sign for FDR 429 on the left. Turn left here, and drive for 0.1-mile to the trailhead sign for Coulton Creek. Park here.

The Hike: The trail climbs up, first through a clear meadow, and then into lovely aspen groves. After about 15-minutes of hiking, you'll be able to enjoy marvelous views of the lush valley below. Then the trail alternates between climbing and leveling off, going through pines, aspens and meadows. Soon you'll cross a timber road, which you'll also encounter a couple more times along the way. After about 1.75-hours of hiking, cross over a little footbridge, under which, by mid-summer, the stream may have dried up. After a few more minutes, you'll finally see and hear Coulton Creek down below you. Cross a side stream and travel along Coulton Creek for a short time. The trail then heads away from the creek, up the other side of a ridge, and levels off, as it passes through a pine forest. You'll soon come to another open area, where you'll again be able to see the creek down below.

The trail then contours along the hillside above the creek, adjacent to and just below an old timber sale area, running north to northeast, then crossing the timber road again. About an eighth-mile past this point, come upon the trail junction with the Cutover Trail-1188A, which crosses over to the Hinman Creek Trail-1177. This trail can be used for a loop hike, if desired – hike [77]. At this point, you should begin to have a clear view of Farwell Mountain ahead of you. The trail then travels through a very wide meadow, which turns northeast for a while, and then north again, toward the mountain.

The official trail ends where it crosses the creek. But you can follow a continuing trail north through the woods, where you'll soon come upon the fattest aspen tree I have ever seen in all my many years of hiking! If you wish, you can follow this trail a little further up, to the base of Farwell Mountain, and then bushwhack your way to the top, if you have the correct topographical map, a compass and the skills to use them. As always, avoid going up the mountain if thunderstorms are in the area.

In the winter, this brown snowshoe hare will turn white – a perfect camouflage.

From this perch, enjoy the view of the boulders and note the 2002 fire damage.

77. Hinman Lake and View - 1177

In the bulb, there is the flower; in the seed, an apple tree.
In cocoons, a hidden promise; butterflies will soon be free.
In the cold and snow of winter, there's a spring that waits to be.
Unrevealed until its season, something God alone can see.
~ Natalie Sleeth

Of Note: Here's a hike with early-season access. The trail crosses Hinman Creek near its beginning, climbs up to a lovely lake, travels next to a spectacular overlook of a huge boulder field, and then finally, to the second crossing of Hinman Creek. At this point, the day hiker turns around and returns, but the backpacker can continue up along beautiful Scott's Run Creek, which heads up a canyon, eventually ending up in Diamond Park.

This is a pretty hike, through evergreens, aspen groves and meadows of waist-high vegetation. Make a quick stop to see the lovely water lily filled Hinman Lake, but then be certain to include the middle stop – to the special perch overlooking a breathtaking view down on a huge boulder-strewn rock field. If time allows, continue to the second crossing of the creek.

Distance: About 4.75-miles, one-way.

Hiking Time: About 2.5-hours one-way, with brief stops at lake and view.

Elevation: Trailhead: 7,800'; Hinman Lake: 8,195'; Viewpoint: 8,714'.

With Children: *Because of the initial climbing, this isn't a good hike for small children. Better to take them on hike [78], from the same trailhead. However, take older, in-shape children to at least the overview, and they'll be as impressed with it as you will be.*

Yampatika Notes: *You didn't expect to see water lilies in the mountains, did you? These are Yellow Water Lilies, and they are a hardy water plant of montane and sub-alpine lakes. They indicate a lake in succession, as they only grow in shallower waters. As lakes recede, water lilies may move in and hasten the lake's succession to a wetland, then a meadow, and maybe eventually to a forest.*

Around 1875, a trapper named Scott wounded a bear, and then did a record run down the canyon to get away from the angry animal. Scott was found badly mauled at Hinman Creek. For his record sprint, the creek in the canyon was named Scott's Run.

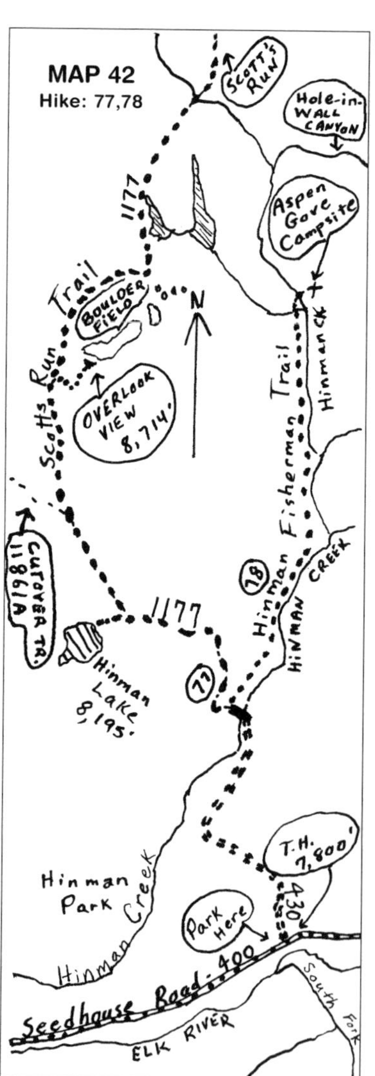

Fishing: *Brook trout in Hinman Creek; no fish in Hinman Lake.*

Map: Trails Illustrated 116; Book map 42.

How to get there: Driving west out of Steamboat on U.S.40, Lincoln, go 1.3- miles past 13th St., until the Airport/Clark Turnoff, Routt 129. Turn right, north, here, and drive for about 18-miles, until just past Clark. Turn right at the Seedhouse Road, FDR 400, and travel 6.1-miles until you see the trail marker for 430. Turn left here and park. If it's not muddy, 4x4 vehicles can drive in a little further, but better not to push your luck!

The Hike: Start out walking on the jeep road for about 20-minutes, through pretty aspen groves. Cross the creek on the footbridge, climb up the bank to the trail, and go left, heading southwest for a few minutes, toward a fence. Just before reaching the fence, turn right and head north/northwest. Hike up through the trees, passing a large pond down on your right. After about a half-hour from the footbridge, come to a fork in the trail. Take the spur trail to the left, off the main trail, climb down a bramble-lined gully, and soon come to Hinman Lake.

After your visit to the lake is complete, take the spur trail back to the main trail, turn left, and continue hiking north through the woods.

After 0.5-mile, on your left, continue past the junction with the Crossover Trail-1188A, which heads over to the Coulton Creek Trail-1188 – hike [76]. Remain on 1177 for about another quarter-mile, until you see a narrow spur trail junction on the right. Take this little spur trail up through the forest for about five minutes, soon coming to the overview mentioned above. Have your lunch here, perched on the rocks, about 1,000' above the magnificent view.

When your visit to the view is finished, retrace your route back to the main trail and turn left to return to the trailhead, or right to travel to the second crossing of Hinman Creek. If you're continuing on, you'll hike through aspens and lodgepole pines for about another two miles, gaining and then losing quite a bit of elevation along the way.

When you reach the creek crossing, rest there before heading back. Or, if backpacking, cross the creek and continue up beautiful Scott's Run, which around 1875 was named after a trapper who was found mauled along the banks of Hinman Creek. He had been running to escape a grizzly bear, which he had wounded, when the creature caught up with him and took its revenge.

78. Hinman Creek Fisherman Trail

I am not against golf, since I cannot but suspect that it keeps armies of the unworthy from discovering trout fishing.
~ Paul O'Neil

Of Note: Especially if you're camping anywhere off Seedhouse Road, this is a pleasant little day hike for a family with small children or seniors who don't want to undertake a vigorous hike. This can also be a good mini-backpack trip for families who want to hike in just a little way, set up a base camp and explore from there, all away from the crowds.

This gentle trail follows closely along Hinman Creek, and takes the hiker through a series of mixed woods and meadows, providing a good variety sampling of wildflowers, trees, and birds native to this area. Expect to encounter deer along the way, if you hike quietly.

The trail ends at a hunting camp in an aspen grove, but the more adventuresome can continue on, bushwhacking up the canyon at bit. Stay high above the creek if you do so. Take along your water-crossing shoes.

Distance: About 2- miles, each way.

Hiking time: About an hour, each way.

Elevation: Trailhead: 7,800'; Aspen grove campsite: 8,100'.

With Children: *This is a good trip for little hikers. The trail climbs so gradually that much of the route seems almost level. The creek is relatively tame and thus, safer with young children. Take water-crossing shoes. If you use this trail for a family backpack trip, read a chapter from my llama book (see below) around the campfire, and make fiction come to life.*

This trail follows the gentle Hinman Creek.

Author's Note: *This hike is the setting for Chapter 10 in my book, STOP SPITTING AT YOUR BROTHER! Life Lessons of a Rocky Mountain Llama, available in Steamboat Springs at Off the Beaten Path, Yampatika, Ski Haus and the Clark Store, as well as from all major retail and on-line bookstores. In the story, Dudley and Sammy llamas take a troop of Girl Scouts on a humorous camping trip on this trail, and they spend the night at the campsite mentioned above, where they are visited by a pack of serenading coyotes. For more information, check my website: www.llamalady.com.*

The German-shepherd-like canid, the coyote, is larger than a fox and gray in color, with a black-tipped, downward pointing tail. They vocalize with yips, trailing howls and with group-serenading yip howling.

Fishing: *Lots of calm spots to fish for brook trout. Please use catch and release.*

Map: Trails Illustrated 116; book map 42.

How to get there: Drive west out of town on U.S.40 for 1.3-miles past 13th St., until the Airport/Clark turnoff, Routt 129. Turn right here and travel about 18-miles, until just past Clark. Turn right on FDR 400, Seedhouse Road. Drive 6.1-miles up 400, and turn left at the marker for 430. Park here. If it's not muddy, 4x4 vehicles can drive back a ways, but don't push your luck!

The Hike: From your car, walk on the jeep road for about a mile through the aspen groves. Use the footbridge to cross Hinman Creek, go straight up the bank and turn right on the trail. (Left goes to hike [77]).

Follow along the creek, heading north, through alternating meadows and woods. You'll need your water-crossing shoes when you ford a tributary stream and hike around some big ponds. About an hour after your original crossing of Hinman Creek, you'll arrive at the main ford, where you'll have to once again use your water-crossing shoes. Cross the creek, climb up the bank in front of you and arrive at your destination – a large clearing in a grove of wonderfully big aspen trees. There is an established hunters' campsite here, perfect for a picnic or for setting up a base camp for further exploration.

79. - 80. North Fork of the Elk River - 1101

A river is more than an amenity; it is a treasure.
~ Justice Oliver Wendell Holmes

The Lord said, "Go out and stand on the mountain in the presence of the Lord, for the Lord is about to pass by." Then a great and powerful wind tore the mountains apart and shattered the rocks, but the Lord was not in the wind...The Lord was not in the earthquake...the Lord was not in the fire. But after the fire came a gentle whisper, a still small voice. ~ I Kings 19:11-12

Of Note: The Diamond Park area was one of the very worst hit areas in the 1997 Blowdown. Commercial logging of these downed trees has been allowed on a large section of this area, and changes were made – and continue to be made – on the trails serving the area. As I write this, these changes continue to evolve. Please check with the Forest Service: 970-879-1870.

There are two hiking trails up the North Fork of the Elk River to Diamond Park. The trail on the eastern side of the river – hike [79] – is my favorite of the two, and one of my most favorite places for an easy family hike in this whole book. Even though hikers must ford a couple streams, the trail's elevation ranges from gentle to moderate, as you hike through a gorgeous lush valley along the eastern side of a most-inviting river. Good campsites and fishing spots abound. Please carefully practice Catch and Release fly-fishing, and leave no trace of your visit.

On the western side of this river is an old jeep road, FDR 431, which is slated to be closed to motorized vehicles and turned into a hiking trail – hike [80] – after salvage logging is completed in the area. It will then be given a four-digit trail number to replace 431 – so please be alert to this pending signage change.

A newly built road bridge at the northern end now links the two trails together. The meadows on the west side of the river may not be as lush as those on the river's east side, but it's still a very nice hike, and there are no water crossings to worry about. I recommend hiking up on the east side [79] and returning back down on the west side of the river [80] for a nice loop hike. If you make this loop, leave your car parked at the new Seedhouse Trailhead parking lot, not at the Lost Dog Road access.

The North Fork is one of three forks that feed the Elk River, so named by early-day pioneers because of the many elk that still roam the area. Trail [79] is part of the Wyoming Trail-1101, and it continues north, past Diamond Park, right up into Wyoming. Turning northeast, onto Trail-1152, takes you along the west side of Diamond Park and then to the beautiful Encampment River area. (See hike [70]).

A section of Trail-1101 north of the new bridge was badly damaged in the

Father David leading a prayer at a St. Paul's Church picnic along the North Fork of the Elk.

The road leading to Diamond Park, now cleared, was heavily damaged by the '97 Blowdown.

'97 Blowdown and is still covered in downed trees. This mile-long section of trail, from the bridge north to Diamond Park, at this writing is scheduled to be salvage logged over the next several years. In the interim, trail users can access Diamond Park by crossing the new bridge to the west side of the river, then continuing north on the jeep road for about a mile. This section of FDR 431, severely damaged by the '97 Blowdown, has somehow been cleared by the Forest Service, and as you'll see, it was a monumental feat!

Trail-1152 is also now cleared of trees, and it runs along a sagebrush-covered side hill west of Diamond Park. Because of downed trees and little use after the Blowdown, 1152 is at this writing faint in spots; however, the Forest Service is now working to re-establish the tread on this path. Please do not hike on the private road that runs through Diamond Park. You will be trespassing if you do.

Both of these North Fork trails come together at the new road bridge. Day hikers can loop these two river trails together and end up back at Seedhouse Road. Backpackers continuing northeast can hike around Diamond Park on 1152. This Main Fork Trail-1152 heads to Gem Lake, Lake Diana and the West Fork Encampment River area – hikes [81], [82] and [70].

Plans are in the works for yet another option for accessing all the trails at the southern end of Diamond Park. The Forest Service has built a new road off of the Lost Dog Road-443, connecting it to the above-mentioned bridge. At the completion of salvage logging in the area, people will be able to drive their cars to a new trailhead junction: the Wyoming Trail-1101 – Main Fork Trail-1152 – Scott's Run/Hinman Creek Trail – 1177. This new trailhead will be at the present-day junction of FDR 431 and FDR 409. When this happens, this road will no doubt become a popular drive-to place for viewing the Blowdown phenomena, plus a way to allow easier access to Gem Lake, Lake Diana and the Encampment River area.

Distance: Depending on the trailhead of origin, about 4 - 5 miles, each way, all the way to Diamond Park.

Hiking Time: Depending on the trailhead of origin, about 2.5 to 3-hours to the bridge.

Elevation: Seedhouse Road trailheads: 7,720'; Diamond Park: 8,727'.

With Children: *Take along water shoes for wet stream crossings on the eastern trail, [79], but other than that, this is a marvelous and pretty much gentle hike for children of all ages. There is much to see and do for the entire length, and there are hundreds of perfect camping sites all along the way for a family backpack trip, fishing and picnicking. Highly recommended, even if you can only hike in for a mile or so. Please practice Leave No Trace camping.*

Yampatika Notes: *Diamond Park was among the worst damaged areas in the October 1997 Blowdown, when strong winds in excess of 120-miles came screaming out of the east, over the Continental Divide. A swath of wind almost five-miles wide and thirty-miles long flattened over four million trees in the Routt National Forest. Because the root systems of these trees were used to winds from the west, these fierce winds from the east uprooted them.*

On your visit to this area, notice the massive root systems of these uprooted trees, and also the deep depressions left in the ground. The soil has been churned up, like a tilled garden, providing a good substrate for new plants to take hold. The depressions capture and provide abundant water. Wildlife has changed, as well, with cavity nesters, especially the three-toed woodpecker, increasing in numbers, while others, like pine squirrels and snowshoe hare, decreasing.

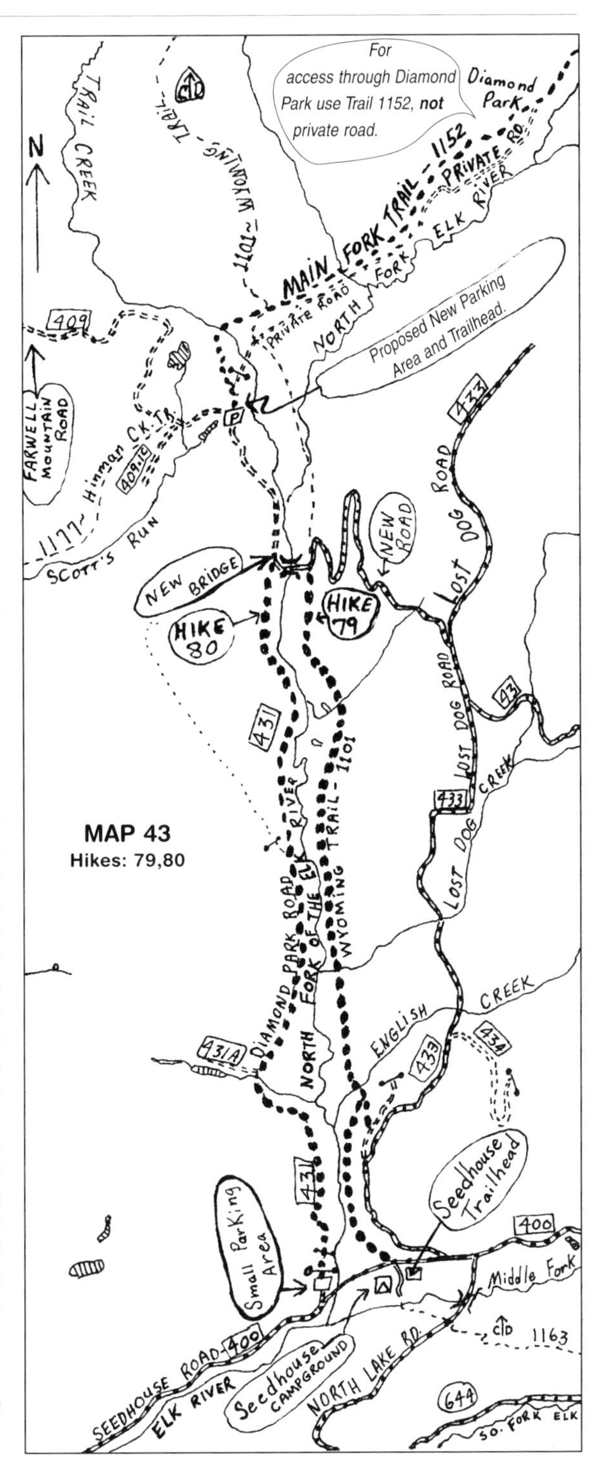

Author's Nature Note: *While camped along the North Fork over the years, I have had a couple bear visits. Luckily, our food was cached and camp clean. Black bears can be black or cinnamon colored, and they can weigh between 175 to 400 pounds. At the shoulder, black bear stand about 3' tall, and can be as long as 5'. Their sense of smell and hearing is exceptional, but their sight leaves something to be desired – which is why I think that when you encounter one, they sometimes stand up on their hind legs and move their heads back and forth, perhaps trying to better focus on you.* *See more information about bears in the Backcountry Safety section of this book, page 17.*

Fishing: *Both sides of the river provide excellent pools for 8-12" cutthroat and brook trout fishing. Please practice Catch and Release fly fishing.*

Map: Trails Illustrated 116; book map 43.

How to get there: Drive west of Steamboat for 1.3-miles after 13th St. to U.S.40, Lincoln, to the Airport/Clark turnoff, Routt 129. Turn right here, north, and drive to just past Clark, about 19-miles. Turn right at Seedhouse Road, FDR 400. The trailhead for the old jeep road 431, [80] is on the left about 8-miles up Seedhouse Road. Before this book is reprinted, this road may be assigned a four-digit hiking trail number, so stay alert.

For hike [79], continue driving for just a bit on Seedhouse Road, and just past Seedhouse Campground on the right, park in the new trailhead parking area on the right. Trail-1101 [79] is opposite this parking area, on the northern side of Seedhouse Road. The trailhead is marked. It heads up through the aspens, and after about 0.75-mile, it meets up with the second access route from Lost Dog Road.

Trail-1101 can also be accessed off of Lost Dog Road, and driving there shortens the hike by 0.75-mile, each way. Drive less than a half-mile past Seedhouse Campground, and on the left, you'll see a sign, "Lost Dog Road, FDR 433;" Turn left here and drive 0.8-mile up 433 to the junction with 433A. Stop and park here. The sign says, "Wyoming Trail-1101 to Diamond Park." Walk on F.S. 433A for about 0.1-mile until you see a sign on your left at the trailhead for 1101. Take this trail steeply down through a wide-open meadow and meet the main trail to the right.

If you continue driving past this point on Lost Dog Road, Forest Service plans are to eventually allow cars to drive all the way back to the new bridge mentioned above, and then, even beyond that to the new Junction Trailhead-1152/1101/1177. For an update on the status of these plans, call the Forest Service – 970-879-1870.

The Hike: The two access trails for 1101 come together and meet at the North Fork River. Early on, keep your water-crossing shoes handy to ford English Creek and Lost Dog Creek. After these two creek crossings, the trail then heads up for about 2.5-miles through rocky woods, and then down through a series of alternating gentle, lush meadows and woods of aspens and spruce. After crossing the new bridge, turn left onto the old jeep road – 431 – if making a loop hike back, or right if continuing up to the trailhead for Trail-1152. Even if making the loop hike back, if you have the time and energy, hike up a bit to the right, toward Diamond Park, to see first-hand the awesome power of the '97 Blowdown.

From the bridge, the hike back down 431 to the Seedhouse Road parking area is 3.6-miles long.

81. Lake Diana - 1152

And the Lord shall guide thee continually...
~ Isaiah 38:11

Of Note: Lake Diana was originally named "Diana's Bathtub" by Forest Service ranger, Frank Rose. Lying just below the Continental Divide, this lovely nine-acre alpine lake offers outstanding views, great fishing, and solitude. At this point, because parts of the trail above Diamond Park can be confusing, and because the spur trail leading up to Diana is not an officially maintained trail, only strong, experienced hikers with good map and compass skills should make this trip.

Please read the description for hike [79] first before planning to make this trip. With the Forest Service recently connecting Lost Dog Road-433 to a newly constructed bridge, which crosses the North Fork of the Elk River, people will at some point be allowed to drive regular cars all the way to the Trailhead for the Main Fork Trail-1152. From this point on, hardy souls will then be able to hike the six-miles to Lake Diana from the trailhead. Previously, a 4x4 vehicle had been required to drive to this trailhead via the old jeep road-431.

Hiking along 1150 to Lake Diana.

Backpackers, too, will find this a convenient way to access the whole wonderful Encampment River area for multi-day trips. Before making plans, check with the Forest Service on this road's status and availability: 879-1870.

For backpack trips, Lake Diana can also be accessed from the Farwell Mountain Jeep Road-409, from the

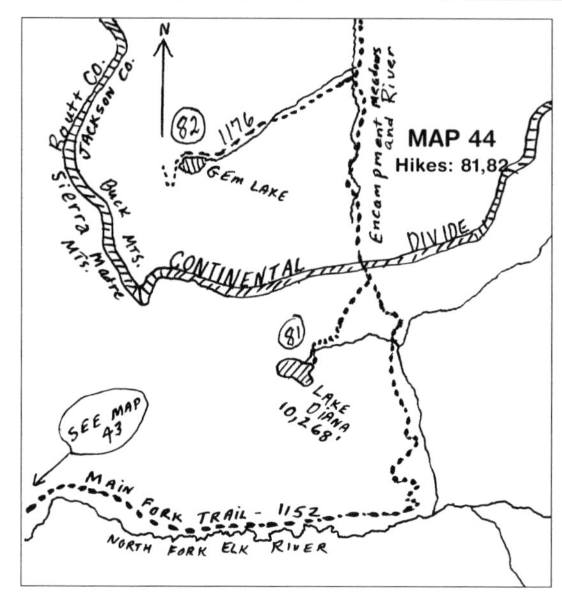

Encampment Trailhead, hike [70] near the Wyoming border, and from the Big Creek Trailhead on the eastern side of Mt. Zirkel, hike [103]. Lake Diana sits just below the top of the Western side of the Continental Divide, while its neighboring lake, Gem, sits just below the eastern side of the Divide.

Distance: Six miles, each way, from the Main Fork Trailhead-1152.

Hiking Time: About 3-hours, each way, from Main Fork Trailhead-1152.

Elevation: Diamond Park: 8,800'; Lake Diana: 10,268'.

With Children: *Only older children who are experienced hikers should make this backpack trip – and then only with experienced adult hikers who know how to read a map and compass.*

Yampatika Notes: *The valley you'll be walking through, alongside the North Fork of the Elk River, is a typical glacially carved valley. Notice the "U" shape to the valley, compared to the "V" shape of a water-carved valley, and the occasional smooth cliff faces. Follow those cliff faces up and you can see how huge these moving masses of ice were. Evidence has been found of glaciers up to 2,000 feet thick!*

Fishing: *Great fishing for native 8-12" Colorado River cutthroat trout; Lake Diana has a 16' maximum depth. Also, there is good fishing in the North Fork of the Elk River along the route. Please carefully practice Catch and Release.*

Map: Trails Illustrated 116; book maps 43 and 44.

How to get there: To get to the Main Fork-1152 trailhead, please use one of the options presented in hikes [79] and [80], the North Fork of the Elk trails – or with a four-wheel-drive, come in on the Farwell Mountain Jeep Road-409. Park in the new parking area, and look for the trailhead sign.

The Hike: Head northeast for a couple miles on 1152, up on a side hill, looping around Diamond Park, which is private property. Do not hike on the private road down in the park. Because of downed trees and low use after the blowdown, and because of numerous game trails, 1152 can be confusing at times, but it has been cleared and the Forest Service is working on making the trail more distinct once again.

Enter the Mt. Zirkel Wilderness, and climb moderately uphill through spruce, aspens, firs and sagebrush shrubs. The trail then heads down and runs close to and parallel with the North Fork of the Elk River. When you reach the junction with the Encampment River, the trail turns sharply north, and you'll then slog up a long stretch of steep switchbacks. Although your legs and lungs will be working hard on this stretch, your efforts will be rewarded with a breathtaking view of the lovely, lovely Sawtooth Range to the southeast. The trail leads you to the end of a high cliff, where you can also enjoy a great view of the Encampment River down below.

Head down the ridge to meet the river, passing by Lake Diana's outlet stream, and climbing up about a half-mile until coming to a fork. Watch for the spur trail on the left – which heads up for about 0.75-mile to the lake from the main trail. This spur trail is neither officially maintained nor signed, but it is generally easy to spot and follow, going through a couple soggy meadows and then turning uphill, where it climbs steeply along the outlet stream's right side. Hike through yet a couple more soggy meadows, cross the outlet stream itself, and arrive at the sparkling turquoise-colored Lake Diana, which sits up in a high shelf of the beautiful Encampment River Valley, just below the Continental Divide. If you're backpacking, there are a few good campsites near the lake. Please observe all Leave-No-Trace rules at this outstanding, pristine lake.

82. Gem Lake - 1152

Praise the Lord from all the earth...lightning and hail, snow and clouds,
stormy winds that do His bidding, you mountains and all hills, fruit trees and cedars,
wild animals and all cattle, small creatures and flying birds.
~ Psalm 148:7-10

Of Note: Gem Lake, at 10,160' and seven-acres in size, is yet another gorgeous remote Mt. Zirkel Wilderness lake, in a rugged sparkling setting just below the Continental Divide, with the steep face of snowcapped Buck Mountain impressively rising above the lake's western end, up on the Continental Divide. Gem Lake's pristine and unusually clear water creates its jewel-like appearance, and thus, too, its name.

Only experienced, strong hikers with good map skills should make this hike. Since this destination follows the same route as to Lake Diana, please read the description for that hike [81] before considering making this hike.

Gem Lake is only about a mile-and-a-half further than Lake Diana, just over the Divide.

On backpacking trips, serene Gem Lake can also be accessed from the Encampment Trailhead, hike [70]), near the Wyoming border, and from Big Creek trailhead on the eastern side of Mt. Zirkel, hike [103].

Distance: About 7 miles, each way, from the Main Fork Trailhead.

Hiking Time: About 4 hours, each way, from Main Fork Trailhead.

Elevation: Diamond Park trailhead: 8,800'; Gem Lake: 10,160'.

With Children: *This is a tough hike, but older, in-shape children, especially those who enjoy fishing and wildflower-strewn meadows, would delight in making this beautiful hike, even if they can't make it all the way up to the lake.*

Fishing: *Excellent for brook trout, to 11"; 26' maximum depth. Please carefully practice Catch and Release.*

Map: Trails Illustrated 116; book maps 43 and 44.

How to get there: To reach the Main Fork Trailhead, please use one of the options presented in hikes [79] and [80]. Call the Forest Service first to check on road status and conditions: 879-1870.

The Hike: Follow the directions in hike [81] to the turnoff point for Lake Diana. At this point, don't turn off for Lake Diana, but continue straight – north – on the Main Fork Trail-1152 for about another mile. A faint trail on the left leads up to Gem Lake. Just before reaching a large rock cairn on the right, watch left for this faint trail. If you reach the cairn, you've gone about ten yards past this spur trail.

Almost immediately, cross over the Encampment River, and then watch for a possible sign pointing you to Gem Lake via Trail-1176. Slog steeply uphill for about a half-mile and reach a lovely wildflower-strewn meadow with photo-op views of towering Buck Mountain. Follow signposts through the meadow, into the woods, and then make a short uphill climb to this wonderful lake.

83. South Fork of the Elk River - 1100 & 1100A

Humankind has not woven the web of life. We are but one thread within it.
Whatever we do to the web, we do to ourselves. All things are bound together.
~ Chief Seattle

For the mountains may depart and the hills be removed,
but my steadfast love shall not depart from you... ~ Isaiah 54:10

Of Note: This is my favorite, easy family-friendly hike. It follows closely along the South Fork of the Elk River. The terrain is gentle, gaining only about 400' in almost four miles. You'll even get to enjoy some very pretty mountain range views, each well worth a photo. This is an especially good hike for birders.

This trail affords you a sampling of just about every tree, wildflower and bird native to aspen meadows in the area. There are numerous, lovely spots to explore all along the river, and great sites for camping. Be sure to filter water, since cows sometimes graze in the area. This trail is also popular with horseback riders and mountain bikers.

Although for the purpose of this book our hike stops before the end of the trail, returning via the same route, the South Fork trail is horseshoe-shaped and ends up at the Hinman

A llamatrek along the South Fork of the Elk.

Campground. If you leave a second car at the campground, and if the river's not too high, you can cross it and complete the horseshoe. This is a good place to take visiting relatives who aren't yet in high-altitude shape. The ride up the Elk River Valley Routt 129 and up Seedhouse Road alone is worth the trip. Take a picnic!

Distance: About 3.75-miles, each way.

Hiking Time: About 1.5-hours, each way.

Elevation: Trailhead: 8,390'; River Crossing: 8,200'; gain and lose about 400' at the high and low points.

With Children: *I highly recommend this hike for children of all ages. It's a gentle trail, with much to offer. Bring a picnic, a bird book, fishing poles, a flower press, binoculars and visiting Grandparents along on this one. If it's a hot day, and not too early in the season, there are many places where supervised children can wade in the cold water.*

Yampatika Notes: *At great stretches of this meandering river way are brightly colored shrubs, dense and hardy. These are mainly species of willows. Their bark ranges from bright yellow and orange, to deep maroon, gray and brown. Most species of willows are salicin or methyl salicylate, which is very similar to aspirin. Chewing on the leaves and inner bark will reduce inflammation and pain. Leaves can be bruised and placed on wounds as an astringent.*

Fishing: *Offers easy fishing access for the entire route. Great for brook trout in the 6-8" range. Please practice careful Catch and Release.*

Map: Trails Illustrated 116 and 117; book map 45.

How to get there: Drive west out of Steamboat on U.S.40 for 1.3-miles past 13th St. Turn right (north) at the Airport/Clark turnoff, Routt 129. Drive about 18-miles until just past Clark,

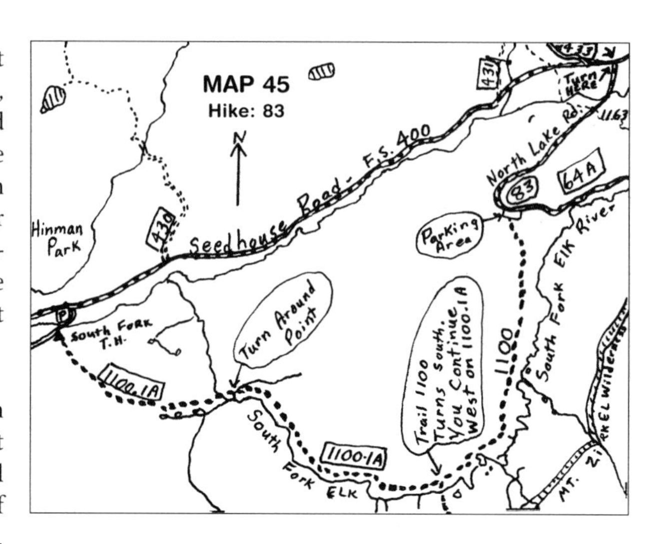

where you will turn right onto Seedhouse Road, F.S.400. Drive up this road for 9.55-miles, until you see a sign for F.S. 443. Turn right onto 443 and drive for 1.7-miles until you see a hiking sign for The Burn Ridge Trailhead-1100. Turn right into the parking lot.

The Hike: Head south on the trail, and after a pleasant 10-minute hike on a level grade through woods of mixed aspens and pines, wildflowers and meadows, arrive at a point where you can first see the river down below on your left. The trail then heads down gradually for a bit, and levels off through abundant lovely aspen groves, pines and meadows. It then pulls away from the river here for a while, as you continue traveling through alternating woods and meadows.

After about 45-minutes of hiking, you'll see a very large rock and a clump of trees off to the left, down at the river. This is a good place to head on down to the water for a picnic or a rest. There's a beaver dam, good fishing and a large clearing for picnicking. You can easily follow the riverbank downstream for about another quarter mile, if you want to explore.

To continue on, head back up to the trail, turn south – left – and hike through a forest of large pines. After a short time, you'll come a fork and trail sign. Stay to the right, going to Hinman Park. Soon you'll come across a gigantic boulder sitting in the middle of the trees, looking completely out of place. It's fun to speculate on when it was placed there by Mother Nature.

Continue hiking through more woods and meadows until finally, after about a total of about 1.5-hours of hiking from the trailhead, you'll come to a clearing where you can see the river down below and a mountain range off to the southeast. After about 10-more minutes, cross a little side stream, where trails go right and left. Say left, and shortly thereafter, reach your destination, a large river crossing. This is where our hike ends, and you can stop for a rest or lunch at the nice campsite to the left of the crossing. Notice the water-level gage in the river.

At this point, hike [83] turns around and returns the way you came. However, if you've left a second car there and you want to continue on to Hinman Park, cross here – there's no easy place to ford, and you'll need your water-crossing shoes. Follow the trail for about another mile until reaching the parking lot for the South Fork Trailhead.

84. Three Island Lake - 1163

The more you ask how far you have to go, the longer your journey seems.
~ Seneca Indian Proverb

All the birds of the air settled on the fallen tree, and all the beasts of the field were among its branches.
~ Ezekiel 31:13

Of Note: The trail that leads up to Three Island Lake was heavily affected by the massive blowdown of trees in 1997. (See notes in front section of book.) Evidence of this natural upheaval is pronounced on this trail, and because of its popularity, it was one of the very first cleared. This hike is an excellent choice for those wanting to see outstanding backcountry views along the way, as well as the results of this dramatic wind phenomenon for themselves. Most impressive are the huge holes left in the ground when gigantic trees were blown over and their immense root systems ripped out. Much of this trail looks totally different now than when it appeared in my first hiking guidebook of the area. Like some angry giant having a temper tantrum, the wind did, indeed, rearrange the forest!

The moderate climb up to this lake has been a favorite destination for hikers over the years, and because of heavy use, camping and fires are prohibited to within a quarter-mile of the lake. Violations are punishable. As always, please leave no trace of your visit.

At 23-acres in size and 40' in maximum depth, pretty Three Island Lake is one of the largest in the Mt. Zirkel Wilderness. It lies snugly in a basin, just below the Continental Divide, and it offers room to spread out and lots of good shoreline for anglers. As its name implies, three forested islands decorate the basin of water

Making a hot lunch to take the chill out of the rainy-day hike up to Three Island Lake.

Just a mile-and-a-half more hiking will take you from Three Island Lake up to remote Beaver Lake, a delightful, small 7-acre lake with more solitude, great fishing and available camp sites. For backpackers, about 2-miles past the turnoff to Beaver Lake, Trail-1163 ends up on top of the Continental Divide, where it meets the Wyoming Trail-1101.

At this writing, the Forest Service is considering the creation of an alternative trailhead, for both the Three Island and North Lake trails, which will also affect the unmarked trails for Dome Lake and the Wolverine Basin lakes. So, before making any of these hikes, check with the Forest Service to see if any trailhead changes have been made: 879-1870.

Distance: Three Island Lake: 3.5 miles, each way; Beaver Lake: 5 miles, each way; to Continental Divide: 7-miles, each way.

Hiking Time: Three Island: About 2 hours, each way; Beaver Lake: about 2.5-hours, each way.

Elevation: Trailhead: 8,330'; Three Island: 9,878'; Beaver Lake: 10,340'.

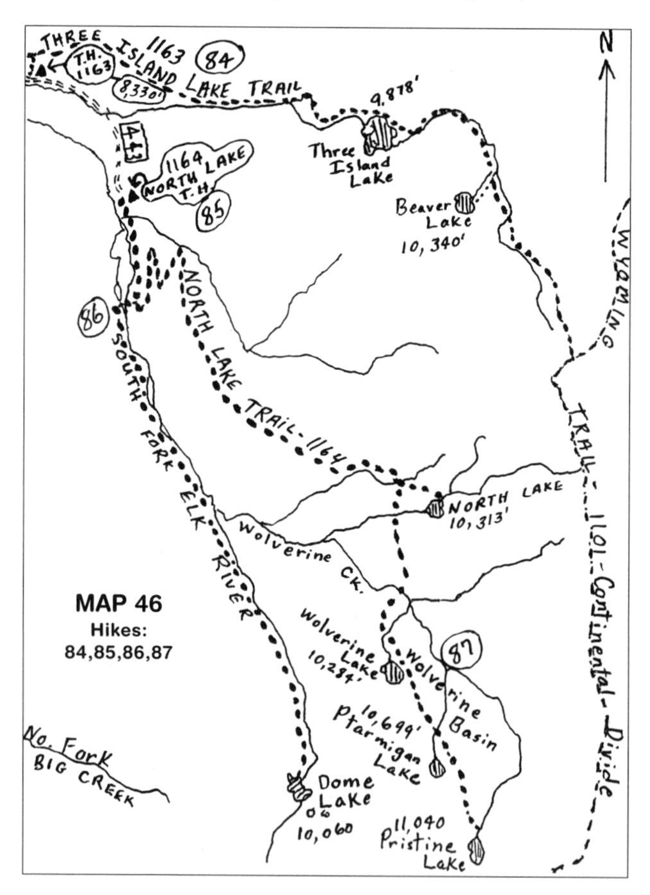

With Children: *There is a moderate to steep climb to the lake, but whether they make it all the way to the lake or not, children of all ages will enjoy making this hike. There are many places to stop and explore all along the route, especially after it begins to parallel Three Island Creek. Be prepared for it to be very buggy in early season weeks.*

Yampatika Notes: *As you walk through these beautiful old-growth spruce-fir forests, especially through the switchbacks before Three Island Lake, you'll probably notice large, round masses in the branches. This is a witch's broom, caused by a parasitic infection. The parasite alters branch growth, reduces vigor of the tree, and inhibits any cone production on the branches it is infecting.*

Fishing: *Three Island: fair to good for brookies up to 12"; stocked with cutthroat; Beaver Lake: 20' maximum depth, great for small brookies in the 8" range. Please practice careful Catch and Release.*

Map: Trails Illustrated 116 and 117; book map 46.

How to get there: Drive west out of town on U.S. 40 for 1.3-miles past 13th St., until the Airport/Clark turnoff, Routt 129. Turn right, north, here, and drive about 18-miles, a mile past Clark, until the Seedhouse Road, F.S.400. Turn right here and drive 9-miles until approximately 0.7-mile past the Seedhouse Campground on the right, turn right onto F.S.443. Drive 3.2-miles to the second signed trailhead for Three Island Lake. The trail begins on the left-hand, north, side of the road. Parking along the road is limited.

The Hike: Climb east up an embankment, switchbacking through chokecherry and aspen trees. At mile 0.25, spur trail-1163.1A, comes into the main trail from the left. Stay right at this intersection, heading east, and begin traversing through alternating wildflowery meadows, aspen groves and evergreen forests. Cross two small streams, and eventually, at mile 1.25, enjoy views of the South Fork of the Elk River Valley.

The magnificent mixture of aspens with spruce, firs and lodgepole pines on this particular stretch of the hike will be an excellent place to enjoy fall colors come late September.

At approximately 1.5-miles into the hike, begin to climb through a thick forest. Uphill switchbacks will take you close to and away from Three Island Creek a number of times, and then around a mammoth boulder.

You'll soon be able to see for yourself the immensity and power of the '97 blowdown. Clearing this trail was a real undertaking, and we can be thankful that our taxes and a lot of hard-working Forest Service personnel made that happen.

After approximately 2.5-miles, the climb becomes more moderate, and then levels off, meandering through a marshy area. At mile 3.0, arrive at the Mt. Zirkel Wilderness boundary, and then about a half-mile later, pass a large meadow on the left, which was once a shallow lake, now filled in. From here, you will have less than an easy ten minutes more hiking, 0.2-mile, to reach the north end of the lake. It's about 0.8-mile around the whole lake.

To visit pristine Beaver Lake, if you have the extra time and energy, follow the trail past the northeast end of the lake, and then head south, toward the Divide. After about a mile-and-a-quarter, look carefully right for a faint, unmarked trail that parallels the Beaver Lake outlet stream, and follow it southwest for about a 10 minute, quarter-mile, hike up to Beaver Lake.

85. North Lake - 1164

We stand somewhere between the mountain and the ant.
~ Onondaga Indian Proverb

Of Note : The hike up to North Lake is a real climb, but the good news is that this helps keep the crowds down. At 5.5-acres in size, North Lake is small, shallow and not as scenic as many nearby wilderness lakes, but it does offer good fishing, camping, solitude and access to the

Continental Divide. It enters the Mt. Zirkel Wilderness early on and travels mostly through old, dense forests of spruce, fir and lodgepole pine, with woods opening into small meadows and pretty views. Because it's less popular with the "masses," North Lake is a good place for an overnight backpacking stay.

At this writing, the Forest Service is considering the creation of an alternative trailhead for both Three Island and North Lakes, which will also affect the trails for Dome Lake and the Wolverine Basin lakes, since they head off trail-1164. So, before making any of these four hikes, check with the Forest Service to see if any trailhead changes have been made: 879-1870.

In wilderness I sense the miracle of life, and behind it, our scientific accomplishments fade to trivia.
~ Charles Lindbergh

Distance: About 4.5-miles, each way.

Hiking Time: Approximately 3-hours up; a bit less time hiking back down.

Elevation: Trailhead: 8,460'; North Lake: 10,313'.

With Children: *Because most of the first mile of this hike climbs up switchbacks, this is not a hike for younger children. But when my own children were about 8 and 11, they enjoyed the challenge toward the end of a summer, when they were in shape from taking many hikes. They especially enjoyed going above the lake to the Divide. There are wonderful, uncrowded places to camp, both near the lake and along the section between the lake and the Divide.*

Yampatika Notes: *After you've climbed the lower set of switchbacks on this trail, notice the forest around you. This is a protected spot harboring old-growth Engelmann-spruce and sub-alpine fir. Draped from their branches are dark brown and light green lichens. These lichens became an important component of a recent acid rain study. The thallus, which is similar to a leaf, absorbs whatever is in the air and in precipitation. The lichens can then be chemically analyzed to determine which specific pollutants are in the area.*

Fishing: *Good for small brook trout, on mostly open shores; 9' maximum depth. Please carefully use Catch and Release.*

Map: Trails Illustrated 116 and 117; Book map 46.

How to get there: [Please read last paragraph of "Of Note."] Drive west out of Steamboat for 1.3-miles past 13th St., on U.S.40 until the Airport/Clark turnoff, Routt 129. Turn right and drive north, about 18 miles, to the Seedhouse Road, just past Clark. Turn right onto Seedhouse Road, F.S. 400, and travel approximately 9-miles until you reach the Seedhouse Campground on the right. Drive 0.7-more miles past the campground. Turn right onto F.S. 443 and travel approximately 4.6-miles to the very end of 443. The last 1.4-miles will be on a very rough road, but if you take it slowly, you should be able to make it in your car. There is abundant parking at the trailhead.

The Hike: The trail begins with a short walk through a level, wooded area. The Mt. Zirkel Wilderness Boundary sign soon appears, and you'll then cross a wide stream. You'll have to use your water-crossing shoes if early in the season. Shortly thereafter, you'll have to ford another smaller stream, and several yards after that, notice a faint, less defined, unmarked trial on the right. This is the non-maintained trail, which strong, experienced hikers take to Dome Lake, hike [86].

Climb a series of steep, short switchbacks. After making a long traverse across, you'll come to a level stretch, after which you'll climb at an even steeper grade than on the switchbacks. This gradually moderates, and you'll then travel easily along the crest of a broad slope for about two miles, in a heavily forested area, making a couple additional easy creek crossings. At about mile 3.5, climb up a series of steep, short switchbacks. At the top of these zigzags, look right to see a large meadow. About 0.2 mile before reaching the lake, the trail heads to the left of this big, grassy meadow. Just before entering a woods at the meadow's far end, notice an unmarked trail leading off to the right, south, which goes to Wolverine Basin, hike [87].

For North Lake, stay left at this intersection, remaining on the main trail. Climb the remaining 0.2-mile and arrive at the north side of the level, grassy shoreline of North Lake. The best campsites are north of the trail, on the north side of the lake.

An additional, easy half-hour climb, just over a mile, will take you gently through pretty open meadows, past a small, unnamed lake, to the top of the Continental Divide, where the trail junctions with the Wyoming Trail-1101. Up there, you'll be treated to wonderful views of surrounding mountain peaks, including the Dome and Lost Ranger Peak – see hike [33].

86. Dome Lake

Shout for joy, O heavens, O earth! Burst into song, O mountains!
For the Lord comforts His people and will have compassion on His afflicted ones.
~ Isaiah 49:13

The mountains have rules. They are harsh rules, but they are there, and if you keep to them, you are safe.
A mountain is sincere. The weapons to conquer it exist inside you, inside your soul.
~ Walter Bonatti

Of Note: This unmarked, rugged trail is neither signed nor maintained, and only experienced hikers willing to bushwhack a bit, climb over some logs, make several water crossings, squish through a few boggy areas and risk being startled by huge cows grazing in the woods should attempt to make it. In some marshy spots, the trail will even disappear for a bit, but the good news is that the route pretty much remains close to the western side of the South Fork of the Elk River, and so should you if you make this challenging hike.

With the gorgeous dome-shaped mountain always ahead of you, an experienced, strong hiker should be able to persevere and arrive safely at the remote ten-acre lake to enjoy its exquisite beauty and solitude. But keep a reassuring map and compass handy.

Because it's so easy to recognize, the Dome seems to pop up in all of the panoramic views on many other Mt. Zirkel Wilderness hikes. On this hike, however, the Dome seems to rise right

The Dome seems to rise up out of the lake.

out of the southern end of a lake, so this is your chance to hike up close to it and put your camera to good use.

Dudley the llama wants to mention that, past the meadows, this is definitely not a good trail for llamas or packhorses – too many downed trees and boggy areas. Please walk gently through the delicate marshland, and as always – Leave No Trace.

Distance: About 5.5-miles, one-way.

Hiking Time: Allow 3-4 hours, each way.

Elevation: Trailhead: 8,460'; Dome Lake: 10,060'.

With Children: *Many years ago, our adventurous, in-shape youngest daughter, about eight at the time, made the trip up to Dome Lake with us, but she was a real trooper! However, a good destination for a simple family backpack trip – less than a mile in – would be to hike just to some lovely, lush meadows, where you may camp and enjoy the river, the meadow, and a delightful view of the famous Dome.*

Yampatika Notes: *There are some rather unusual plants along this hike. As you encounter small, shaded springs with mossy rocks, look for the delicate triangular-leaved Oak Fern. In the broad marshes, look for a diminutive cream-colored Ladies Tresses Orchid. Take a good whiff. Yummy! On the last rocky, steep slope up to the lake, look for the leathery leaved Christmas Fern and the short shrub of White Rhododendron, with its single white creamy flowers hidden under the leaves. Please do not collect any of these plants.*

Fishing: *Good fishing for brook trout in the South Fork of the Elk River; fair fishing for large 8-12" Colorado River cutthroat in the lake itself, which has a 12' maximum depth. Please practice careful Catch and Release.*

Map: Trails Illustrated 117 (doesn't show trail); U.S.G.S. Mt. Zirkel and Mt. Ethel; Book map 46.

How to get there: Please follow the instructions to the North Lake trailhead in hike [85]. Note: Forest Service may change trailhead location. Check first.

The Hike: Start up trail-1164, toward North Lake. After walking for about a quarter-mile through the heavily-wooded spruce and fir forest, you'll reach the Mt. Zirkel Wilderness sign. Ford a small stream, and then hike up the first switchback. On the second switchback, which now heads away from the small stream, the trail will fork, with the left fork going to North Lake, and the less-distinct right fork heading to Dome Lake. To discourage its confusion with the main trail, sticks and brush may have been placed on the trail – making it difficult to see. This faint trail to the right heads through the forest and downhill for a bit, until reaching the South Fork of the Elk River. This crossing will be tricky if the water is still high and cold, so water-crossing shoes are a must. You'll be making other smaller water crossings, so keep the shoes handy.

After the large water crossing, another quarter-mile of easy hiking takes you through the trees to the lush meadow area mentioned above in "With Children," and your first impressive view up the valley of the Dome itself.

The tricky part comes after this, though – through a second meadow with many downed trees to maneuver and marshy areas, which seem to swallow up signs of the trail. At this point, bear to the right, above the meadow, and look for the trail once again in the trees, on the other side of this meadow. The trail begins to climb, but then becomes harder to find. At this point, if you lose the trail, remain close to the river until you once again locate it.

At about mile 2.0, the trail enters yet another meadow, with numerous downed trees to maneuver around or over. At this point, hike uphill to your right. Look for an open space between the steep slope on the western end of this meadow and a patch of trees, and head toward and through it. The trail now drops down again on the other end of the meadow and enters more trees. Hereafter, the trail heads southward along the river, and it should be relatively easy to follow it for the rest of the way to the lake.

Four miles into the hike, enjoy the site of the river cascading through a narrow canyon, as the trail continues to follow the river, while you hike slightly uphill. About a half-mile before the lake, look for a talus slope on the right, and be prepared to negotiate Blowdown debris. Here begin a steep climb, until you finally reach Dome Lake. And....Wow!

87. Wolverine Basin Lakes

Wolverine, Ptarmigan, Pristine

In God's wilderness lies the hope of the world – the great, fresh unblighted, unredeemed wilderness.
~ John Muir

If you know wilderness in the way that you know love, you would be unwilling to let it go...
this is the story of our past and it will be the story of our future.
~ Terry Tempest Williams

Of Note: The wolverine is noted for its strength, cunning, fearlessness and voracity, and no animal except humans hunts this animal. Supposedly, during the early 1900's, an area hunter killed the last Wolverine in Routt County in this basin. The unfortunate critter's name was Wally, and it is said that the wolverine's ghost still makes nocturnal visits to campsites.

You don't have to be a fisherman or wolverine hunter to love this place, however. This is one of my favorite camping destinations in the whole Mt. Zirkel Wilderness, in spite of Wally Wolverine's midnight hauntings. Three pristine wilderness lakes in a remote valley wait in line to offer fabulous fishing, good campsites, and seclusion. And just after the third one, it's only a half-mile up to the Continental Divide, with its joyful, exhilarating vistas.

Only strong, experienced backcountry hikers should make this hike, since, at this writing, the trail is neither marked nor officially maintained. Here and there, you may have to use your map and compass to determine your whereabouts. Downed trees and boggy areas require caution if taking horses or llamas on this trail.

Fishermen friends of mine use llamas to transport "belly boats," and in them, they can float around and fish every inch of all three lakes – a nirvana for Catch and Release fly fishermen!

You can access this area from either North Lake or from the Wyoming Trail-1101. Backpacking fishermen generally include a quick quarter-mile trip up to North Lake on the way in or way out of Wolverine Basin. Fishermen who don't generally hike or backpack should be in good physical shape and acclimated to high altitudes before visiting this area, or any high altitude destination. Please leave no trace of your visit to these lakes.

Distance: Wolverine Lake: 5-miles, each way; Ptarmigan Lake: 5.75-miles each way; Pristine Lake: 6.5-miles, each way.

Hiking Time: About 2.5-hours up to the first lake, Wolverine.

Elevation: Trailhead: 8,330'; Wolverine Lake: 10,284'; Ptarmigan Lake: 10,699'; Pristine Lake: 11,040'.

With Children: *Hikers of all ages strong enough to backpack up to this area, or those with pack animals, will relish spending time in this area.*

Fisherman Chuck uses llamas to carry his belly boat up to fish Wolverine Lake.

Sparkling Pristine Lake, situated just below the Continental Divide.

Yampatika Notes: *If ever there was a place a wolverine could still thrive in, it would be in this remote basin. Called the "skunk bear" or "little bear," the wolverine is a scavenger in the summer and winter, and it preys mostly on small animals in the summer. Its powerful jaws allow it to crush bones to extract the marrow and tear apart frozen winter carcasses. Because they are very agile, wolverines are able to climb trees. Intelligent animals but shy around humans, wolverines are one of the most misunderstood animals in North America.*

Author's Nature Note: *On this alpine tundra hike, you may encounter ptarmigans, small grouse-like birds that somehow manage to survive in an inhospitable environment year round. The bird adapts well to its surroundings by being a camouflaged mottled brown and black color in the summer months – blending in with rocks – and then turning pure white and growing feathers on its feet in the snowy winter months. Around Ptarmigan Lake, hens lays six to eight buff-colored, lightly spotted eggs in ground nests made of leaves, feathers and grasses. If you're lucky, you may get to watch – from a distance, please – baby chicks scamper around behind their mama birds.*

Fishing: *Wolverine Lake: 7-acres, 25' max. depth; good for 12-16" cutthroats; has a good beach; Ptarmigan Lake: 7.3-acres, 16' maximum depth; good access; deep shoreline; cutthroats. Pristine Lake: 9.7-acres; 55' maximum depth; excellent for 8-12" brook trout. Please practice careful Catch and Release fishing.*

Map: Trails Illustrated 117 (doesn't show trail); U.S.G.S. Mt. Zirkel and Mt. Ethel; Book map 46.

How to get there: Please follow driving directions to the North Lake Trailhead in hike [85]. Note: Forest Service may change trailhead! Check if you aren't sure: 879-1870.

The Hike: Please follow the hiking instructions in hike [85] to the point where the trail to Wolverine Basin splits off the North Lake Trail-1164. The trail to the basin is not marked, so watch carefully. From the turnoff, you'll hike about another 1.2-more miles to reach Wolverine Lake. The area was greatly impacted by the 2002 wildfires, so beware of the danger of snag trees.

Glacier Lilies.

Turn right on this spur trail, and hike along the eastern end of the big meadow, in a southerly direction. Heading through the lush meadow, the trail appears a bit faint at times, but it becomes more distinct when it reaches the trees. Head down steeply, where you'll soon meet and ford North Lake's outlet stream. About 0.75-mile after splitting from the North Lake Trail-1164, arrive at and cross Wolverine Creek, which collects drainage from all three lakes above it.

The last half-mile of the trail to Wolverine Lake climbs gradually up through a forest of spruce and fir, and downed trees may at times obscure the trail. Especially if using pack animals, you may have to skirt around the deadfall. If so, keep your map and compass handy, and use it if you begin to wander too far off the established trail.

Arrive at the northern end of shimmering Wolverine Lake, which is mostly surrounded by spruce and fir trees. There's a delightful sandy beach on the southeastern shore, and the best campsites await your tent in the woods on the ridge/shelf on the northeast side of the lake.

To get to Ptarmigan Lake from Wolverine Lake, about a half-mile hike, continue walking in a southerly direction above Wolverine's southeastern end, where you'll soon see a small pond on the right. Look for a rock cairn marker on the right, which will guide you to the continuing faint trail, which now goes into the trees on the right, about 350-feet past the pond. The trail then heads through the woods for about 0.5-mile, until reaching a soggy meadow that sits at the bottom of a steep slope. Look for a steep rocky face on the left, Ptarmigan Lake's outlet stream to the right of that, and then at the slope of trees lying straight ahead of you. At the bottom of that slope, look carefully for another rock cairn, head for it, and you'll once again pick up the established trail. The last section of the trail after this remains distinct for the rest of the climb up to Ptarmigan Lake. Look for good campsites in the woods on the lake's eastern side. Don't be surprised to see ptarmigan birds, which nest around this lake – and thus the name, Ptarmigan Lake.

The trail continuing from Ptarmigan to Pristine Lake, about a mile-long, is easy to see and follow, as it climbs up the hillside to timberline and open tundra. When the trail fades, look for Wolverine Basin's southern wall, and point your feet toward the rusty-colored section of rock, which you can see just above the wall's gray cliffs. At 11,040', Pristine Lake sits high above timberline, and it is one of the Mt. Zirkel Wilderness' highest, and I think, most beautiful lakes. The views from Pristine Lake are superb, and as soon as you see the unspoiled emerald-colored lake, you'll realize that it is aptly named.

From Pristine Lake, the hike up the final half-mile to the Continental Divide's Wyoming Trail – 1101 requires a tough scrambling over rocks on the lake's southeastern side, and then a steep climb up a slope to a saddle on the Divide. It's well worth the effort, if you can spare the time and energy. And as always, please Leave No Trace at this special, pristine place.

88. Mica Lake - 1161 & 1162

May the road rise up to meet you. May the wind be always at your back.
May the sun shine warm upon your face. May the rain fall soft upon your fields,
And until we meet again, may God hold you in the palm of His hands.
~ An Irish Blessing

Of Note: Mica Lake is a glorious little 6-acre gem among the many hundreds of high mountain lakes and ponds in the Mt. Zirkel Wilderness. This sparkling alpine lake is a tarn – a small glacial bowl lying at the head of a glacial valley in a cirque – a natural, glacially carved amphitheater. And this is also my husband's favorite day hike in this book. Because the hike up to this basin is more difficult, Mica Lake attracts far fewer people than Gold Creek and Gilpin lakes, which share the same trailhead at the end of Seedhouse Road. During early July, the beauty of the wildflowers along the way will overwhelm you!

Unless you're in good hiking shape, it's not an easy climb to make, with more than 2,000 vertical feet awaiting you. But the scenery is spectacular for most of the whole route, and the lake itself is surrounded on three sides by part of the Sawtooth Range, Little Agnes Mountain, and the haunting beauty of 12,059' Big Agnes Mountain, with its jagged peaks and small craggy towers – horns – rising dramatically up and down, into the clouds. So, your strenuous hiking efforts will be well rewarded! And once up at the lake, if you have some extra time and energy, you can hike up to the col – the saddle – on the lake's northern side for an exquisite panoramic view of Mica Lake below and the surrounding and more distant peaks, such as Dome and Lost Ranger. Avoid hiking up the saddle if lightning threatens.

The basin receives heavy snows, so the trail may open later than most. Mica Lake and Mica Creek take their name from the mica deposits, which come down with the snowmelt and can be found in the creek and lakebed. Along the way, you'll be able to see firsthand some of the dramatic devastation imposed on this area by the October '97 Blowdown, when acres and acres of trees were pushed down by severe winds coming from the east. Much of this blowdown debris burned in the 2002 wildfire, and you'll see the aftermath along the way.

Distance: About 4-miles, each way.

Hiking Time: About 2.5-hours up and 2 back down.

Elevation: Trailhead: 8,460'; Mica Lake: 10,428'.

With Children: *This is not a hike for young children, but older, in-shape children can – with an early start, a little encouragement and some rest stops – make it up to the lake. The trail provides a great variety of terrain, many colorful wildflowers in early July, delightful Mica Creek to follow along the way, and wonderful photo opps.*

Yampatika Notes: *Mica is a very common mineral in our local rocks. Large sheets of mica were mined in the area and used for windowpanes and oven doors. Look at almost any rock and you'll find black or clear shiny pieces, some large, some small, which peel off like pieces of paper. Mica, generally light pink feldspar with mirrored surfaces, and quartz, which comes in many colors – clear white, rose, red and smokey – are the main mineral building blocks for the granite, schist, gneiss, and many other rocks found in the Park Range.*

Climb up the saddle to get a spectacular look at Mica Lake and surrounding vistas.

Fishing: *Mica Lake has an 11' maximum depth; good for brookies and an occasional large rainbow; treeless shores facilitate fly fishing; most successful fishing during early morning or early evening hours. Please practice Catch and Release.*

Map: Trails Illustrated: 116; Book map 47.

How to get there: Driving west out of Steamboat on U.S.40, drive 1.3-miles from 13th St. until the Airport/Clark turnoff, Routt 129. Turn right, north, here and drive about 18-miles, just past Clark to the Seedhouse Road, FDR 400. Turn right here and drive 11.9-miles to Slavonia, the end of the road and the joint trailhead for Mica, Gilpin and Gold Creek Lakes. Read and follow the information on the kiosk.

The Hike: Head up the trail, and in a few minutes, cross over a little stream, see the remains of an old cabin on the right, and then quickly come to the junction of the trails – right going to Gold Creek and left going to Mica and Gilpin lakes. Sign the register, and then go left on 1161, climbing gently through aspens and firs, and notice Gilpin Creek down far below to the right. After about a quarter-mile, you'll pass a series of beaver ponds on the left. These would be fun to explore with children. Every year the beavers try to re-route the hiking trail to suit their needs.

The terrain levels off, going through more aspens, pines and lovely meadows. Cross a series of small streams. Enter the Mt. Zirkel Wilderness about 1.2-miles from the trailhead. About a quarter-mile further, reach the junction of the Mica Lake and the Gilpin Lake trails. This junction now sits in the middle of the aftermath of an angry whirlwind, with severe '97 Blowdown destruction strewn everywhere. The boulder on the right that used to catch your attention as you arrived at this junction is now covered with dead trees and debris. So watch carefully for the trail sign on the left, and turn left onto 1162. Expect to see many uprooted trees and huge exposed root systems along all the rest of the remaining 2.5- miles to the lake.

Walk on level terrain for about 0.2-mile, and then ascend steeply up the hillside for the next 1.5-miles, through a mixed forest of fir, spruce and lodgepole pine. Enter the Mica Basin and notice Mica Creek down far below you on your right. After moderating a bit, the trail passes an inviting, scenic waterfall, the perfect place for lunch and a rest.

From here, the trail turns to the left, heads on up, and then winds around rock outcrops. After this, it levels again and heads once more toward the creek. You'll soon have to ford Mica Creek, and especially in early summer, you'll need to use water-crossing shoes. Early in the season, you may also want to keep them on for the marshy area just past the ford, as well.

Hike the next mile in a northerly direction, with Mica Creek now on your left, through alternating woods and open grassy areas. Cross a couple more side streams, and then climb steeply up the last half-mile until you reach the level valley floor and this pristine, amphitheater-like glacial lake. When you first see the beautiful mountain range in front of you, don't be deceived. You still have a ways before reaching the lake. Once there, campsites are easy to find in the area above the lake. Please practice Leave No Trace camping.

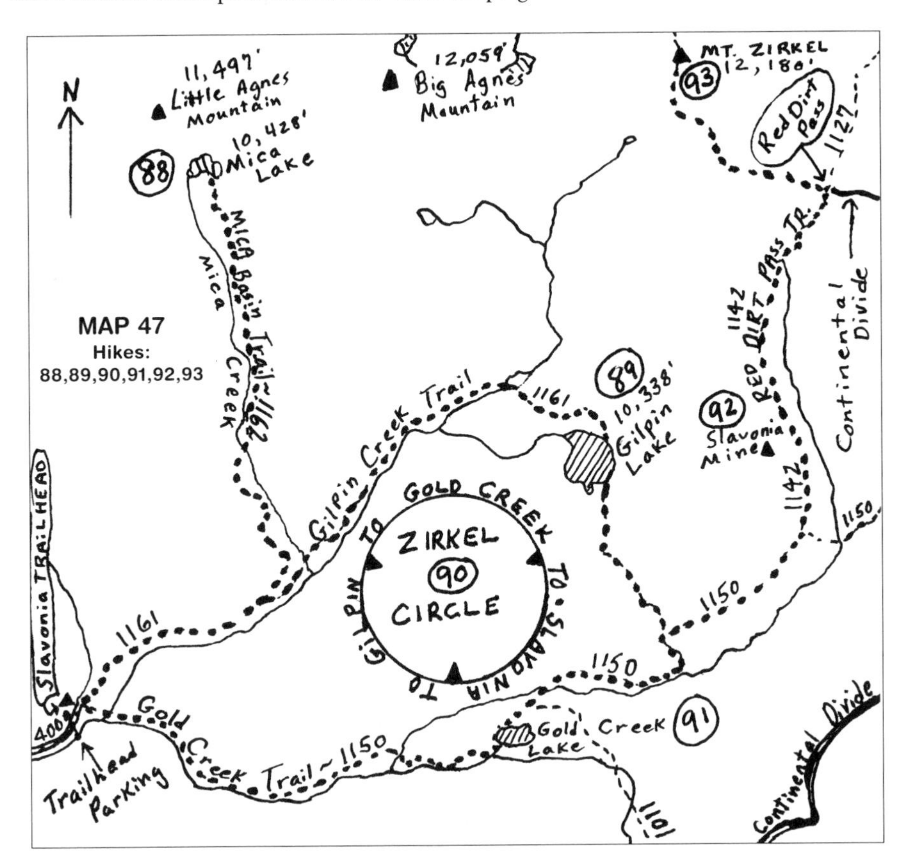

89. Gilpin Lake - 1161

When thro' the woods and forest glades I wander, and hear the birds sing sweetly in the trees...
When I look down from lofty mountain grandeur, and hear the brook and feel the gentle breeze...
Then sings my soul, my Savior God to Thee, How great Thou art, how great Thou art!
Then sings my soul, my Savior God to Thee, How great Thou art, how great Thou art.
~ Stuart K. Hine

Of Note: Because of its great beauty – see this book's cover – Gilpin Lake is one of the most-visited hiking destinations in the Mt. Zirkel Wilderness, especially on weekends. Because the Forest Service is trying to undo damage from past overuse and abuse, there are restrictions on camping and fires within a quarter-mile of the lake. Please observe these rules – tickets are issued to violators. If it's solitude you're after, this is probably not the hike for you.

This lake was named after William Gilpin, Colorado's first territorial governor. The trail up to it follows closely along Gilpin Creek and passes through stands of trees, meadows of wildflowers and numerous avalanche paths that have left eerie stands of dead trees in their wake. Here and there, along the way you'll also get to see pockets of tree damage inflicted by the '97 Blowdown.

Twenty-nine acres in size, 60' in maximum depth, Gilpin is a large lake that offers breathtaking views of the Sawtooth Range, Big Agnes, Little Agnes, and dark, deep blue-colored water below. I consider the view from the ridge above the lake to be the rival of any view in all of Colorado, including from atop the summit of Mt. Zirkel itself. As always, avoid being up top if lightning threatens.

If you don't mind bumping into lots of people on the trail and are anxious to partake of the lake's spectacular beauty, your camera will be put to much good use on this hike, since the lake is one of the most picturesque in all of Colorado. If you choose to make this hike, please be certain to leave no trace of your having visited.

Distance: 5-miles each way to the lake; another 0.5-mile to the saddle above it.

Hiking Time: About 3.5-hours, each way.

Elevation: Trailhead: 8,460'; Gilpin Lake: 10,338'; Top of saddle: 11,164'.

With Children: *This is a lovely hike for all children, although because it's a long hike, many will be able to go only part of the way. If you start early and take rest stops, older, in-shape children should be able to make it all the way to the lake and back in a very long day.*

Yampatika Notes: *There was a gold mine on the east side of Gilpin Peak, believe it or not! In 1887, it consisted of a small cabin and a hole. Three individuals by the names of Pritchett, Dever and Williams were antsy to begin their mining careers in March 1887, but when they arrived at the cabin, it was gone! They finally found it under four-feet of snow. There was no appreciable gold found that summer, so the mine was abandoned.*

Fishing: *The fish in Gilpin are reputed to be "smart" and difficult to catch; but there are fat brook trout in the 12-16" range, and some get careless. Best fishing is found on the rocky side opposite the trail side. Please practice Catch and Release fly-fishing.*

Hikers climbing up the Gilpin Lake Saddle.

Map: Trails Illustrated 116; Book map 47.

How to get there: Driving west out of Steamboat on U.S.40, go 1.3-miles from 13th St. until you get to the Airport/Clark turnoff, Routt 129. Turn right, north, here and drive about 18-miles, just past Clark, to the Seedhouse Road, FDR 400. Turn right onto Seedhouse and drive for about 11.9-miles to Slavonia, the end of the road and the trailhead parking area for several destinations. Park here. Read the kiosk information, and then head up the trail.

The Hike: In a very short time, cross over a little stream, and soon thereafter, the trail splits. Sign the register, and then go left, to Gilpin Lake.

Climb gently through aspens and firs, and notice Gilpin Creek down far below to the right. After about a quarter-mile, look for a series of beaver ponds on the left. These would be fun to explore with small children. The trail levels off and goes through more aspens and pines and lovely meadows. Cross a series of small streams and enjoy many varieties of wildflowers along the way.

Enter the Mt. Zirkel Wilderness about 1.2-miles from the trailhead. About a quarter-mile further, pass by the junction of the Mica Lake and Gilpin Lake trails. This junction now sits in the middle of the aftermath of a very angry whirlwind, with severe '97 Blowdown destruction strewn everywhere. The boulder on the right on which people used to sit at this junction is now inundated with dead trees, debris and 2002 fire remains.

Stay right at this junction, remaining on 1161. The trail now climbs and then moderates a number of times, through pines and meadows. Cross over fast-flowing Mica Creek and then start up some steeper switchbacks, followed by a more gradual grade. Finally hike out of the trees to a wonderful view of mountain peaks off in the distance. Enjoy the vast array of flowers in this area during early July.

Climb through more pinewoods until reaching an open, flat area with a stream running through it. Come to an old, wide avalanche area with deadfall and standing dead trees. Climb up through more pines, switch backing for a bit, and then find the trail leveling off. You'll soon need to cross Gilpin Creek, so dig out the water-crossing shoes.

If you're planning to camp overnight, this is a good time and place to scout out a campsite on either side of the creek or in the trees to the right after fording the creek. Remember to stay 100 feet away from the creek and trail. From this point, the last 0.75-mile stretch of switchbacks climbs 500 feet through the woods, until reaching the northern end of spectacular Gilpin Lake, surrounded beautifully by peaks on three sides. Please respect this very special place and Leave No Trace of your having ever been there.

From the lake, the climb up to the top of the saddle between Gilpin and Gold Creek Lakes will add another half-hour of hiking, but as I say above, the view from that vantage point is beyond compare. To make the climb, follow the trail around the eastern shore of the lake and switchback up, near the southeast end, all the way to the crest of the saddle. Then prepare to be overwhelmed by the beauty!

90. The Zirkel Circle - 1161 - 1150

The Gilpin - Gold Creek Loop

Get these glorious works of God into yourself – that's the thing!
~ John Muir

Your love, O Lord, reaches to the heavens, your faithfulness to the skies.
Your righteousness is like the mighty mountains, your justice like the great deep.
~ Psalm 36:5-6

Of Note: This is the number-one classic Steamboat residents' hike – an eleven-mile-long loop day hike from the Slavonia trailhead, up along lovely Gilpin Creek to spectacular Gilpin Lake, then up the saddle to one of the best views in the whole Rocky Mountains, over that saddle and down to Gold Creek Lake, and finally, down along the ever-so-pretty Gold Creek trail, back to the Slavonia Trailhead. The hike is totally tiring and totally exhilarating!

And if you're in good hiking shape, it's not to be missed. But because of the hike's popularity, don't expect to find much solitude on this adventure.

Start the hike very early in the day, for there will be many worthwhile places where you'll want to "stop, smell and photograph" the roses along the way, so to say. Go well prepared for any emergency – weather or otherwise. (Read Backcountry Safety information in the beginning of this book.) Take along lots of drinking water or a filter and plenty of film for your camera. Get off ridges if lightning threatens.

Rounding the turn on the Zirkel Circle.

Distance: Eleven-mile loop, total.

Hiking Time: Although you can probably hike this quicker, give yourself at least six good hours to do it "right."

Elevation: Trailhead: 8,460'; Ridge above Gilpin Lake: 11,164'.

With Children: *Older, in-shape children should enjoy this challenge.*

Fishing: *Many places to fish along the way, but if you want to get back before dark, you probably should make this a "keep-moving" kind of hike. So save the fishing for another day.*

Map: Trails Illustrated 116; Book map 47.

How to get there: Please follow the driving directions to the Slavonia Trailhead in the Gilpin Lake hike [89].

The Hike: Follow the directions in the Gilpin Lake hike [89] to the top of the ridge between Gilpin Lake and Gold Creek Lake.

Descend south on switchbacks down through the woods on 1161 until it connects with the Gold Creek Trail 1150. Go right at the junction. (Going left takes you to Mt. Zirkel, hike [93].) Shortly thereafter, the trail turns west and parallels the creek for a little while, and then crosses it, which, if the water is running high, may require the use of your water-crossing shoes to ford.

The trail levels here, and you will soon remain right at a junction with the Wyoming Trail on your left, until reaching a low rise. Continue for a few more hundred yards, arriving at the north shore of Gold Creek Lake. Follow the Gold Creek Trail-1150 west, back down to the trailhead at Slavonia. For additional information about trail-1150, please read the description for hike [91].

91. Gold Creek Lake - 1150

Now he walks in quiet solitude, the forests and the streams, seeking grace in every step he takes.
His sight has turned inside himself to try and understand, the serenity of a clear blue mountain lake.
~ John Denver ~ Rocky Mountain High

Life is what happens when you're too busy making other plans.
~ Unknown

Of Note: Gold Creek Lake is one of the most popular destinations for area hikers. Because of past overuse and abuse, there is no camping or fires allowed within a quarter-mile of the 8-acre lake. Tickets are issued to violators. Beyond the restricted area, good campsites can be found in the small meadows northeast of the lake.

Because of a difficult water crossing, this is not a hike to take too early in the season. If you're seeking solitude, this also isn't the hike to take, since you'll probably pass many people along the way. The trail to the lake parallels Gold Creek for three miles, up a narrow, steep-sided forested valley, and the creek scenery along the way, I think, is as good as it gets anywhere! The area is thickly forested with fir, spruce and lodgepole pines, and here and there, you'll see uprooted dead trees from the '97 Blowdown, especially just above the lake itself, where it looks like a mentally-disturbed developer's bulldozer has wrecked havoc – but Mother Nature's wind accomplished all the carnage. In early July, and somewhat throughout the whole entire summer, wildflowers thrive and show off their gorgeous colors. Cooling trees provide shade along much of the route. The area around Gold Creek Lake is my favorite place for finding delicious, edible mushrooms – though, don't you try it if you don't know what you're doing!

There is one very tricky fording of Gold Creek, which the Forest Service has recently tried to improve. But the water here is almost always high, and a log crossing isn't always available or reliable, so water-crossing shoes are a must to have with you for this challenge. Don't go searching for a better place to cross – there aren't any, and you may end up lost! If the log is too wet or the water too high, you'll have to either wade across or turn around and save the lake for another day. When fording, using a sturdy walking stick can help you keep your balance, and people generally leave them conveniently on either side.

The first 2.5-miles climb moderately, but the last half-mile requires a climb up a series of steeper switchbacks.

If your ability, time or energy is limited, or if the water is still too high to cross, you can take a wonderful hike just on the first mile-and-three-quarters of this trail, to a large flat boulder overlooking a sparking, cascading 35-foot waterfall. Plan to have lunch here.

Enjoying a rest stop at Gold Creek Lake.

An early-day explorer to the area, Charles Franz, named Gold Creek and Lake in the late 1800's. Gold was at one time mined in the creek and put through sluice troughs in Slavonia, the present trailhead.

To use the Gold Creek hike as part of an eleven-mile loop hike with Gilpin Lake, the "Zirkel Circle," see hike [90].

Distance: A tad over 3-miles, each way.

Hiking Time: About two hours up and a little less coming back down.

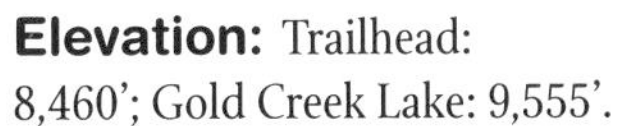

Elevation: Trailhead: 8,460'; Gold Creek Lake: 9,555'.

With Children: *I highly recommend the first section of this trip for hikers of all ages, even if you can only reach the waterfall mentioned above. Beyond the waterfall, the creek crossing and steeper last section will be too tricky for youngsters or seniors, especially early in the season. But at the waterfall, you'll have easy access to explore the creek, and you'll get to enjoy everything but the lake.*

Fishing: *Gold Creek Lake has a 34' maximum depth; fishing is good for brook trout in the 6-9" range; best fishing off the rock outcrops on north side. Please practice catch and release fly-fishing.*

Map: Trails Illustrated 116; Book map 47.

How to get there: Driving west out of Steamboat on U.S. 40, go 1.3-miles from 13th St., until reaching the Airport/Clark turnoff. Turn right, north, here, and drive about 18-miles, just past Clark, to the Seedhouse Road, FDR 400. Turn right here and drive for about 11.9-miles to Slavonia, the end of the road and the trailhead parking for several hikes. Park here, read the information at the kiosk, and then head up the marked trail.

The Hike: Soon cross a little stream. Sign the register, and then go to the right at the trail junction of 1150 and 1161. Hike on 1150 through a level area of meadows and aspens, soon crossing Gilpin Creek over a small footbridge. Travel through an evergreen woods, and then more meadows and aspens. Just after passing the Mt. Zirkel Wilderness boundary sign, at about mile 1.0, the trail starts to climb gradually. The trail curves gradually right, to an overlook with an outstanding view of Gold Creek down far below it. Be especially careful with children here, since it would be a deadly fall down the cliff.

After a bit more hiking through woods, the trail soon begins to parallel the creek more closely. Traverse across an area of boulders, and then climb along a wall through another open area. If the water isn't too high or dangerous, ford Gold Creek at the tricky crossing mentioned above – however best you can – and walk through the woods for a wee bit longer until another much easier water crossing. A few minutes later, you'll begin a steeper climb up the last half-mile to the lake.

Because the lake is surrounded by many spruce trees, over the coming years, sadly we will begin to see the devastating results of a spruce beetle epidemic, both along the trail and at the lake itself. The '97 Blowdown made the area ripe for such an infestation. Luckily, however, most of the trees are fir and won't be affected. And such are the ways of Mother Nature!

Update: *The 2002 Wildfire burned much of the blowdown debris on surrounding hillsides in this area.*

92. Slavonia Mining Camp

Trails 1150 and 1142

The mountains will bring prosperity to the people, the hills the fruit of righteousness.
~ Psalm 72:3

Stand at the crossroads and look; ask where the good road is, the godly paths you used to walk on in the days of long ago. Travel there, and you will find rest for your souls...
~ Jeremiah 6:16

Of Note: Some hardy souls make this 14-mile roundtrip hike in a long day, but since I personally can use pack llamas, and since my joints are wearing out, I prefer to make this interesting destination my overnight base camp. From there, early the next morning, I then hike to the top of Mt. Zirkel, the next hike in this book.

The Slavonia Mining Camp is reached from the Slavonia trailhead, which might sound a bit confusing, since, many years ago, they used to mine gold near the trailhead parking area as well. But these are two different places, one on either end of this hike.

This is a good opportunity to visit one of the few old mining camps in the Mt. Zirkel Wilderness. In the early 1900's, wagons transported miners and supplies up a rugged dirt road to these diggings, which sit at 10,000 feet. Many years later, the remains of the rough wagon road became the hiking trail to this historic destination. Rusted machinery – a hydraulic-powered compressor, rusty rail carts and rails – along with meager cabin remains, all older than most of today's senior citizens, can be investigated and explored. Unfortunately, present-day visitors have also left some modern-day garbage, as well.

The camp is about 2.5-miles past Gold Creek Lake, and surrounded by Engelmann spruce and sub-alpine firs. With easy access to the creek, it's the perfect place to spend an overnight, and then begin an early-morning 2.5-mile trek northwest, climbing above timberline to the top of glorious 12,180' Mt. Zirkel, the namesake for this whole wilderness!

Distance: Almost 7-miles to the mining camp, each way.

Hiking Time: About 3-hours to the camp, each way.

Elevation: Trailhead: 8,460'; Slavonia Mining Camp: 10,000'.

With Children: *This is too long a day hike for children, but if you can safely cross Gold Creek (page 240), this makes a delightful several day backpack trip for families with older children.*

Fishing: *Plenty of fishing for brook trout in Gold Creek along much of the entire route, both before and after Gold Creek Lake, as well as in the lake itself. Please practice catch and release fly-fishing.*

Map: Trails Illustrated 116; Book map 47.

How to get there: Please follow the directions to the Slavonia trailhead in the Gold Creek hike [91].

Old cabin remains at the camp. *(Photo: Elaine Dermody)*

The Hike: Follow the directions to Gold Creek Lake, hike [91]. Once at the lake, walk around the left side of it for about a quarter mile, and then pick up the trail to the mining camp, on the north side of the lake near the large outcrop of rocks. Shortly thereafter, stay left at the junction with the Wyoming Trail-1101, and soon cross a tributary creek. Especially early in the season, this creek may be high, and an easy way to cross on logs may not be available, so keep your water-crossing shoes handy just in case.

About a mile from the lake, drop down and walk parallel with the creek, enjoying the view ahead of you of Flattop Mountain. The trail thereafter begins to climb, until, after 1.5-miles, you reach another trail junction. Left goes to Gilpin Lake on 1161 on a reverse of hike [90], but the right fork is what you want to follow, northeast, along a ridge toward Red Dirt Pass, following the Gold Creek drainage to its headwaters below this pass. At about mile 2.5 from the lake, come to yet another junction. The right goes to Ute Pass, and the left fork, which you want to follow, now turns north and becomes the Red Dirt Pass Trail-1142. About a quarter-mile after this junction, you'll reach the old mining camp on the left. Good campsites abound. Please leave no trace of your ever having visited the area.

93. Mt. Zirkel Summit

All these things my hand has made...
~ Isaiah 66:2

Silently, one by one, in the infinite meadows of heaven,
blossomed the lovely stars, the forget-me-nots of the angels.
~ Longfellow's Evangeline

Of Note: Although Mt. Zirkel is the tallest peak in the Park Range, because it is "only" 12,180-feet high, the peak is ignored by most of the "fourteener" people, those who seek to climb all of the mountains in Colorado which are over 14,000-feet high. Yet, the majestic vistas to be gained by this strenuous, yet not-technical, climb are every bit as magnificent as those viewed from atop the taller peaks. And because it isn't a "fabulous fourteener," the crowds-to-the-top are virtually non-existent, and a hiker can enjoy the views from the top in relative solitude.

Mt. Zirkel was named in 1874 to honor the contributions of Ferdinand Zirkel, an early-day explorer who helped establish a common classification system for American and European rocks.

Make this hike early in the day to avoid lightning storms. Avoid the top at all costs if lightning threatens. And since it can be extremely windy up top, make sure you take a down vest and wool hat with you. Although not a technical climb, extreme caution must be used at all times when climbing from the base to the top peak.

Although there are several routes to reach the Mt. Zirkel summit, the traditional one I recommend is the longest, but because all but one-mile of it is on established trails, it can be hiked faster than the other routes. So, time wise, they are about the same.

From here, it's much further to the top of Mt. Zirkel than this photo leads you to believe!

Distance: From Slavonia Trailhead: 8.6-miles, each way; from Slavonia Mining Camp: 2.5-miles each way.

Hiking Time: From the mining camp, about 2-hours up and 1.5-hours back down.

Elevation: Slavonia Trailhead: 8,460'; Slavonia Mining Camp: 10,000'; Mt. Zirkel summit: 12,180'.

With Children: *This is not a technical climb, so older, in-shape children should relish making this ascent from the mining camp. But with younger children, unless they fit in a backpack, it's probably best to leave them supervised at the camp until your return.*

Yampatika Notes: *Because of its 12,180' height, Mt. Zirkel creates its own weather, as it catches clouds and weather systems rolling by. There is much for geologists to study in the peak's bizarre mixture of gneiss, schist and greenstone. Mt. Zirkel is part of the Zirkel-Big Agnes-Sawtooth Uplift, a classic faulted anticline. Simply put, underground pressure pushes rock layers up into a huge fold or a series of folds called anticlines. But if the fold has a fault in it, it breaks as it rises, and an anticline is created, with steep cliffs to one side and gentle uplift to the other.*

Map: Trails Illustrated 116; Book map 47.

How to get there: Please see the driving directions to the Slavonia trailhead in the Gold Creek hike [91].

The Hike: Please follow the directions from the Slavonia trailhead up to Gold Creek Lake [91], and then from there, to the Slavonia Mining Camp [92]. Engelmann spruce and subalpine fir trees dominate the area.

Spectacular view from the top of Mt. Zirkel, with Gilpin Lake on the left.

From the mining camp, continue north, switch backing up the Red Dirt Pass Trail – 1142 for about 1.5-miles to the Red Dirt Pass, 11,540', about 500' above timberline. Especially early in the season, be prepared for wet marshy areas, but the trail will generally remain distinct even in these areas. The wildflowers in this area are outstanding in number and color. The Red Dirt Pass is on the Continental Divide, and it offers impressive views of the Frying Pan Basin area, north beyond the Pass, and of the Gold Creek drainage and the Ute Pass area to the south – other places to visit on other trips!

From the Pass, you'll have to climb yet another 800 vertical feet on alpine tundra, for almost a mile to the summit. Leave the established trail at this point, turning left, and traverse northwest for a few hundred feet, up a broad grassy ridge, to a high plateau. Looking up, you'll see three spires – horns – on the top of the promontory, a few-hundred feet apart from each other – two sub-peaks and the actual Mt. Zirkel summit itself. (See photo on page 245.)

After walking across the flat plateau to the base, probably against strong, heavy winds, carefully climb over very large boulders to the top of the first of the two sub-peaks. A very narrow trail then leads across an exposed ridge to the highest peak, Mt. Zirkel. Use extreme caution throughout this ascent. Work your way slowly up to the third and highest peak, and look for a trail register under a rock for you to record your visit. If it's not too windy, spread out your map and use your compass to identify everything you see. Don't forget your camera!

Perched up here, you'll feel like you're on top of the world! But remember: to quote Arlene Blum, "You never conquer a mountain. You stand at the summit for a few moments; then the wind blows your footprints away."

MT. ZIRKEL
ROUTT National
U.S. Department of Agriculture
16063WZ
COLORADO

94. Percy, Round and Long Lakes - 1134

Two roads diverged in a wood, and I, I took the one
less traveled by, and that has made all the difference.
~ Robert Frost

Of Note: Percy, Round and Long Lakes are three of the most family-friendly lakes in the Routt National Forest, with fairly easy access and good fishing and camping. They can be reached via several hikes in this book, from all directions, and if you're backpacking, you can easily add several nearby lakes onto your itinerary.

Hike [22] takes you in from the west, from Fish Creek Reservoir up on Buffalo Pass, to Long Lake.

Hike [23] takes you in from the west, from Fish Creek Reservoir up on Buffalo Pass, to Long Lake, and then to Round and Percy Lakes.

Hike [38] takes you south-to-north, from Fishhook Lake off Rabbit Ears Pass, and then up to Lost, Elmo, Round, Percy, and Long lakes.

This hike [94] directs you from the eastern side of the Wilderness Area to these wonderful lakes. The trail gains 1,200 feet in elevation in about 3.5-miles, so it's a moderate to steep climb. But your efforts will be worth it.

Distance: 3.5-miles to Long Lake, one-way.

Hiking Time: About 2-hours, each way up; less going back down.

Elevation: Trailhead: 8,845'; Percy: 10,035; Round: 10,060'; Long: 9,880'.

With Children: *Because of the initial climbing, this approach is not the ideal way to go in with small children, but older, in-shape children should be able to make it easily enough. With younger children, try one of the other approaches from the western side. These lakes provide wonderful resources for successful family camping experiences.*

Yampatika Notes: *See hikes [22] and [23].*

Fishing: *Percy: 17-acres; 23' maximum depth; good for brook along eastern shore; Round: 16-acres, 40' maximum depth; good for small brook trout; Long: 40-acres, 32' maximum depth; good for brook to 12" along northern shore. See hike [38] for information on the other lakes.*

Map: Trails Illustrated: 118; Book map 48.

Percy and Round Lakes provide excellent camping opportunities.

How to get there: From Steamboat Springs, drive east on U.S.40 over Rabbit Ears Pass. Turn left onto CO14 and drive for an additional approximate 20-miles north until Jackson CO26. Watch for a sign "To Coalmont." Turn left here and head west, and then north, until 26 intersects with 24. Turn left onto 24 and follow it to the Grizzly Campground, about 12-miles from CO14. Drive west past the Grizzly Campground on Buffalo Park Road and turn left onto the Hidden Lakes Road, FSR20. Drive past the Hidden Lakes Campground, and past Crosby Creek to the trailhead sign for 1134 on the left, 1/3-mile north of Colorado Creek. Head west on 1134.

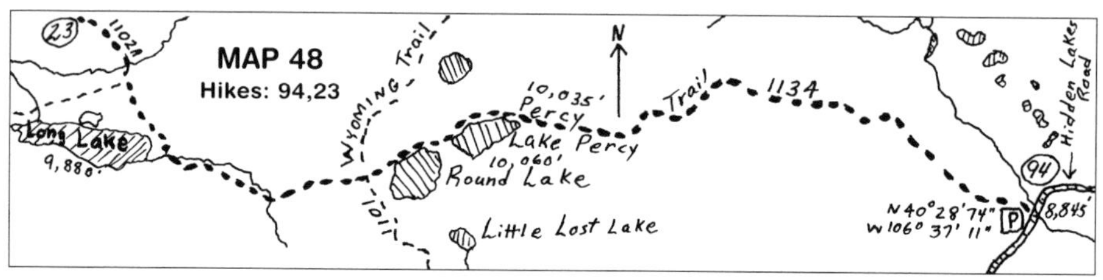

The Hike: The trail up to Percy Lake meanders uphill through forests of spruce-fir trees, climbing gradually toward the Continental Divide. Both Percy and Round Lakes are nestled together in high mountain meadows, surrounded by thick stands of spruce and fir trees. Good campsites are available at both lakes. Be prepared to share the trail with horseback riders, dirt bikes and ATV's, especially on weekends.

95. Newcomb Park - 1132

Don't strew me with roses after I'm dead, when life claims the light of my brow.
No, flowers of life will cheer me instead, so give me my roses now.
~ Thomas Healey

Of Note: The first two miles of this very mellow hike are appropriate for families with small children. The trail meanders along a gentle creek through open meadows of sagebrush and willow trees. Then it leaves the creek bottom and rambles alternately through lodgepole pine forests and large meadows of sedge and tufted hair grass. Cattle graze the area, and one is likely to spot a few of them along the way.

Newcomb Park is a good place to take grandparents and out-of-shape relatives when car camping on the eastern side of the Mt. Zirkel Wilderness Area, at either Teal Lake or Grizzly Lake Campground. The first two miles of this hike are level and travel mostly through open meadows – perfect places to enjoy a vast array of July wildflowers, birds, deer and busy chipmunks. The whole 9.5-mile trail is the remains of an old jeep road that begins to climb after the first two miles, and eventually gets steeper and ends up on top of the Continental Divide near Buffalo Pass. Hike [25] describes the trail from its western end to Round Mountain Lake.

Distance: 2-miles or 4.5 miles for a short or longer hike, each way.

Hiking Time: Variable; about one hour each way if making short hike.

Elevation: Trailhead: 8,760'; At mile 2.5: 8,800'; Round Mountain Lake: 9,860'; top of Continental Divide: 10,605'.

With Children: *The first two miles offers a perfect hike for little ones. Before leaving Steamboat for this hike, stop in at the marvelous Yampatika Nature Store at 10th and Lincoln and purchase some fun nature study books and supplies to use with children on this wonderful children's hike.*

Fishing: *Newcomb Creek and Round Mt. Lake both good for brook trout.*

Map: Trails Illustrated 117 (to be updated spring '01); Book map 49.

How to get there: Drive east on U.S.40 for 25 miles over Rabbit Ears Pass. Turn left onto CO14 and drive for an additional approximately 20-miles north until Jackson CO26. Watch for a sign "To Coalmont." Turn left here and head west, and then north, until 26 intersects with Route 24. turn left onto 24 and follow it to the Grizzly Campground, about 12 miles from CO14. Continue past the campground and turn right on FSR615. Follow it for about 4 miles, passing Tiago and Teal Lakes, and continue to a sign on the left, "Newcomb Creek Trailhead." Turn left here and drive for another 0.25-mile to the trailhead. There are several good car campsites here also, but no water supply.

The Hike: Immediately enter the Mt. Zirkel Wilderness, crossing a stream, and travel through a series of lovely large mountain meadows – the first one filled with willow trees. Gentle Newcomb Creek flows parallel to the left of the trail. Spruce and fir trees line both ends of this meadow. After hiking for about a mile and a quarter, the trail climbs up a small hill and then enters a large grassy meadow, where you can now catch a view of Round Mountain to the west. Pass through some cooling woods, through yet another meadow, and then through some aspen trees, until reaching a very large meadow, which hosts an inviting small pond on its southern side. At about two miles from the trailhead, the trail crosses Newcomb Creek. After enjoying the creek, turn around here and

Newcomb Park provides a great place for a fall family backpack trip.

return for the short version of this hike. This creek, by the way, is generally difficult to cross until early July.

If continuing on to Round Mountain Lake, cross the creek and climb another 1,000 feet in 2.5 miles until reaching the lake. If you're backpacking, yet another 2.5-miles of gradual climbing will take you up through Engelmann spruce and sub-alpine fir, to the Continental Divide Trail-1101. (See hike [25], page 84.)

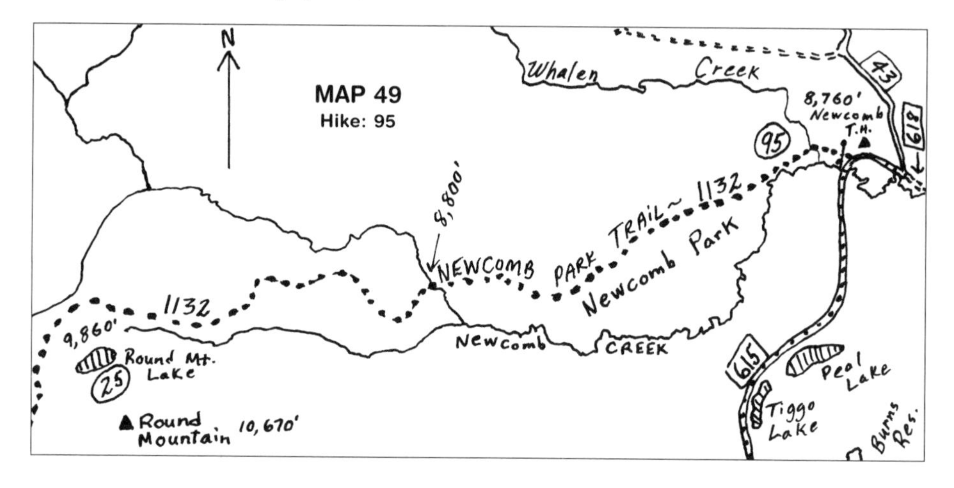

96. Rainbow Lake - 1130

When the rainbow appears in the clouds, I will see it and remember the everlasting Covenant between God and all living creatures of every kind on the earth.
~ Genesis 9:16

Of Note: Having looked down on Rainbow Lake from atop the Continental Divide more times than I can remember over the years, admiring its impressive size and beauty from afar, I finally traveled over to the eastern side of the Mt. Zirkel Wilderness and actually hiked to this glorious lake for the very first time in preparing this book. Upon arriving at the lake, I discovered that it lived up to its reputation. It is, indeed, a huge, gorgeous, glorious deep blue-colored lake in an exquisite setting, and if you live in Steamboat Springs, it is definitely worth the long drive over to its trailhead. But if you can't backpack in, plan to at least car camp for a night so that you'll have a full day to enjoy this special place.

Rainbow Lake is the largest lake in the Mt. Zirkel Wilderness, covering almost one hundred acres and having a 91' maximum depth. Adding to its attraction is the fact that it also makes a wonderful place to base camp and visit other nearby lakes and peaks, such as Mt. Ethel, Lost Ranger Peak and Slide, Upper Slide, and Roxy Ann Lakes. The hike itself, on trail-1130, is a

Sammy and Dudley visit gorgeous Rainbow Lake.

shady, gradual, scenic trek, and the snow-covered eastern flank of Mt. Ethel provides a photo-perfect spectacular backdrop on the lake's western side. The altitude gain of about 1,100 feet is spread out along 3.3-miles, making it a fairly easy to moderate climb.

The lake is a very popular destination and likely to be crowded, especially on weekends. But its vast size and nearby satellite lakes, Middle and Lower Rainbow, make it easy for one to seek out and find solitude. Please leave no trace of your visit.

Camping is restricted between the trail and the lakes, and allowable sites are identified on the kiosk at the trailhead. Violators are ticketed! There may be competition for the trailhead parking and lake camping sites on busy weekends. Don't forget your fishing equipment or your camera. And especially early in the season, don't forget your bug repellant!

Distance: About 3.3-miles, each way.

Hiking Time: About two hours, each way.

Elevation: Trailhead: 8,760'; Rainbow Lake: 9,854'.

With Children: *Older, in-shape children should be able to easily make this hike. Take fishing poles, sketchpads, a disposable camera and other activities, and make a whole day of it at the lake. This also makes a nice family-backpacking destination with older children. Plan on a few rest stops along the way.*

Flishing: *Good fishing for rainbow and cutthroat trout in all three Rainbow Lakes.*

Map: Trails Illustrated 117; Book map 50.

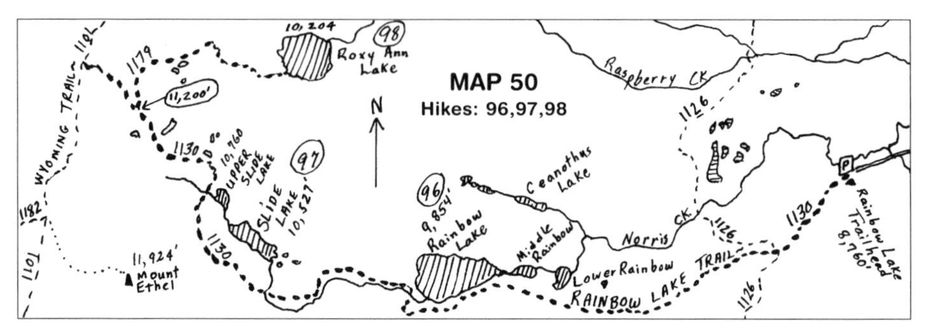

How to get there:

Coming from Walden: Take CO14 east from Walden for about a quarter-mile. Turn right, west, onto Jackson CO12, and drive for about 5 miles, at which point you'll keep left. The road now becomes Jackson CO18, and you'll take this about 4.5-miles to its Y-intersection with Jackson CO5. Turn left, south, onto CO5.

** Set your odometer. The pavement now becomes a well-maintained dirt road. In 1.8 miles, CO5 turns left, but you should remain going straight, with the road now turning into CO22 at this point. About 4.3-miles after you turned onto 5 from 18, there is one unmarked fork. Bear right at that Y, which appears to be the main route. At about 6-miles since turning onto 5 from 18, the dirt road now narrows, climbs dramatically and becomes much rougher. Just drive slowly and carefully. You will start to pass a series of small cabins and hunting camps, and at 7.2-miles from 18, you will enter the Routt National Forest. The trailhead is about 0.1-mile further. Parking is abundant, with room for horse or llama trailers on the left, but plan to arrive early if it's on a weekend or holiday, since this is a very popular hike. Read the signs at the kiosk, and then begin your hike.

Coming from Steamboat: Drive east on U.S.40 over Rabbit Ears Pass for about 25 miles from downtown Steamboat. Turn left onto CO14 (set your odometer), and drive 21.8-miles to the town of Hebron. Continuing north past Hebron for 5.1-miles, turn left onto Jackson CO9. There is no warning for this road, so watch your mileage carefully, especially since you'll be turning from a 65 MPH paved road onto an improved dirt road, so use caution when slowing down to look for it. There is a sign as you turn confirming that you are now on 9. From here, after 3.0-miles, 9 ends at a T at Jackson CO18. Turn left, west, onto 18, which is paved. Take this 4.5-miles until its Y-intersection with Jackson CO5. Turn left onto CO5.

From this point, please follow the same driving directions marked as ** in the "From Walden" directions above.

The Hike: The wide, rocky trail begins its climb gradually through woods of aspen and pines. Notice the valley to the north, formed by Norris Creek, which drains out of the Rainbow Lakes. After about 0.7-mile, arrive at the junction with the Grizzly-Helena Trail-1126, which skirts the whole flank of the eastern half of the Mt. Zirkel Wilderness, north and south, intersecting most trails heading west.

Continue straight on the Rainbow Lake trail-1130. Pretty soon you'll begin to hike along the crest of a very long ridgeline, through aspen and brush. The ridgeline attracts refreshing cool breezes. Traverse along the southern slope of the ridge, where you'll be treated on your left to a marvelous view of North Park, the Gorge Range on clear days, and even the famous Rabbit Ears, way off in the distance. Also note on one section of the ridge how aspens grow exclusively on the left, southern side, and sub-alpine firs and Englemann spruce dominate the northern side, on the right – dramatic proof that aspens prefer sunny south facing slopes, while the evergreens prefer the cooler, northern slopes.

After hiking about 0.4-mile from the junction with 1126, you'll walk over a flat area on the crest of the ridge for a bit, and then begin to travel on the slope's lush, north side, which is covered with cooling spruce and firs. After the first two miles from the trailhead, the trail levels out a bit and continues west. At mile 2.6 from the trailhead, the trail drops slightly, and after about another half- mile of easy walking, it runs parallel to and slightly above the shoreline of Middle Rainbow Lake. Continue on for just a few hundred more yards to reach a side trail across a meadow to the southeast end of beautiful Rainbow Lake. Feast your eyes and take out your camera! And please leave no trace of your ever having been there.

97. Slide Lakes - 1130

All religions are but stepping-stones back to God.
~ Pawnee Indian Proverb

Of Note: At just over seven-miles one way, exquisite Slide and Upper Slide Lakes are too long a day hike for most people. However, if you have pack animals or can backpack in, these scenic lakes, tucked into a rugged basin above Rainbow Lake, are definitely worthy of a visit. And from a base camp at either of the Slide Lakes, you can continue on to various other day hike destinations, such as Roxy Ann Lake, the Continental Divide, Lost Ranger Peak, Pristine Lake, etc., all covered in this book.

Two-miles further up from the larger over-crowded Rainbow Lake, you'll find much more solitude and additional disbursed camping sites at Slide Lake. With its inviting deep blue-green-colored water, Slide Lake takes its name from the mountain which seems to rise up out of the water on the lake's northeast shore, and which has shed huge chunks of itself down the mountain's side in the form of impressive rock slides. A hike up to the 10,527' high Slide Lake will also take you alongside an outlet stream that uniquely flows down a huge sheet of smooth bedrock, which also serves as the stepping-stones up to the lake. Upper Slide Lake is about another mile-and-a-quarter hike away from Slide Lake

Distance: About 7.25 miles, one-way.

Hiking Time: About 4 hours in; a little less going back.

Elevation: Trailhead: 8,760'; Slide Lake: 10,527'; Upper Slide: 10,760'.

With Children: *Even with pack animals, this is too tough a hike for most children; older backpacking Boy Scout troops, however, with rests along the way, make it all the time.*

Yampatika Notes: *Take a slow, meticulous walk on the boulder fields around the lake and explore a world most people overlook. On the rocks are crusty patches of colorful lichens. Count the number of colors, shapes and sizes you find. Lichens, "the house," are a fungus, and alga, the food provider, set in a symbiotic relationship, sometimes where the fungus definitely wins. Of the three main types of lichens, crustose, fruiticose and foliose, the crustose are the most common on rocks. Lichens begin an important process. To create better surfaces with which to hold onto, the lichens produce acids that slowly etch the rock. Particle by particle, the rock catches in niches, until enough is supplied for a seed to land and grow, providing valuable organic matter. Within a couple thousand years, grasses become plentiful, and flowering plants may be pushing their way in. Thus, lichens are the ultimate pioneers.*

Fishing: *Lower Slide: 27-acres, 65' maximum depth; Upper Slide: 8.6-acres, 35' maximum depth; both lakes provide excellent fishing for brook and plump cutthroat trout to 15"; hike over to the rocky northeast shore of Slide for best results.*

Map: Trails Illustrated: 117; Book map 50.

How to get there: Please follow driving instructions to trailhead presented in hike [96], for the Rainbow Lake Trailhead.

The Hike: Please follow hiking directions to Rainbow Lake in hike [96].

From Rainbow Lake, continue on the trail around the lake's south side for about a mile-and-a-quarter, and cross Norris Creek, the lake's inlet stream, at its west end. The trail now crosses many feeder creeks, and then it switchbacks up a steep incline, through a spruce-fir forest, and alongside a pretty waterfall. Arrive at the top of a ridge and enter a meadow, which may be very wet. Continue through several meadows, which have the scenic east face of the rugged Mount Ethel behind them.

Slide Lake is named for the rocks which slide down to its shore from the mountainside.

About a mile and a half after leaving the western side of Rainbow Lake, come to the junction of two streams, and cross the Slide Lake outlet stream, which cascades down a huge section of bedrock to the right. After crossing this outlet stream, leave the main trail, turning right, north, and hike steeply up the bedrock, following the stream for about a quarter-mile to the eastern end of Slide Lake. There is no sign directing you up this way, and no defined trail on the bedrock, but you can simply follow the stream up. Disbursed campsites can be found in the trees near the south and east sides of the lake. And please leave no trace of your visit.

To continue on to Upper Slide Lake, return to the main Rainbow Lakes trail-1130 by following the outlet stream back down the bedrock, and then turning right, north to northeast, on the main trail. Hike up the main trail for another 1.25-miles until reaching the western shore of Upper Slide Lake. The Rainbow Lake Trail continues beyond Upper Slide Lake, taking you first to the intersection of the trail to Roxy Ann Lake, next to the Divide, and then to various other destinations from there.

98. Roxy Ann Lake 1130 & 1179

Only an extraordinary person would purposely risk being outsmarted
by a creature often less than 12" long, over and over again.
~ Janna Bialek

Of Note: At 63-acres in size, stunning Roxy Ann Lake, 10,204 feet high, is the second largest and one of the prettiest lakes in the Mt. Zirkel Wilderness. It's a ten-mile hike in from the trailhead on the eastern side of the wilderness area, via trails 1130 and 1179, and so it definitely requires a tough backpack trip in and an overnight – if not at Roxy Ann itself, then from a base camp at Rainbow or Slide Lakes. But the difficult trek into this lake will reward a hiker with an up to 126' deep, clear blue-water lake, sandy beaches, wonderful fishing opportunities and some cold-water swimming on a hot day.

Parts of the trail are boggy, steep and rocky, and so only strong, in-shape backpackers should make this trip. The trail is rarely maintained. Dudley the llama wants you to know that the difficult, steep hike down 1179 to the lake is not for pack animals.

If you're hiking along the Continental Divide-Wyoming Trail-1101, you can also reach this lake. The turnoff to 1130 will be marked between Mt. Ethel and Lost Ranger Peak, and then a large pole cairn will direct you from there to 1179 and Roxy Ann Lake.

Distance: 9.5 miles, one-way total from the Rainbow Lake-1130 trailhead; 1.75 miles from the junction of 1130 and 1179.

Hiking Time: About 5-6 hours in, depending on the weight of your pack!

Elevation: Trailhead: 8,760'; Jct. of 1130 & 1179: 11,200'; Roxy Ann Lake: 10,204'.

Roxy Ann is the second largest lake in the Mt. Zirkel area.

With Children: *Recommended only for older, very strong teens.*

Fishing: *Cutthroat, golden and native trout are numerous, big and fat, but a challenge to catch at times. Good luck! Please practice careful catch and release.*

Map: Trails Illustrated: 117; Book map 50.

How to get there: Please follow driving instructions to Rainbow Lake Trailhead-1139 in hike [96].

The Hike: Please follow hiking directions to Rainbow Lake [96], then to Upper Slide Lake [97].

Remain on trail 1130, past Upper Slide Lake, hiking uphill for an additional 0.75 mile, at which point you'll see the pole cairn marking the intersection of 1130 and 1179. Turn right onto 1179 at this junction and descend through rocky outcrops and wet, boggy meadows. Watch for rock cairns and signs to help you navigate where the trail seems to fade. Hike through clumps of Englemann spruce and firs in a rocky landscape. You won't get a view of the lake until you've hiked almost a mile from the turnoff.

Be prepared for steep pitches and rough, slippery sections. If multiple user trails confuse you, choose the most distinctive one, though all will take you eventually to the lake. After crossing the inlet stream, descend for yet another quarter-mile before reaching the western end of this lovely lake. Please leave no trace of your visit.

99. Lost Ranger Peak

From the Eastern Side of Mt. Zirkel Wilderness Area

Beyond a wholesome discipline, be gentle with yourself.
You are a child of the universe no less than the trees and the stars; you have a right to be here.
And whether or not it is clear to you, no doubt the universe is unfolding as it should.
Therefore, be at peace with God, whatever you conceive Him to be.
And whatever your labors and aspirations, in the noisy confusion of life, keep peace in your soul.
With all its sham, drudgery and broken dreams, it is still a beautiful world
~ *Max Ehrmann*

Of Note: There are four approaches to Lost Ranger Peak: two from the western side of the Mt. Zirkel Wilderness Area – via Buffalo Pass and North Lake (hikes [32] and [33]) – and two from the eastern side of the Wilderness, via Lost Ranger Trail and the Rainbow Lake Trail. Because this is such a "must" destination for serious hikers seeking to truly take in and digest all that the area has to offer, each possible approach is presented in this book. Unless you're a superman, however, all of these hikes must be made as day hikes from a base camp at one of the nearby lakes.

To help avoid confusion, I have gathered together all approaches to Lost Ranger Peak and placed them in an earlier section of this book. So, please read the introduction presented before hike [32].

From the eastern side of the wilderness area, Hike [34] in this book will guide you from the Rainbow Lake Trailhead and Hike [35] will guide you via the Lost Ranger Trail-1131.

Maps: Trails Illustrated 117; Book map 51.

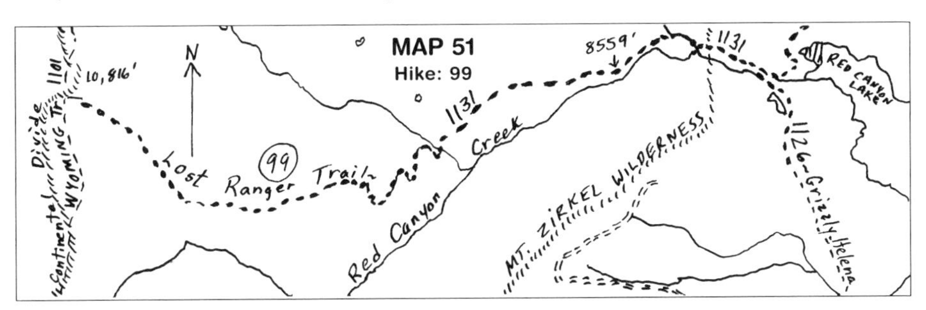

But ask the animals, and they will teach you, or the birds of the air,
and they will tell you; or speak to the earth, and it will teach you,
or let the fish of the sea inform you.
Which of these does not know that the hand of the Lord has done this?
In his hand is the life of every creature and the breath of all mankind.
~ *Job 12:7-10*

Trailhead for:

100. Lake Katherine 1129 & 1157
101. Big Horn Lake - 1129 & 1040
102. Lone Pine Trail - 1129 to Continental Divide

The words of God are not like the oak leaf which dies and falls to the earth, but like the pine tree which stays green forever. ~ Mohawk Indian Proverb

The following three hikes, to Lake Katherine, Big Horn Lake and a route up to the Continental Divide via trail-1129, all share the same trailhead off FSR640, as well as the first mile and a half of trail-1129. The following driving instructions will work for all three hikes:

How to get there: From Steamboat Springs, drive south on U.S.40 over Rabbit Ears Pass. After driving about 25 miles from downtown Steamboat, turn left onto CO14 and drive for another 40 miles. Turn left at the stop sign before Walden, where CO125 joins CO14 from the right. Drive 0.6-mile more until the "Welcome to Walden" sign. Turn left here, onto Jackson CO12W. A sign also points this way to Delaney Butte Lakes. After 5 miles, 12W curves right, and then three miles further, 12W curves left. Two miles further, curve right at the junction of a road that heads left to Delaney Butte Lakes. Two miles after the previous junction, the pavement ends at a "T." Turn left at the T onto Jackson CO16. Drive through the private property and past the buildings belonging to the Lone Pine Ranch, and five miles from the T, enter the Routt National Forest. Jackson CO16 now becomes FSR640, and after 2.5 miles on 640, reach the trailhead for 1129, passing two trailhead signs for 1126 south and 1126 north. There are numerous car campsites near the trailhead, any one of which would make a good base camp for day hiking to the three destinations served by this one trailhead. Since many vehicles pass by these campsites, it's best to lock up any valuable camping gear in your car before heading out for a day hike.

The Hike: To begin any one of the three hikes, follow the trail marked 1129 at the very end of the road. Begin to climb moderately uphill, along Lone Pine Creek, through very tall, cooling old growth evergreen trees, alternating with small, lush, sometimes wet meadows. Wooden boardwalks constructed to help hikers navigate through early-season boggy areas cover some of these meadows. Note on your right an old avalanche path, now covered with new-growth aspens, ceanothus and fir trees. At 0.75-mile into the hike pass the Mt. Zirkel Wilderness sign. At about 1.2 miles, notice an area of avalanche debris, as you head downhill to the left. At about 1.5 miles from the trailhead, notice a sign on the right, "Continental Divide," with an arrow pointing right. Turn here if you wish to head up to the Divide, but if you're going on to Katherine or Big Horn Lakes, remain on the main trail for just a few more yards until you come to the junction sign for the other two destinations.

Please note: At this trail junction, while hiking 1129 for this book, I encountered a black bear eating beside the trail. Dudley and Sammy llamas let out a loud llama alarm noise, and the bear took off a-runnin'! So be certain to cache your food up in a tree if camping in this area.

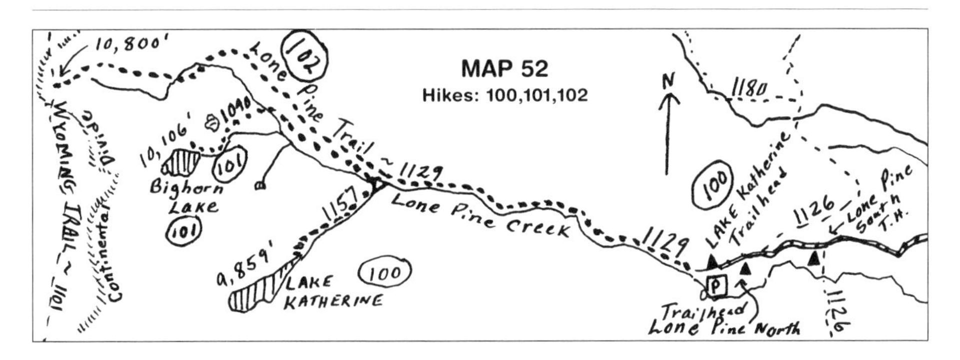

100. Lake Katherine - 1129 & 1157

Our task must be to free ourselves – by widening our circle of compassion to embrace all living creatures and the whole of nature and its beauty.
~ Albert Einstein

Of Note: It's best not to make the hike to this popular, gorgeous lake on a weekend – you may feel like you're on a mountain freeway if you do. But during the week, this relatively easy hike is a 'classic' for the eastern side of the Mt. Zirkel Wilderness. I counted only three decent allowable campsites anywhere near the lake, so it's also best just to day hike to the area, enjoying its large, deep, turquoise-colored mystical lake. Katherine sits at the bottom of an impressive glacial cirque, and it has a poster-worthy mountain rising about 1,000' above the lake to the top of the Continental Divide. Please leave no trace of your visit to this special place.

Since there are a number of water crossings, it's best to make this trip later in the summer season, but not during hunting season, when the area gets inundated with elk hunters.

Distance: 2.5-miles, each way.

Hiking Time: 1.5-hours, each way.

Elevation: Trailhead: 8,960'; Lake Katherine: 9,859.

With Children: *Since this is a relatively short hike, the few steep places shouldn't discourage any in-shape children from making the trip, though you should build in some time for a couple rest stops. This destination provides a most-beautiful setting in which to take some special photos of your children.*

Yampatika Notes: *On the cliffs above Lake Katherine are several permanent snowfields. Found in the north and east facing cliffs, these large chunks of ice could be remnants from the last Ice Age, which retreated about 10,00 to 12,000 years ago. The brilliant blue color comes from the fact that blue wavelength of light is passed farther through the ice than other colors. Hence, the color of ice we see is blue.*

Fishing: *Maximum lake depth: 115'; good for lake and brook trout. Rumor has it that big mackinaw lurk in some of the deeper holes of the lake. Please practice careful catch and release.*

Maps: Trails Illustrated 116 and 117; Book map 52.

How to get there: See driving instructions on page 260.

The Hike: The first part of the hike to Katherine shares the same first section of trial 1129 as two other destinations (see above). About 1.5-miles from the trailhead for all these hikes, trail-1129 heads off to the right. The sign says "Continental Divide," and an arrow points the way. At this sign, do not turn right, but continue straight ahead of you for just a few more yards, and you'll soon see the trail marker at the junction of the Lake Katherine trail-1157 and the Big Horn Lake trail-1040. The sign directs you left to Katherine and right to Big Horn. If early in the season, about 250 yards after this junction, you may need your water-crossing shoes to cross Lone Pine Creek, just above its confluence with Katherine's outlet stream to the right. The crossing here can be difficult from mid-May through mid-July.

For about the last half mile to the lake, the trail climbs rapidly through some thick stands of old growth firs and spruce, gaining almost 450 feet in elevation. Near the top, on your left, notice very old log and boulder debris strewn along badly eroded stream banks. Arrive at the top of the lake's outlet stream, at its northeastern finger, and note the large hole in the middle of the remains of a very old stone and mortar water storage dam. In 1961, a large rush of lake water pushed through the dam and rushed down the creek bed, leaving the tree debris and erosion mentioned above. If you are backpacking there are just a couple allowable campsites off in the trees on the northeast side of the lake, and one near the remains of an old shelter cabin on the other side of the outlet stream and dam. Be prepared for the possibility that these few sites will already be occupied. When you first view the lake itself, your reaction is likely to be something akin to, "Wow!"

Make sure you take your camera to Lake Katherine!

Big Horn Lake is a great destination for families with either older kids or with kids still small enough to be carried.

101. Big Horn Lake - 1129 & 1040

See I am sending an angel ahead of you, to guard you along the way to bring you to the place I have prepared.~ Genesis 23:20

Of Note: Big Horn is yet another spectacular high mountain lake in the Mt. Zirkel Wilderness, typically surrounded by spruce and fir trees and sitting below high-rising talus-strewn ridges. It is 13.8-acres in size and 59' in maximum depth. Like Rainbow and Katherine Lakes, Big Horn's easy access and outstanding alpine setting make it a very popular destination, and so it is best to hike it during the week, except during hunting season when it will be crawling with elk hunters, no matter what the day.

Allowable good campsites along the trail and at this lake are few and far between, so it's best to base camp below and visit the lake on a day hike. There are numerous revegetation areas near the lake, so campers should pick their site carefully. If using it as a day hike destination, try to get there early so that you can spend the whole day exploring and being inspired by Big Horn's delightful water and shoreline. Although it's only a three-mile hike to big Horn, there are a number of particularly steep sections along this trail, especially near the end. So I would recommend it for only hardy hikers. Please leave no trace of your visit.

Distance: 3.3-miles, each way.

Hiking Time: 1.75 hours, each way.

Elevation: Trailhead: 8,960'; Big Horn Lake: 10,106'.

With Children: *Because of the several very steep sections and uncleared downfall, this is not a particularly good hike for most children. However, with a little help on these sections, since it is only 3.3-miles long, very strong, experienced young hikers can successfully and happily make the trip. Once there, unless the weather is bad, the lake will be a total joy for people of all ages.*

Another spectacular high alpine lake, Big Horn sits behind a high–rising, talus–strewn ridge.

Fishing: *Good for cutthroat trout up to twenty-inches. Please practice catch and release.*

Map: Trails Illustrated: 116 & 117; Book map 52.

How to get there: Please follow driving instructions on page 260.

The Hike: After about 1.5 miles from the trailhead, 1129 heads off to the right, up to the Continental Divide. At this sign, do not turn right, but continue straight ahead for just a few more yards, and you'll soon see the trail marker at the junction of the Lake Katherine Trail-1157 and the Big Horn Lake Trail-1040. The sign directs you left to Katherine and right to Big Horn, which is where you will head. The Big Horn Lake trail, 1040, will now take you uphill for about another mile. Be prepared for some very steep sections near the top. Just before your arrival, pass a large pond on the left, after which you'll arrive at the northeast side of the lake, near the outlet stream. While the west side of the lake is rocky, there are forests on the northern and southern shores. A few allowable campsites exist up in the trees, to the right of your arrival site, which is closed for camping because of past overuse. Notice the view of the Continental Divide off in the distance, behind and above the lake. Please leave no trace of your visit.

102. Lone Pine Trail - 1129 to Continental Divide

He climbed cathedral mountains, he saw silver clouds below,
He saw everything as far as you can see.
~ John Denver ~ Rocky Mountain High

Of Note: The first part of this trail is used mostly as an access to Katherine and Big Horn Lakes, but if you head north on it where it junctions with the other two, it will take you up to the Continental Divide, where majestic vista views await the eye. The second half of this hike is a steep ascent, and in some places, you'll even have to use your hands to help you go up arduous switchbacks, so it's not a hike for the faint-of-heart – nor for llamas, which do not have hands. A series of beautiful alpine meadows just below the divide provide backpackers with

The Lone Pine Trail takes you up to the Continental Divide.

plentiful campsites, wonderful vantage places from which to gaze at a billion stars at night, including numerous shooting stars which streak across the black sky to entertain you.

Distance: About 4.4-miles, each way.

Hiking Time: 2.5 to 3 hours, one way up.

Elevation: Trailhead: 8,960'; Atop the divide: 10,800'.

With Children: *When hiking 1129 for this book, I met a dad, a mom and an eight-year-old daughter who successfully made this trip as a day hike from their Lake Katherine base camp. They took quite a few breaks and had to help the child on the steep parts, but she seemed perfectly happy and none-the-worse for wear afterwards. So, children who are used to hiking will take this one in stride if you go at the child's pace.*

Map: Trails Illustrated 116 & 117; Book map 52.

How to get there: Please see driving instructions in the introduction to these three hikes.

The Hike: Please see hiking instructions for the first part of this hike in the introduction to the three hikes which share this same trailhead, on page 260.

At about mile 1.5 from the trailhead on 1129, arrive at a sign saying "Continental Divide" and an arrow pointing the way. Turn right, following the arrow, and begin a steep northwest ascent up to the divide. Cross Lone Pine Creek twice along the way, passing through a series of beautiful alpine meadows. Switchback steeply up to meet 1101, the Wyoming Trail. And then take in the breathtaking beauty. Backpackers may wish at this point to drop down the western side of the Divide for an easy visit to Beaver and Three Island Lakes, or to Gold Creek or Gilpin Lakes.

103. Bear Lakes - Ute Pass Loop - 1126 & 1128

Sing songs of the sunrise into the night.
The stars as your timepiece make it all right.
Make friends with the darkness, talk to the moon.
And when the light lifts, you can let out a tune.
~ John Denver – Cowboy's Delight

Warning: *You should either be an experienced hiker, or be with experienced hikers, if you decide to hike up on the Continental Divide. You need to have with you a good compass, the appropriate topographical maps, and the skills to use them. And you should also be well equipped for possible bad weather, which can be more severe and unpredictable up on the Divide.*

Of Note: Here's a challenging 14-mile backpack loop for only hardy, experienced hikers that will take you up to two remote, picturesque, dark-blue-colored alpine lakes, surrounded by spruce and fir trees, past the remains of an old mine, and then high atop the Continental Divide, where you can enjoy sweeping views of the north slopes of Bear Mountain, as well as look back to the south and east to see outstanding views of the Bear Creek Valley. This loop hike originates on a section of the Grizzly-Helena Trail-1126C-D, heads up the Bear Creek Trail-1180 and intersects and continues on the wide Ute Pass Trail-1128 to many nearby lake and mountain peak side-trip destinations, such as Gold Creek Lake down on the western side of the Divide. This route heads up the eastern flank of the Mt. Zirkel Wilderness Area, and along the way, there is good fishing, beautiful vistas and much solitude. Adding to their beauty, the lakes rest below tall talus-covered ridges. At the mid-way point, several good campsites exist in the trees between Upper and Lower Bear Lakes.

Distance: About 14-miles roundtrip loop.

Hiking Time: 8-9 hours total.

Elevation: Trailhead: 8,870'; Bear Lakes: 10,343'; Ute Pass: 11,000'.

With Children: *Only strong, in-shape teenaged children could make this pack trip.*

Fishing: *Good fishing for up to 12" cutthroats on the northern shore of Upper Bear Lake, with even bigger cutthroats and browns in Lower Bear Lake.*

Map: Trails Illustrated 116 and 117; Book map 53.

Hiking through a lush forest on the Bear Creek/Ute Creek Trip.

How to get there: From Steamboat Springs, drive east on U.S.40 over Rabbit Ears Pass. After driving about 25 miles from downtown Steamboat, turn left onto CO14. Drive for another 40 miles, and

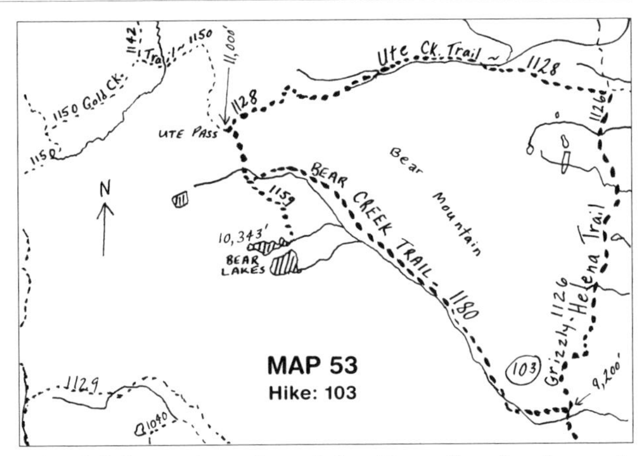

turn left at the stop sign before Walden, where CO125 joins CO14 from the right. Drive 0.6 mile more until the "Welcome to Walden" sign. Turn left here, onto Jackson CO12W. A sign also points this way to Delaney Butte Lakes. After five miles, 12W curves right, and then three miles further, 12W curves left. Two miles later, curve right at the unction of a road that heads left to Delaney Butte Lakes. Two miles after the previous junction, the pavement ends at a "T." Turn left at the "T" onto Jackson CO16. Drive through the private property and past the buildings belonging to the Lone Pine Ranch, and five miles from the "T," enter the Routt National Forest. Jackson CO16 now becomes FSR460, also known as the Lone Pine Road. The Grizzly-Helena Trail intersects Lone Pine Road in two spots – one going north and one going south. For the purposes of the above hikes, you will begin at the section of the Grizzly-Helena Trail-1126 called the Lone Pine North" trailhead on the right, which is 1.3 miles past the National Forest boundary. There are several good car campsites available along this road and also further up, past this trailhead, where the road ends at the Lake Katherine-Big Horn Lakes trailhead.

The Hike: Follow this section of the Grizzly-Helena Trail North for 1.5-miles, as it winds uphill through large aspen groves and then heads down to a crossing of Bear Creek. At the intersection with the Bear Lakes Trail-1180, turn left, and travel on 1180 west and then northwest. The trail very quickly enters the Mt. Zirkel Wilderness. At mile 0.5 from the turnoff, you'll pass by the remains of two old miners' cabins and the old abandoned Bear Creek mine, which is located at the top of the tailings pile, several hundred feet up above you. If you climb up to look at the mine, please remember that it is unsafe to enter old mines. The trail now climbs gradually westward, thorough intermittent stands of spruce and fir trees, crossing numerous pretty meadows. At this point, enjoy great views of the southern slopes of Bear Mountain. After hiking about 2.5-miles past the mine, the trail levels out quite a bit, and if it becomes too faint, follow rock cairns across this level section. At the far end of this flat section, the main trail begins to switchback steeply up a hillside, but just before the base of the hill, look for the trail to the pristine, glimmering Bear Lakes on your left.

This spur trail, 1159 on the map, heads somewhat faintly down an open grassy section for about 0.75-mile, and then it becomes more distinct. Watch for a large rock cairn that shows you where the trail now enters the trees. If the trail fades in the wet meadows, it's generally easy to find it again on the opposite end of each of these meadows. The trail soon winds downhill to the first Upper Bear Lake, which sits at 10,343' high, is 10-acres in size, and 37' at its deepest, and then on to Lower Bear Lake, which sits at 10,320' high, is almost 16-acres in size, and almost 60' at its deepest.

After your visit to the lakes, to continue on to the top, retrace your steps back to the main trail, turn left and head up Ute Pass. Nearing the pass, the trail becomes quite steep, as it threads up a series of tough switchbacks, heading first through the remaining forest before reaching timberline and the Continental Divide. (Please read the warning on page 81.)

After enjoying some time on the top, or after returning from some side trips down to western side lakes, follow rock cairns on the far west section of the flat part on the top of the pass to first find, and then continue on down, the Ute Creek Trail-1128. This trail heads northeast over the higher portion of the Pass at the west end of Bear Mountain. The trail makes several large switchbacks above timberline, and then goes into a dense spruce fir forest, following, and then eventually crossing, Ute Creek two times before it reaches the Grizzly-Helena Trail. Walk south for about 2.5-miles on this trail before reaching Bear Creek, and then another 1.5-miles until the trailhead of origin.

104. Twin Lakes via Grizzly-Helena-1126 & 1174

Everyone to his own.
The bird is in the sky, the stone rests on the land.
In water lives the fish.
And my spirit is in God's hand.
~ Johannes Scheffles

Of Note: The trailhead leading up to Twin Lakes is less than two miles from the boundary of the Mt. Zirkel Wilderness, but the roads shown leading up to it run across private property and do not allow public access. That's the bad news. The good news is that, since you have to access this and several other trails via the longer Grizzly-Helena Trail, the extra mileage and efforts tend to keep the crowds away from these two adjoining lakes, which lie in a magnificent photo-worthy setting. So, if you are a strong, experienced backpacker looking for beauty, solitude and some good fishing, Twin Lakes is one hike that will provide you with all three.

Distance: 9-miles, each way.

Hiking Time: 5-hours, one-way.

Elevation: Trailhead: 8,870'; Twin Lakes: 9,865'.

***Fishing**: Lake and brook in Lower Twin; Upper Twin good for brook to 12". Please practice catch and release.*

Map: Trails Illustrated: 116 & 117; Book map 54.

How to get there: Please follow the driving instructions to the trailhead on page 267. Several hikes share this trailhead. If you're coming from the north, you can access this trail via the northern end of the Grizzly-Helena trail, driving 660 south out of the Big Creek Lake area.

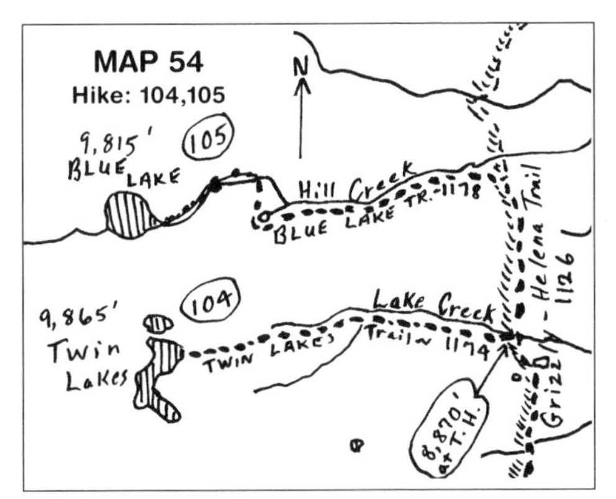

The Hike: Head uphill on this section of the Grizzly-Helena Trail for a mile, through a thick aspen grove. Then descend down for a half-mile to cross Bear Creek. Continue past the turnoffs for the trails to Bear Lake and the Ute pass, and then look east for some great distant views. Seven miles from the trailhead, take the turnoff west for the Twin Lakes Trail-1174. This part of the trail rambles westward for 1.5-miles, following Lake Creek, mostly through thick-forested areas. As you approach Twin Lakes, the skies open from the trees, and you are presented with an awesome view of Flattop Mountain. Arrive at the larger, lower lake, 23-acres, 39' deep, and enjoy watching the beautiful cascading waterfall flow down the mountain on the lake's western shore. Since most of the lake's shores are either boulders or delicate alpine tundra, it's best to look for campsites east of the lake, up in the forest, or in the ridge of trees situated between the upper and lower lakes. The smaller upper lake is only 4.3-acres in size and has a 21' maximum depth.

105. Blue Lake via Grizzly-Helena-1126 & 1178

The heavens are yours, and yours also the earth;
You created the north and the south.
~ Psalm 89:11

Of Note: Like its nearby neighbors, Twin Lakes, Blue Lake requires a long access trek on the Grizzly-Helena Trail, but because of this, an experienced backpacker can enjoy exquisite beauty in solitude at this very deep, blue-colored lake. If you're in the Big Creek Lake area, you can access the Grizzly-Helena trailhead from the north and cut down on the hiking mileage. Blue Lake is surrounded on three sides by a steep cirque, which adds to its outstanding, rugged beauty. It is 21-acres in size and has a whopping 132' maximum depth. Please leave no trace of your visit.

Distance: 10-miles, one way, from the south.

Hiking Time: 6 hours, one way in.

Elevation: Trailhead: 8,870'; Blue Lake: 9,815'.

With Children: *Too long and difficult a backpack trek for children.*

Fishing: *The deep waters hold good fishing for lake, brook and rainbows. Please catch and release.*

Map: Trails Illustrated: 116 & 117; Book map 54.

How to get there: Coming from the south, please follow the driving directions to the Grizzly-Helena trailhead for hike [94]. This is the same trailhead for several hikes. Coming from the north, follow 660 out of the Big Creek Lake area to the Grizzly-Helena trailhead.

The Hike: From the south, head uphill on this section of the Grizzly-Helena Trail for a mile, hiking through a thick aspen grove. Then descend down for a half-mile to cross Bear Creek. Continue past the turnoffs for the three trails to Bear Lake, Ute Pass and Twin Lakes, and about a mile after the Twin Lakes turnoff, arrive at the turnoff for Blue Lake-1178. The Blue Lake trail is wide and gentle for the entire 1.7-additional miles, and it parallels Hill Creek before dropping down to the lake. Enjoy watching the outlet stream from Peggy Lake, about a mile above blue Lake, flow down the southwestern shore of this lovely, lovely lake. The best campsites are located to the northeast of the lake, but they can accommodate only small groups.

Hikes accessed at Big Creek Lake

106. Red Elephant Nature Trail-1125
107. Big Creek Falls-1125
108. Seven Lakes-1125

Of Note: There are three hikes that can be made out of the Big Creek Lake Campground, located at the northeastern side of the Mt. Zirkel Wilderness, and they complete this guide to hikes based out of Steamboat Springs, Colorado. Each of the three hikes leads into the other two. Quite fittingly, they were the last three hikes that I made in preparation for writing this book. A late-September snowfall turned the trip into quite an adventure for me and my five companions – my human friend, Pat Wessel, and four llamas, including Dudley and Sammy and two young guys from the herd.

This was the very last opportunity I had to make these hikes for this book, and I was determined to do it, bad weather forecast or not. I figured if we were well prepared for bad weather with supplies and good equipment, we could handle just about anything. Pat, being as enthusiastic as I am about hiking, decided she would bravely face the challenge with me. Little did we know... Read about our adventure in the "Of Note" section of the last hike.

The drive from Steamboat to the Big Creek Campground takes you through the broad plains of North Park. Outstanding views can be seen of nearby mountain ranges, including the Never Summer Range, the Rabbit Ears Range, the Park Range, and the Medicine Bow Range. North Park is an immense stretched-out basin, and you can travel through this area and see only miles and miles of rangeland. In the area's most recent history, in the 1800's, the Ute Indians hunted buffalo and other animals in the park. Fur trappers came next, and then the gold miners. Those that remained started many of the ranches we see today. The area becomes a hunter's paradise during hunting season. And people with cameras come to this prime moose habitat to try to capture these magnificent beasts in photos. You may also see antelope.

Yampatika Notes: *The large, lush riparian areas support good populations of moose. Historically, prior to 1978, moose were occasional visitors to Colorado. In 1978 and 1979, they were re-introduced into North Park. The population has steadily increased and is moving into new territories, including our valleys in northwest Colorado. In the summer of 2000, a moose was seen enjoying himself in the Yampa River in downtown Steamboat Springs.*

A moose's main food in winter is willows and other woody browse, and in summer, they will forage grasses and other aquatic plants. They are typically solitary animals, except for cows with calves. They are very large, unpredictable animals, so never approach one under any circumstances. Visit: www.mooseworld.com

How to get there:

Directions for driving to the trailhead for the above three hikes:

From the bottom of Rabbit Ears Pass, where County Road 20 intersects with U.S.40, drive east over the pass for 17.5-miles, to the intersection with CO14. Turn left, north, here, and at mile 50.6 of the total, arrive in Walden. From Walden, take CO125 north until Cowdrey, at mile 60. Turn left, west, in Cowdrey, onto 6W, and continue until mile 78.2, where you'll intersect with FSR600; turn left, south, here, and drive 6 more miles, until at mile 83.7, arrive at Big Creek Lakes Recreation Area. Go to the campground at the west end of Big Creek Lake, to the right, and find the Red Elephant Nature Trail sign and brochure box at the kiosk. This is also the joint trailhead for the hikes to Big Creek Falls and to Seven Lakes.

If you happen to be visiting the Hog Park area, near the Wyoming border (see Hike [70]), you can also reach this trailhead by following Route 80 east from Hog Park to the town of Pearl. Turn right here onto FSR600 and drive 6 more miles until the trailhead. From Steamboat Springs, driving north through Hog Park and then south to the trailhead is ten miles shorter than going south and then north through Walden. But different strokes for different folks!

106. Red Elephant Nature Trail

You can muffle the drum, and you can loosen the strings of the lyre.
But who shall command the skylark not to sing? ~ Kahlil Gibran

Of Note: This nature trail is a gentle, Forest Service-manicured wide footpath, and a three-mile round trip walk through delightfully cool woods of fir, spruce, lodgepole pine and some aspens. Twenty-five numbered stations, instructed by a free brochure, teach you about the inter-relationship of the forest ecosystem of plants, animals, microorganisms and nature's processes, such as forest fires and predation. There are generally brochures in a box at the trailhead, but just to be sure, you may also stop at the Forest Service office in Walden, on your left just as you leave town, to pick one up and peruse all the other free materials there. The level trail takes you to the northwest edge of Upper Big Creek Lake and returns you the way you came.

Distance: Three-miles, round trip.

Hliking Time: About two hours roundtrip.

Elevation: Trailhead: 8,997'; Upper Big Creek Lake: 9,009'.

With Children: *This is an excellent hike to make with even toddlers and young children, especially if they are interested in studying nature. The interpretive brochure offers good drawings and simple information written in layperson's terminology. Take a lunch and eat it at the lake before returning.*

Fishing: *Big Creek Lake: 350-acres in size and 57' in maximum depth, is good for catching rainbow, brown and brook trout; Upper Big Creek Lake: 101-acres and 31' in maximum depth, is good for brown trout.*

Map: Trails Illustrated: 116; Book map 55.

How to get there: See directions above.

The Hike: Take a brochure from the box and begin the hike. The trail is very wide and travels through a mixed forest of fir, spruce, lodgepole pine and some aspens. Along the way, you'll stop at twenty-five different stations, where you can learn first hand about the area's trees, birds, animals, plants, water and insects. Before reaching the lake, you'll come to a fork with a signed trail that leads to Big Creek Falls and Seven Lakes. Stay left here, and continue on to the lake. Once there, let your imagination help you make out the shape of an elephant on the large reddish peak to your right.

Upon your return, if your energy permits, turn left at the fork and add a side trip up to Big Creek Falls to your day. (See next hike). It's well worth the effort.

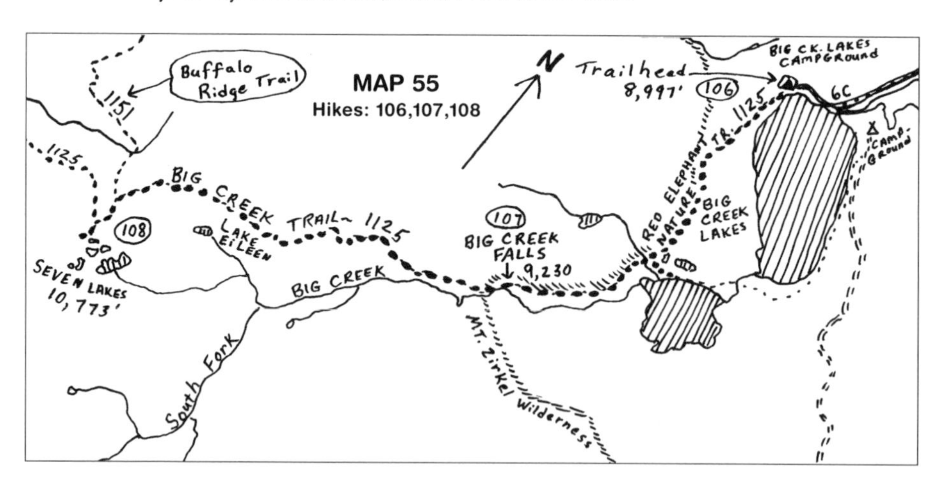

107. Big Creek Falls

In the world, there is nothing more submissive and weak than water, yet
for attacking that which is hard and strong, nothing can surpass it.
~ Lao-Tzu

Cascading water at Big Creek Falls.
(Photo: Michelle Willford)

Of Note: This is a five-mile roundtrip hike, first along a section of a wide-path nature trail, and then up through a continuing mixed forest to an exquisite, cascading waterfalls, situated just inside the Mt. Zirkel Wilderness boundary. Along the way, keep your camera handy for some very impressive views of Big Creek Lake down below. Because of its relatively easy access and special beauty, don't expect to find solitude on this hike, especially on weekends. But if you have the time, you can continue on past the falls for another 0.5-mile or so, where the level trail continues closely beside the creek and offers the visitor many more small, percolating, bubbly mini-waterfalls to enjoy, and with fewer people to share them with. These mini-falls are much larger in summer's early weeks.

Distance: 2.5-miles, each way.

Hiking Time: 1.25-hours, each way.

Elevation: Trailhead: 8,997'; Big Creek Falls: 9,230'.

With Children: *This is an excellent hike to make with children, grandparents and visiting relatives, even if they can't make it all the way up to the picturesque falls. Most of the hike is through very cooling woods on a level path, with much to explore along the way.*

Yampatika Notes: *You may hear a screeching "cheerek cheerek" as you walk past the second of the Big Creek Lakes up to a spectacular view point. Osprey have nested on the southwest shore of the smaller Big Creek Lake for several years. Later in the summer, the fledglings can be seen dive-bombing and playing with the rest of the family. These white-bodied, dark-backed hawks with a broad cheek patch are fishers. They will hover over water and plunge feet-first to grab a fish.*

Fishing: *The fishing is good in Big Creek Lake, and brook trout are known to hide in the Creek. There are many good spots to try your luck in Big Creek itself, especially just after the waterfalls.*

Map: Trails Illustrated: 116; Book map 55.

How to get there: Please follow driving directions on page 271

The Hike: Start up the Red Elephant Nature Trail, a wide and gentle footpath through cooling woods. At mile 1.5, the trail forks, with the one to the left the continuing nature trail (hike [106]) and the one to the right going up to the waterfalls. After hiking about a mile from this fork, you'll reach the Mt. Zirkel Wilderness boundary sign, and immediately thereafter, the glorious twin waterfalls, which are most impressive in early summer, when the runoff is at its highest level. The falls are directly adjacent to the trail, and you'll hear them before you actually see them. Unless your camera is malfunctioning, you almost can't take a bad photo of this very special place. For me, the falls sing out, "Praise God from whom all blessings flow!"

108. Seven Lakes - 1125

Nature has no mercy at all. Nature says, "I'm going to snow. If you have on a bikini and no snowshoes, that's tough. I am going to make it snow anyway!"
~ Maya Angelou

The Lord will keep you from all harm. He will watch over your life;
The Lord will watch over your coming and your going – both now and forevermore.
~ Psalm 121:7-8

Of Special Note: On our hike up to the Seven Lakes, nature, indeed, had no mercy, but thankfully, the Good Lord also watched over "our coming and our going"!
This was the very last hike I made in preparation for this book. It was toward the end of September 2000, and the weather didn't look too promising. But it was a "now or never" situation for me, if I were to include it in this guide. And so my brave friend, Pat, and I decided to give it a go, thinking we could always just turn around and return if things got too bad. Besides, we had the use of four llamas, so we could take plenty of food and supplies and bad weather gear. We could always honker down and wait out anything – or so we thought.

Cold rain poured on us the entire 6.5-miles up – not a good omen. Upon our arrival at Seven Lakes, everything we had on was damp-to-wet, including Pat's Forest Service issued Gortex rain jacket. We hurriedly set up our camp in the rain, and had little time to investigate the seven lakes. We would save that for morning. Luckily, we had along and set up a very large tarp, which sheltered us and allowed us to keep our gear and supplies somewhat dry, as we sat under it to cook and eat our meal. Cleaning the dinner dishes, we watched anxiously as the cold rain turned into a wet, heavy snow, and the temperature plummeted. We brought the llamas in close together among the trees for shelter and headed for our tent and warm, dry sleeping bags.

The next morning, we emerged from the sagging tent to discover more than a foot-and-a-half of snow on the ground – and more was coming down. A cold wind made matters worse, and we very quickly realized that the llamas no longer had access to grass. We fed them the little bit of oats that we'd brought along for their treats, but in that cold, up at such a high altitude, and

Lindsey and Jennifer Adler playing on the boulders at Seven Lakes.

drenched from the previous day's unrelenting rain, the llamas seemed famished. The two young guys even shivered. And the little bit of firewood available up at the lake was far too wet for us to even build a warming fire for ourselves. So, given all that, we decided to pack up and head out.

Unfortunately, in the heavy rain of the evening before, we hadn't paid too much attention to our bushwhack route in, and now, under all that snow, we weren't at all sure where the trail was. Our anxiety level continued to rise.

As we trudged along in the deep snow, I have to admit that I walked along in total faith and hope--in our map, in our compass, and in the Good Lord above! After about a half-hour of walking, we finally recognized a little sign on a tree that we had passed on our way in the day before, and both Pat and I hollered out in pure joy!

Hiking down the whole 6.5-miles through the snow, the white woods were quite beautiful, though by then, everything we owned – including our cameras--was wet. Finally, arriving back at the trailhead, we tethered the llamas in a meadow in which the grass was deeper than the snow, and they ate ecstatically – going from snowy famine to feast. We broke out the backpack stove, and hot food and drinks had never tasted so good!

Amazingly, both Pat and I agree that, because it had a good outcome, we enjoyed our adventure greatly, proving once and for all that fanatic hikers often have strange ideas about what constitutes 'fun.' We both plan to return to the area again, only next time, in mid-July or so. Dudley says, "Count us out, lady. We don't go where you feed us snow!"

Of Note: As its name implies, the Seven Lakes Basin contains seven high mountain alpine lakes of differing sizes, six very shallow and the seventh lake, the largest and the deepest, at 14-acres and 25' deep. These magical water bowls are kettle lakes, remnants of glacial action, and

This photo of Pat Wessel was taken at Seven Lakes only two weeks after the photo of the Adler children on page 275 was taken there.

they sit in a mostly open, lovely meadow area. There are quite a few stands of trees in which you can find very nice campsites.

The hike up to the lakes will take you partly along the nature trail (hike [106]) and past Big Creek Falls (hike [107]). This is a moderate-to-difficult backpack trip, since it involves some long stretches on very steep switchbacks. And at 6.5-miles each way, it pushes the day's limit for most hikers.

After spending a night at Seven Lakes, if you want, you can easily then continue on through dense spruce-fir trees down to the Main Fork Trail. From there, you can visit Encampment Meadows, Gem Lake and Lake Diana, if you turn south, or West Fork Lake if you turn north and then west. Another fork in the trail will take you to Davis Peak.

Distance: 6.5-miles, each way.

Hiking Time: About 4-hours up; about 3.5-hours back down.

Elevation: Trailhead: 8,997'; Seven Lakes: 10,773'.

With Children: *Unless you have pack animals, this is too tough a trip for children. My friends, the Adlers, took their two youngsters on a weeklong llama trek and spent a good day and a night camped at Seven Lakes. But that was a couple weeks ahead of my own trip there, before the early snows began to fall.*

Fishing: *Good trout fishing in Big Creek along the way; The largest of the seven lakes, at 14-acres, 25' maximum depth, is stocked every other year with trout, and it offers fair fishing for cutthroats to 14" in size.*

Map: Trails Illustrated: 116; Book map 55.

How to get there: Please see driving instructions to the Big Creek Campground in the introduction to this section.

The Hike: Follow hike [107] to Big Creek Falls. The trail continues past the falls through forests of Englemann spruce and sub-alpine fir at a moderate grade. About 0.25-mile past the falls, the trail drops close to the creek and offers good access to the water for about the next half-mile. But then it pulls away from the creek and begins to slowly climb, until you are challenged by a series of steep switchbacks about a mile beyond the falls. You'll gain 750' in about a half-mile. One saving grace of this climb is the fabulous views to be had by looking back down the valley to Big Creek Lakes, North Park and Red Elephant Mountain. After climbing to 10,350', you'll cross over the top of a knoll, and then gratefully discover that the trail now levels off quite a bit, with a series of slight descents, rises and then level sections leading through a lovely forest.

Look for several wonderful meadows on your left. In early July, these will be bedecked by colorful wildflowers. Reach a junction fork with a sign directing you north toward Davis Peak-1151, and Encampment Meadows-1125. Go left, south, toward Encampment Meadows, climbing moderately once again through forests and past many small inviting meadows. Shortly past this junction, the trail forks once again, with this sign directing you to either Encampment Meadows or Seven lakes. Go left at this junction, south, and you'll almost immediately enter the big Seven Lakes basin. Follow a well-defined path eastward around all the smaller lakes to reach the largest lake. To the south, you can look up to see the Continental Divide running along the crest of a ridge above Seven Lakes. Please leave no trace of your visit.

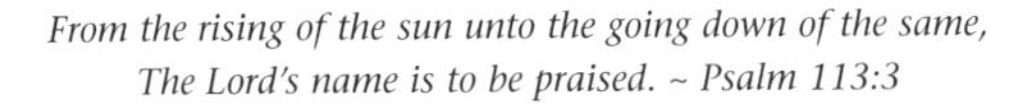
From the rising of the sun unto the going down of the same,
The Lord's name is to be praised. ~ Psalm 113:3

Golden fall aspen leaves quake and sparkle in a setting sun.

Fears are legitimate topics
STEAMBOAT PILOT
Hot real estate market hard to resist
Officials take
direction from

STEAMBOAT SPRING
LEGEND HAS IT THAT THREE FRENCH TRAPPERS
FIRST NOTED THIS UNUSUAL SPRING IN THE YAMPA
VALLEY. THE SPOUTING SPRING, ACCOMPANIED BY
A "CHUGGING" SOUND, REMINDED THEM OF A STEAMBOAT.
HENCEFORTH, SINCE THE EARLY 1870'S, THE TRAPPERS,
GUIDES, AND MINERS CAME TO RECOGNIZE AND KNOW
THIS FUTURE TOWNSITE AS "STEAMBOAT SPRINGS".

Forest Service Volunteers

For fifteen years, Sam and Helen Bayliss and their little dog, Nic, served as campground hosts at Fish Creek Falls. They welcomed thousands of visitors, provided assistance, information, first aid, collected parking fees, and helped maintain the facilities. Many years ago, I first met Sam on my way up to Long Lake, as he was trimming back branches from the trail. My first encounter with Helen was when she came running after me, chastising me in her no-nonsense New England voice for not having my dog on a leash. And we soon became great friends. When Sam was in his early seventies, he and I twice climbed up 13,500' Notch Mountain together, to take in the great view of Mt. of the Holy Cross. He had no trouble keeping up with me either time. But Alzheimer's Disease has now taken its toll on him, and sadly, the summer of 2000 had to be their last year at Fish Creek Falls. All of us who have enjoyed their friendship and loyalty over the years will miss their presence. Thank you, Helen and Sam, for your friendship and your dedicated service.

Sam, Helen and Nic Bayliss.

Become a Volunteer

Volunteers are central to helping the Forest Service accomplish its mission. Besides becoming campground hosts, the types of work a volunteer may perform are many and varied. Your talents and skills will be matched with your work preference in order to provide an experience that satisfies you and helps accomplish something meaningful. You may work on a part-time, full-time or one-time-only basis. Some of the jobs include: answering phones and greeting visitors at the ranger stations; planting trees and seeding damaged areas; presenting environmental education programs; building and repairing fences, nesting boxes, picnic tables and other structures; building and maintaining trails; restoring damaged stream banks and burned-over areas. Call the Forest Service for more information: Steamboat: 970-879-1870; Walden: 970-723-8204; Yampa: 970:638-4510. For an application and more information about hosting positions, you can also check: http://www.ournationalforests.com

Trailcrew – our tax dollars at work. Thanks for your hard work, guys!

There are also opportunities for volunteers to be trained for the Friends of Wilderness – volunteer field rangers who help patrol trails and assist in managing and protecting wilderness areas on the Routt National Forest. Call 879-1870 for more information.

Afterthoughts

Wow! I actually finished writing this book! Creating it has been a true labor of love. Taking these 108 hikes took up at least two full summers and autumns of my time, and doing so put thousands of miles on my car's odometer. I went through many, many tanks full of gasoline, and sitting for hours and hours at my computer has put I-hate-to-say-how-many extra pounds on my body. But it's finally finished!

When the first "Hiking the 'Boat" was published in 1992, it covered only thirty hikes. But over the years, I found myself discovering more and more wonderful places to hike, and I wanted to share them all with hikers who live in or visit the Steamboat Springs area. This has now become a reality with the publishing of "Hiking the 'Boat II."

Writing such a thorough book was possible only because our children are now young adults, and also because I now have two llamas to carry my heavy supplies for me on overnight trips – something my body no longer allows me to do for myself. Except for a few little secret places that all hikers seem to have, I've tried to include in this book everything I could find worth hiking in the entire greater Steamboat Springs area. I'm sure there are other hikes out there that I somehow missed, but those will just have to wait for some other next-generation writer, I think.

I tried to be very generous with Hiking Time:, hoping to keep the time required more the average of the fastest and slowest hikers. I know there will continue to be people who will come up to me, happily telling me that they made a hike in far less time than I suggested. That's O.K. I prefer that to discouraging neophyte hikers with unrealistic times. Anyway, most experienced hikers can guess their own required time just by looking at and considering the mileage, elevation gains, how often they like to stop, and the weight they have to carry on their backs. When I read an article in the July 16, 2000, *New York Times* quoting a Star class sailor, Mark Reynolds, racing for gold in the Summer Olympics, I had to laugh. He was talking about how sailors hang out over the edge of a sailboat to make it go faster – i.e., 'hiking the boat.' "The harder you hike the boat, the faster you go," Reynolds stated. Now if you just turn that around, ain't it the truth!

I've tried to include many fun photographs of family and friends in this book to help bring the hikes to life for people who, for one reason or another, aren't able to make the hikes, but still take pleasure from just reading about them. I also wanted this book to help preserve good memories for all those who made these hikes with me and who appear in the photos.

To the best of my knowledge and ability and at this printing, the directions in the book are accurate, but no doubt about it – men, time and nature will change things here and there, if they haven't already. Signs fall down or get moved or reworded – or disappear altogether. Trailheads get moved, and trails get re-routed or closed by avalanches, blow downs or forest fires. Time takes it toll on all hiking guidebooks, it seems.

If you do discover changes or corrections, please write to me so that I can keep this book periodically updated: Aspen Tree Press, P.O. Box 775051, Steamboat Springs, CO 80477. And if you ever have any doubts about anything presented in my book, please call the local U.S. Forest Service and ask them about it. Remember, they do this full time! Steamboat: 970-879-1870; Walden: 970-723-8204; Yampa: 970-638-4516.

I hope HIKING THE 'BOAT II will help and encourage you to spend more time outdoors, hiking on the trails in this gorgeous, gorgeous environment. Please be good to the land – leave no trace of your visits and follow all posted regulations. They are there for a purpose. And before you head out, please take the time to read, digest and follow the Backcountry Safety information in the front of this book.

Finally, dear readers and friends, I pray that the Good Lord will watch over your coming and your going, and that you will enjoy many safe, happy, memory making hikes!

"Memories! Taken many years ago when our backs were strong, our stomachs lean, our children were tiny, my hair was long and my shorts were short!"

MT. ZIRKEL
WILDERNESS
ROUTT National Forest
WILDERNESS

THE CLARK STORE
U.S. POST OFFICE
Clark Colorado 80428